AF544800

GREAT LONELY PLACES *of the* TEXAS PLAINS

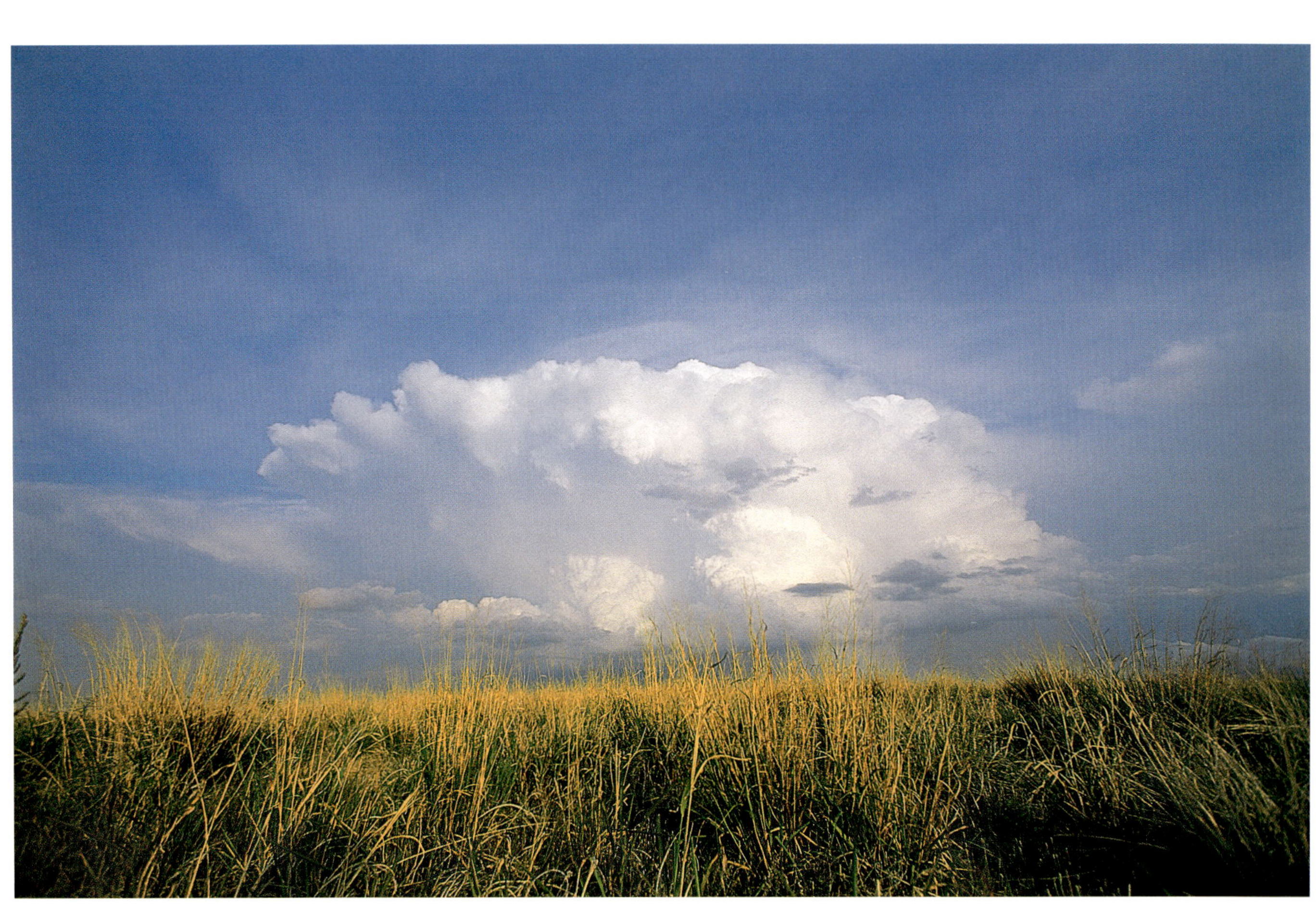

GREAT LONELY PLACES *of the* TEXAS PLAINS

Poems by Walt McDonald

Photographs by Wyman Meinzer

TEXAS TECH UNIVERSITY PRESS

This book was typeset in Adobe Jenson. The paper used in this book meets the minimum requirements of ANSI/NISO Z39.48-1992 (R1997). ∞

Designed by Laine Markham and Barbara Werden

Manufactured in China at Everbest Printing Company

Library of Congress Cataloging-in-Publication Data
McDonald, Walter.
Great lonely places of the Texas Plains / poems by Walt McDonald ; photographs by Wyman Meinzer.
p. cm.
ISBN 0-89672-506-5 (alk. paper)
1. Plains—Texas—Pictorial works. 2. Country life—Texas—Pictorial works. 3. Texas—Pictorial works. 4. Texas—History, Local—Pictorial works. 5. Plains—Texas—Poetry. 6. Country life—Texas—Poetry. 7. Texas—Poetry. I. Meinzer, Wyman. II. Title.
F387 .M43 2003
976.4'00945'022—dc21
2003007171

03 04 05 06 07 08 09 10 11 / 9 8 7 6 5 4 3 2 1

Texas Tech University Press
Box 41037
Lubbock, Texas 79409-1037 USA
800.832.4042
ttup@ttu.edu
www.ttup.ttu.edu

For Carol and the children

WMcD

To the people, sky, land, and history

that fuel our appreciation

for the Plains

WM

NO MORE A STRANGER, NOR A GUEST,
BUT LIKE A CHILD AT HOME.

Isaac Watts

"My Shepherd Will Supply My Need"

1719

PREFACE

Natives of West Texas, we have both devoted careers to seeing and celebrating these plains, but we hadn't realized how much our work spoke to each other's until Judith Keeling at Texas Tech University Press suggested we work together.

The seventy-seven pairs of color photographs and poems you find here aim to capture some of the moods and images of wilderness and people on the great lonely places it has been our delight and privilege to know.

Wyman already had a cache of photographs, some from earlier books, and traveled hundreds of miles for more. Walt chose from hundreds of poems to connect with Wyman's color images: poems not yet in books, some from earlier books, and some he wrote or revised when stirred by especially intriguing photos. Then together we selected favorite pairs.

We matched poems with photos not to illustrate actual persons, but as celebrations of the Plains. In doing so, we kept only the photos and poems that together and on their own both startled and delighted, that shocked and jostled. Throughout the selection process came the delight of recognizing our common heritage in those lonely but great places of the Plains, those unexpected and too often unnoticed details that sometimes get lost between horizon and sky, those people we've loved and learned from.

Some poems goaded stories that seemed to lurk behind the photos; some voiced haunting encounters with the landscape, or celebrated the people who boldly made and make the Plains their home. Every poem in the book is fiction, freely invented, its content coming from Walt's imagination. Just as millions live out their own stories on the Plains, Walt's poems come from many voices, many points of view. Every photograph speaks to Wyman's fascination with the land and sky, and with man's struggle, past and present, to thrive in a place of uncompromising temperament. Some of the images celebrate the natural history that defines our Texas Plains. Others honor forgotten peoples whose faint marks upon the landscape are all that document their heroic struggle for lasting presence in an oceanic region. Always, we tried to connect poems with the spirit of the photographs.

We paired some photos with poems because of similar textures or setting. Sometimes, though, we risked a radical connection or contrast, a juxtaposition that worked for us like a simile. Yoking poems with photos of faces or landscapes, we found surprising insights about our feelings for the vast, wide Plains.

Gladly, we offer these pairs of poems and color photographs as testimony to the kinship of all of us who inhabit our territory. We hope you'll share our sense of awe in these dramatic colors of sprawling landscapes and sky, the calm and vigorous people who have thrived under these thousand miles of stars, accepting the risks, the splendor of it all.

Walt McDonald
Wyman Meinzer

CONTENTS

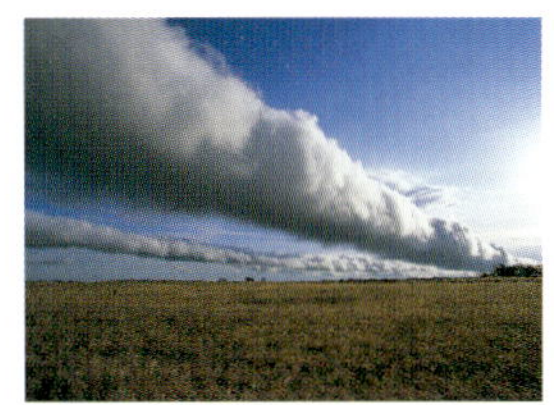

A ROUND HORIZON WITHOUT A TOWN

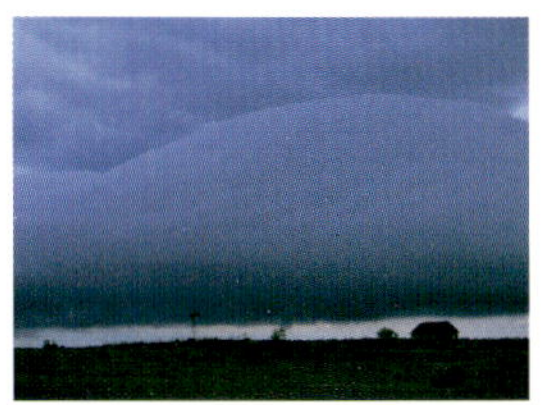

PRAYING FOR RAIN ON THE PLAINS

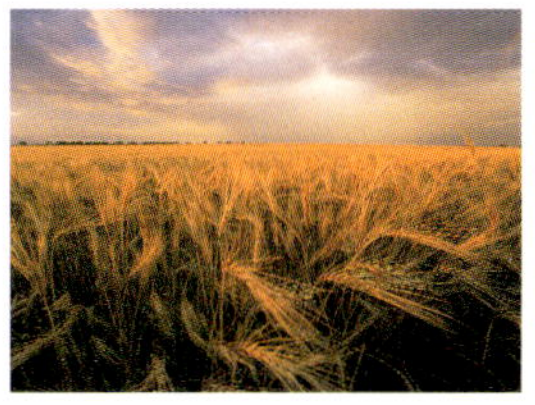

PRAIRIE WAS A TABLELAND OF PRAISE

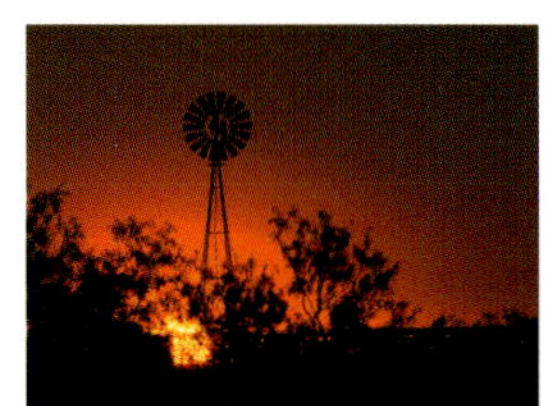

WINDMILLS LIKE CATHEDRAL WINDOWS

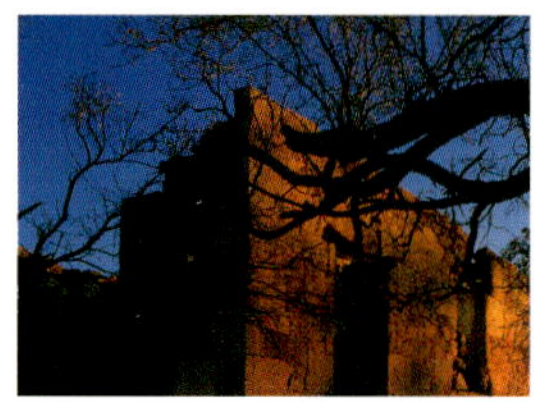

THE DUST WE'RE MADE OF

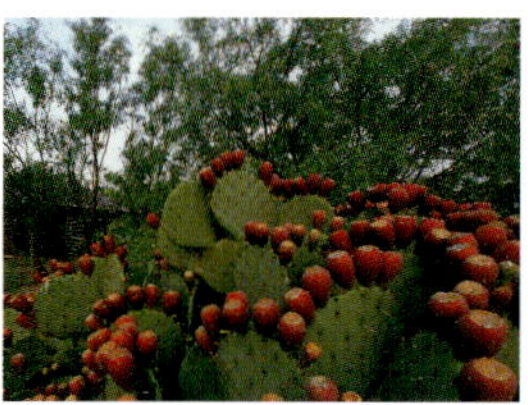

GARDENS OF SAND AND CACTUS

ACKNOWLEDGMENTS

I'm deeply grateful to editors of the following publications in which earlier versions of these poems first appeared, some with different titles:

Archipelago: "Where the Train Slows Down"
Ascent: "Between the Moon and Me"
The Atlantic: "Heirlooms"
Borderlands: "Tasting the Night Air Gladly"
Chelsea: "Diamonds in the Carnegie Museum"
Christian Century: "This Could Be Eden"
Cincinnati Poetry Review: "Calling First Stars by Name"
College English: "Finding My Father's Hands in Midlife," "Leaving Sixty"
Concho River Review: "The Art of Growing Old"
Confluence: "Grandmother's Wagon Trail Diary"
Descant: "Mornings," "Springtime in Texas"
Descant (Canada): "The Perks of Being a Greenhorn"
Electronic Poetry Review: "In Spring, the Cedar Waxwings"
Eleventh Muse: "Let Thunder Rattle the Glass," "Taking Charge"
Fiddlehead (Canada): "Loading the Summer Cattle"
First Things: "The Waltz We Were Born For"
Gettysburg Review: "Praying for Rain on the Plains"
Hawai'i Review: "Two Years after World War II"
JAMA: "Wherever the Puff Goes"
Kenyon Review: "My Father on His Shield"
Manoa: "Harvest"
Midwest Quarterly: "Ten Miles in Every Direction"
Mississippi Arts & Letters: "Black Wings Wheeling"
Mississippi Review Online: "Aunt Florence and the Kalahari"
Missouri Review: "Cool Water Gushing from the Earth," "Where Buffalo Grass Grows Loud if We Listen"
The Nation: "When the Children Have Gone"
The New Criterion: "Under Blue Skies"
New England Review: "Rembrandt and the Art of Mercy"
New Letters: "Leaving the Scene"
New Orleans Review: "On a Saturday Afternoon in the Country"
New Southern Literary Messenger: "All That Aches and Blesses"
New Texas 99: "Prairie Was a Tableland of Praise"
New York Review of Books: "Digging in a Footlocker"
Nimrod: "Hardscrabble June"
North American Review: "The Winter Daddy Died"
North Dakota Quarterly: "Frogs Croaking Their Love Songs"
Offcourse: "Chains We Didn't Hang," "A Round Horizon without a Town"
Ohio Review: "No Matter Where We've Been"
Old Red Kimono: "Out in the Pasture at Dusk"
Oxford Magazine: "Soaring at Lubbock"
Pacific Review: "Buying the Last Half Section Back"
Paris Review: "Rocking for Days in the Shade"
Phi Kappa Phi Forum: "The Pleasures of Coffee Together"
Poet Lore: "In Gusty Winds This Wild"
Poetry: "The Dust We're Made Of" (also in *The Poetry Anthology*, 1912–2002), "Old Pets," "The Songs We Fought For," "Wishing for More than Thunder"
Poetry Northwest: "What the Wind Delivers"
Poetry Webring Review: "Granddaughters of the Plains"
Poet's Canvas: "After Decades Away, Ulysses Sounded the Same"
Prairie Schooner: "Uncle Oscar and the Art of Carving"
Roanoke Review: "The Force that Grew the Grain"

Salt River Review: "Big Dogs after War"
Seattle Review: "Patting Each Other's Hands"
Seems: "Mother's Chihuahuas"
Sewanee Review: "Bowing to Skies in a Hat," "Crossing the Road," "Luck of the Draw"
Shenandoah: "Nights on the Brazos"
Southern Poetry Review: "Mesas I Never Took the Time to Climb"
Starry Night Review: "Aunt Fanny and the Neighbors' Nags," "Whatever Old Cowboys Tell Us, They've Already Done"
Westview: "Clouds Drifting Thin around Us"
Windsor Review (Canada): "Hardscrabble, Tooth and Claw," "Summer Nights"
Writers' Forum: "In Fields of Rattlesnakes"; also in *Aabye's Baby* (UK)

I'm especially grateful to the editors and presses that published earlier books with several of the poems included in *Great Lonely Places of the Texas Plains:*

Witching on Hardscrabble (Spoon River Poetry Press, 1985).
The Flying Dutchman (Ohio State University Press, 1987).
After the Noise of Saigon (University of Massachusetts Press, 1988).
Rafting the Brazos (University of North Texas Press, 1988).
Night Landings (Harper & Row, 1989).
The Digs in Escondido Canyon (Texas Tech University Press, 1991).
Where Skies Are Not Cloudy (University of North Texas Press, 1993).
Counting Survivors (University of Pittsburgh Press, 1995).
Blessings the Body Gave (Ohio State University Press, 1998).
All Occasions (University of Notre Dame Press, 2000).

WMcD

Many of the images contained here would still be residing in my files had it not been for the poetic genius of Walt McDonald and his willingness to share his work with me. I share Walt's appreciation for our expansive Plains and have, during my years of travel, collected photographs on the basis of sheer affinity, whenever a composition or particular light caught my eye and seemed to define a moment or place irresistibly. Before Walt and I could make our final selections, however, I was compelled to hit the road once more, to create other images that conveyed the spirit of the Plains. With the help of people like Alvin Lynn, Tom Bivins, the Cogdell family and a host of other plainsmen and women, I collected what I thought to be an excellent selection of work that would do justice to our Texas Plains. I could not have completed the work offered here without the help of friends from all points of this expansive region.

WM

1

A ROUND HORIZON WITHOUT A TOWN

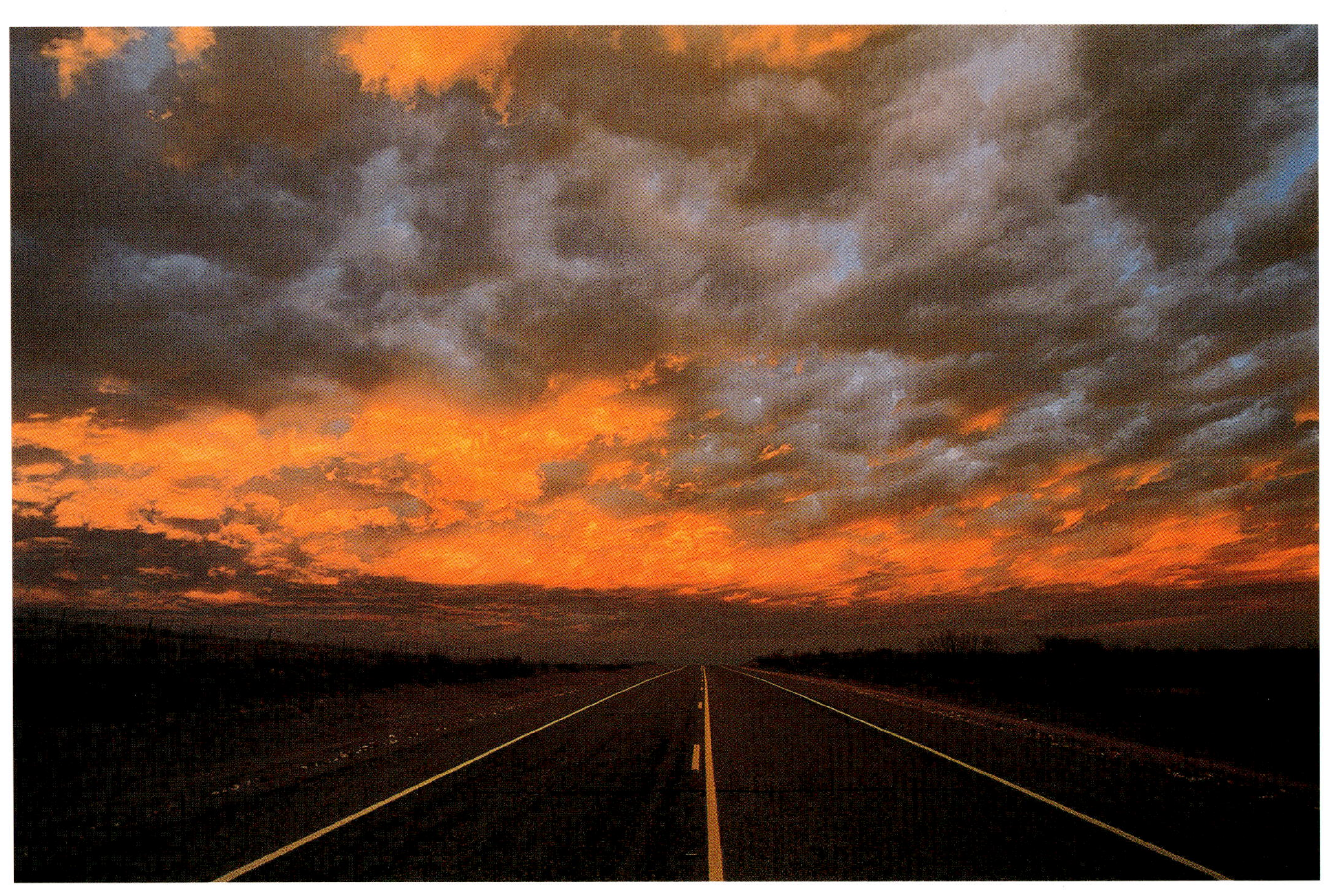

TASTING THE NIGHT AIR GLADLY

We race the harvest moon past posts,
the highway and barbed wires
strung between towns, hours on the road
and still two hundred miles. Jackrabbits

hit the lights and vanish, sometimes an owl
on a strand of fence. We see it rise,
flapping wide wings away. A lonely woman's song
calls us to the world of others, radio waves

that ricochet all night. Grandchildren we adore
are sleeping in Dallas, arms around big pandas
and baseball gloves we gave. A week
is never enough, gone like asphalt miles

behind us. When we pull over to stretch
and let the other drive, we taste the night air
gladly under stars, the vinegar-sweet aroma
of mesquites, the tang of cactus. And there,

off there in darkness, a flash, another light
we'll puzzle over, always wonders to talk about
after all these years, taking turns behind the wheel
or dozing, chasing a centerline.

OLD PETS

Hawks in wide, hardscrabble skies track mice
in fields we say we own. We feed too many pets
our children raised by hand and abandoned.
Old bulls aren't worth the hay to save them,

but I don't throw away a glove because it's ugly.
Look at them, old goats and horses fat in the pasture.
That palomino's lame, the oldest mare on the Plains,
drools when I rub her ear, can't hear unless I whisper,

leans on me like a post, slobbering oats from my glove,
swishing her tail. This abandoned barn was weeds,
the padlock missing. Thieves hauled good metal off,
nothing but someone's dream holding a roof over stalls,

the cows long slaughtered. Owls watched the plunder of doors
in silence. A man with children built this barn
to last, but not one stayed to carry on his herd.
We had to track them down to sign. And now the barn is ours,

and pastures fenced by barbed wires dangling from posts,
and most of those are broken. We might as well breed wolves
or trap for bounty snakes that kill our calves.
We could sell the rattlers' venom for research,

and wolves are bred for national parks in Montana
so why not here? Dawn, I shake my head at my schemes
and saddle up, time for rounding strays
and dumping hay to old pets bawling at the barn.

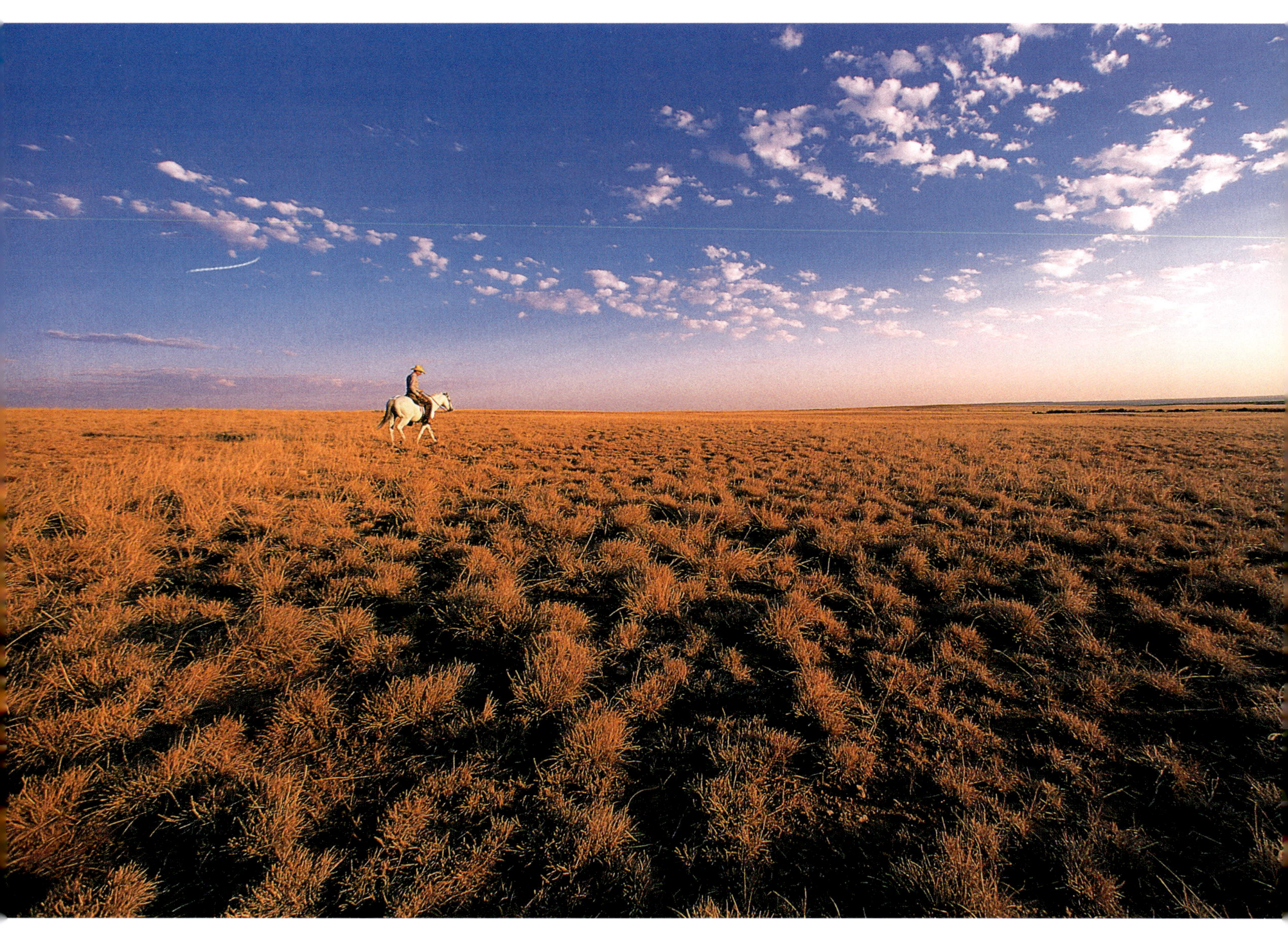

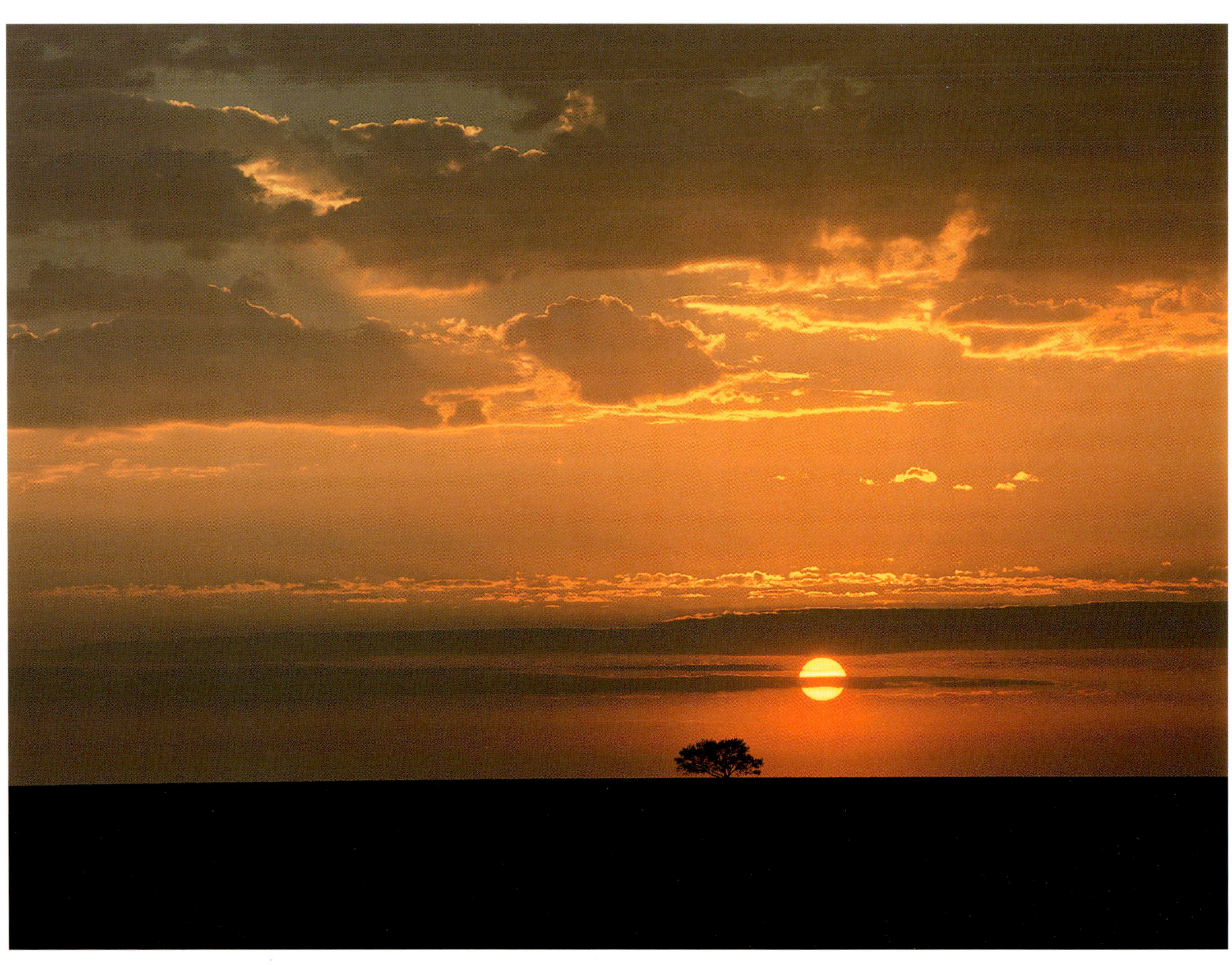

TEN MILES IN EVERY DIRECTION

Fields offer distance we can't escape,
pastures the back of God's hand.
Sandstorms remind us to behave, *slap slap,*

time's running out. Eternity's not far,
ten miles in any direction we can see
on feet made of clay. On the Plains,

we're silt without rivers, parched
with the heaped other dust. The sun
burns hotter here, sunrise ten miles away.

The horizon holds it down
for five minutes, then lets it go
like a helium balloon, floating west all day

past the jet stream. Prairie never lets us
forget we live on a hill called here.
At dusk, the sun ten miles away

torches grass fires and clouds,
fat Angus steers burned black,
the nearest neighbors' barn roof

blazing silver for seconds,
snuffed out like a candle
by a silent click of God's clock.

ROCKING FOR DAYS IN THE SHADE

In another parched summer,
Comancheros gone, we rock
on our heels by the spring,
watching buzzards circle like clocks,

calling their lazy cousins to lunch.
We sip iced tea, rolling cold glasses
on our skin. Not one thick cloud
for months, the weeds so brittle

goats snap them off like sticks.
We wonder, are we here by choice?
Great-grandfather left the cavalry
for this? After renegade bullets and arrows

he stayed in Texas where topsoil was sand
and free. He said he needed sun to heal.
The only blood he lost in forty years
dried on rocks already red.

These goats are not his goats.
Imported rams he bred were sterile,
cotton the way he kept from starving.
When he stumbled on this canyon

in smelly blues on horseback,
chasing the last straggling
Comanchero raiders
off the plains of Texas,

he retired—a hidden range,
enough water to bathe in,
far enough from others
to build a shack with a back porch

and do whatever he wanted,
rocking for days in the shade,
watching buzzards thirsty for his blood,
daring anything to make him leave.

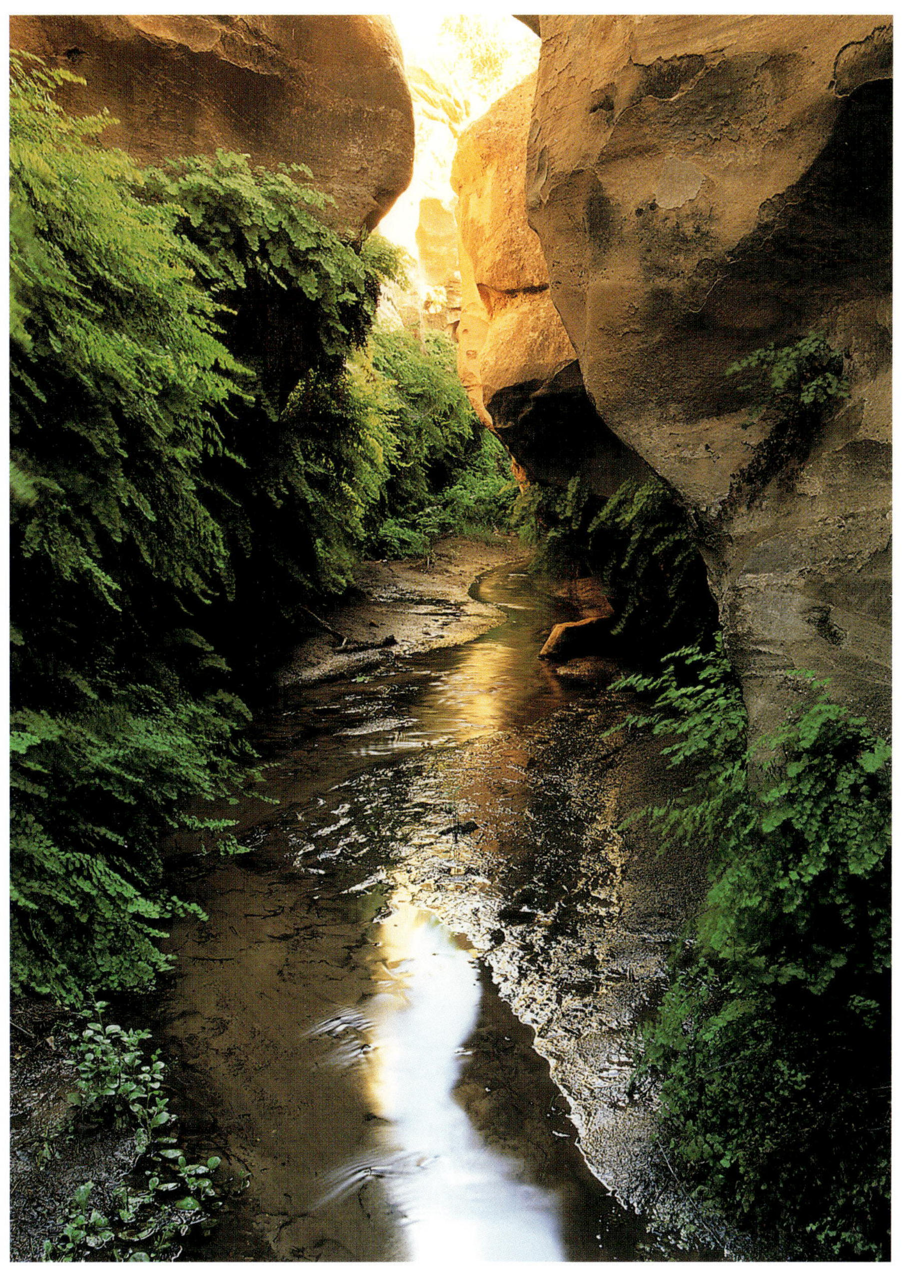

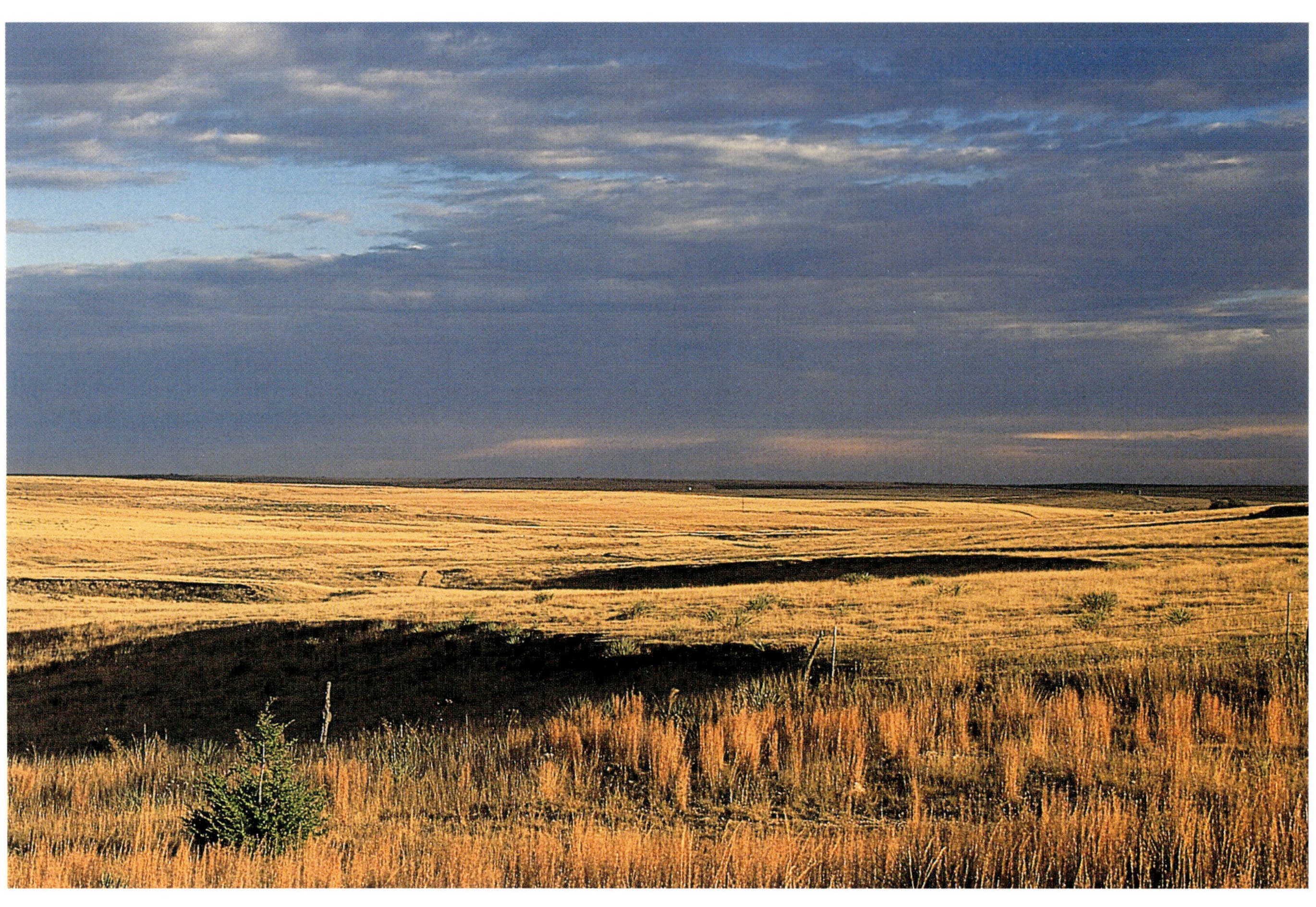

A ROUND HORIZON WITHOUT A TOWN

The prairie on any day is endless,
too much to take it in between blinks.
My wife and I aren't Atlas
toting the world. We carry the cosmos,
not a globe but stars and rocks

in a billion different directions,
if we could track them, like canoeing
the Brazos River after a rain,
ripples and flow forever changing.
Horizon is fragile on the Plains.

Grazing cattle shift, the buzzards glide,
vast details that don't match. Boots
and horses' hooves turn the globe,
and skyline scrolls. We raised four babies
on the Plains. They toddled off and fell,

shoved up and now they're gone.
Explorers learned the signs,
established trails highways bypass.
Step any direction and pastures shift,
a herd of antelopes galloping

while binoculars change hands,
strap quickly off and my wife
lifting them with a twist to fit
her eyes, counting four pronghorns
or five, not the ten I claimed I saw.

HARDSCRABBLE, TOOTH AND CLAW

Packs roam the plains, attacking abandoned pets.
Caught in the fields, most cats survive.
They scratch the eyes of dogs, the pack
maddened by blood. I've come across cats
before the buzzards found them, and blind dogs

stumbling and whining. Owls don't ask
who did it. My wife's green eyes
glean kittens from our fields like picking lint
off cashmere. Today, we found another sackful
by the road, a litter tossed from a car,

scraps for the buzzards. When we're in time,
my wife nurses cats with eyedroppers,
milk from a Jersey. They grow up
gladly in our barn, stalking mice on claws
grown perfect, their purring mouths all fangs.

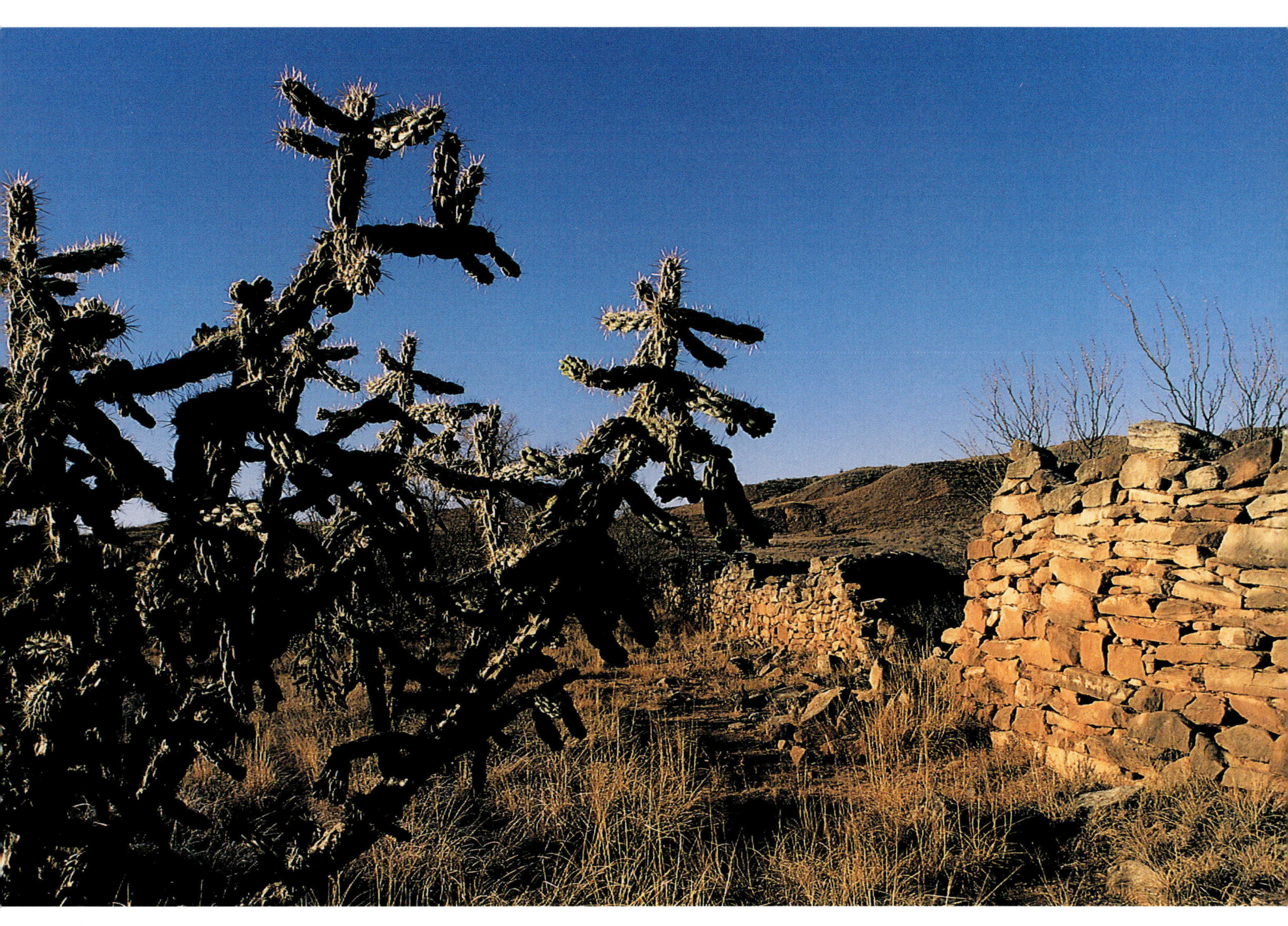

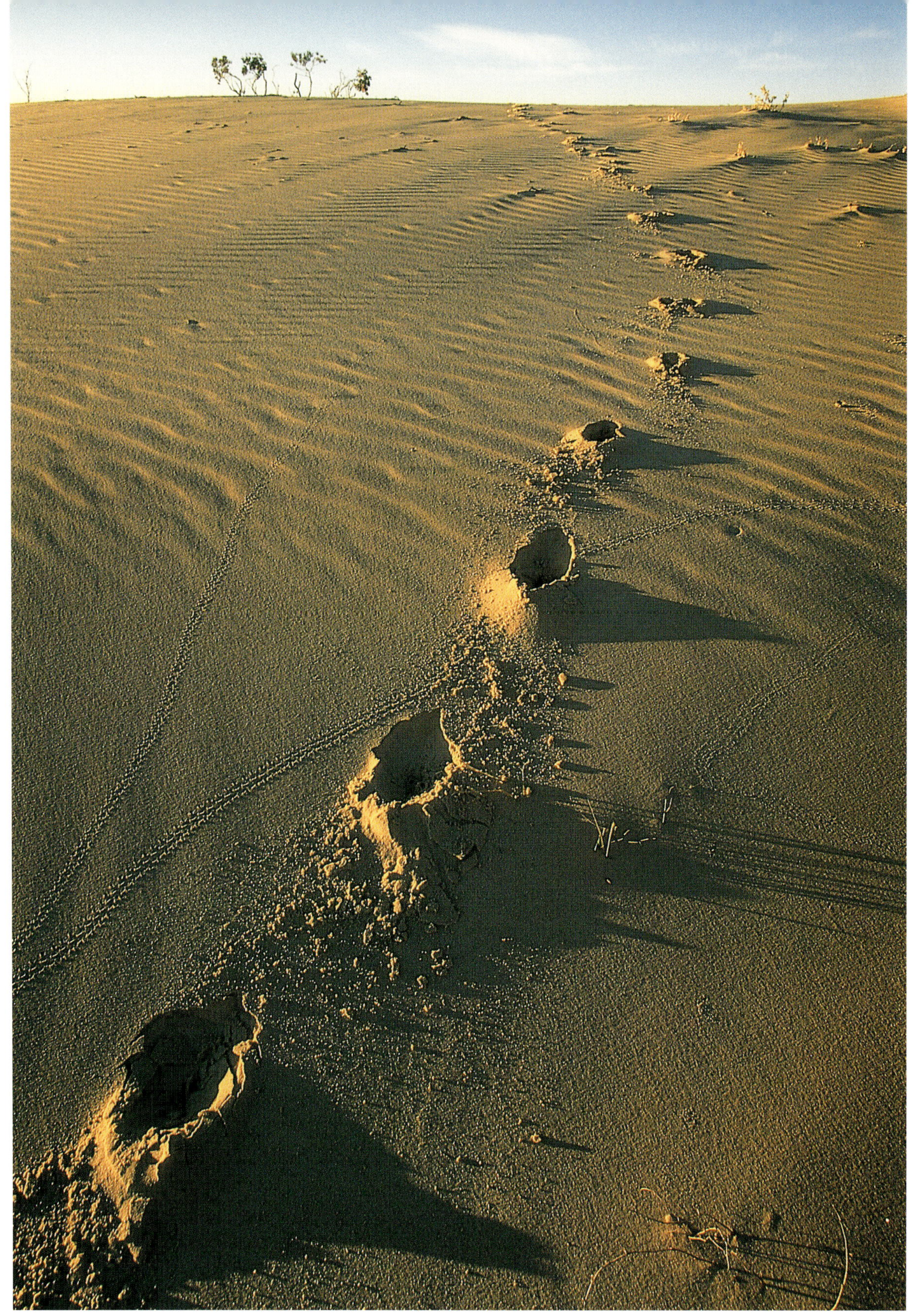

WHAT THE WIND DELIVERS

Living on wind, hawks ride out the drought.
Rodents with round eyes and rapidly beating hearts
stay in at night, ball up in burrows and dream of seeds.

A terrapin, dragging on bent legs hard as stones
his armor ridged with diamonds, sometimes seems
the only moving thing on earth too dry for plows,

a miner lost in the desert, bearing his claim
on his back, slow as rain clouds wind may bring.
Lower, slower over the sand, another is slithering,

drinking the dust, the dry ground perfect
for shedding skin, diamonds emerging on his back
bright as his eyes, which know the way to live is hard

and ancient as stones, is simply to go on searching,
rattle tip-up and silent, tongue testing the wind, the wind
knowing where, the wind always delivering.

WHEREVER PUFF GOES

I am bones and veins, a slab of meat
shrink wrapped. Even rawhide withers,
plump bacon dries, and home-smoked
venison, taped tight, evaporates.

So skin wrinkles, sags under jowls
and eyes, throats pucker like meat
in the freezer. Old age should bulge
with wisdom firm as bones,

but I am tallow soft as English sausage,
the gristle butchers slice
before plopping a pound of sirloin
on the scales. I'll never be granite,

but sand, the sift on plastic
after coffee beans are ground,
the sticky stuff on a spoon.
Lord of more than a pound

of brain and a voice box, I'm breath
under pressure, a coffee can
pierced by a blade that spins
until the lid pops loose.

Wherever puff goes, leaving dregs
when the last cup's gone, I'll follow,
wherever You are. I don't know where
or when, but know I'll go there soon.

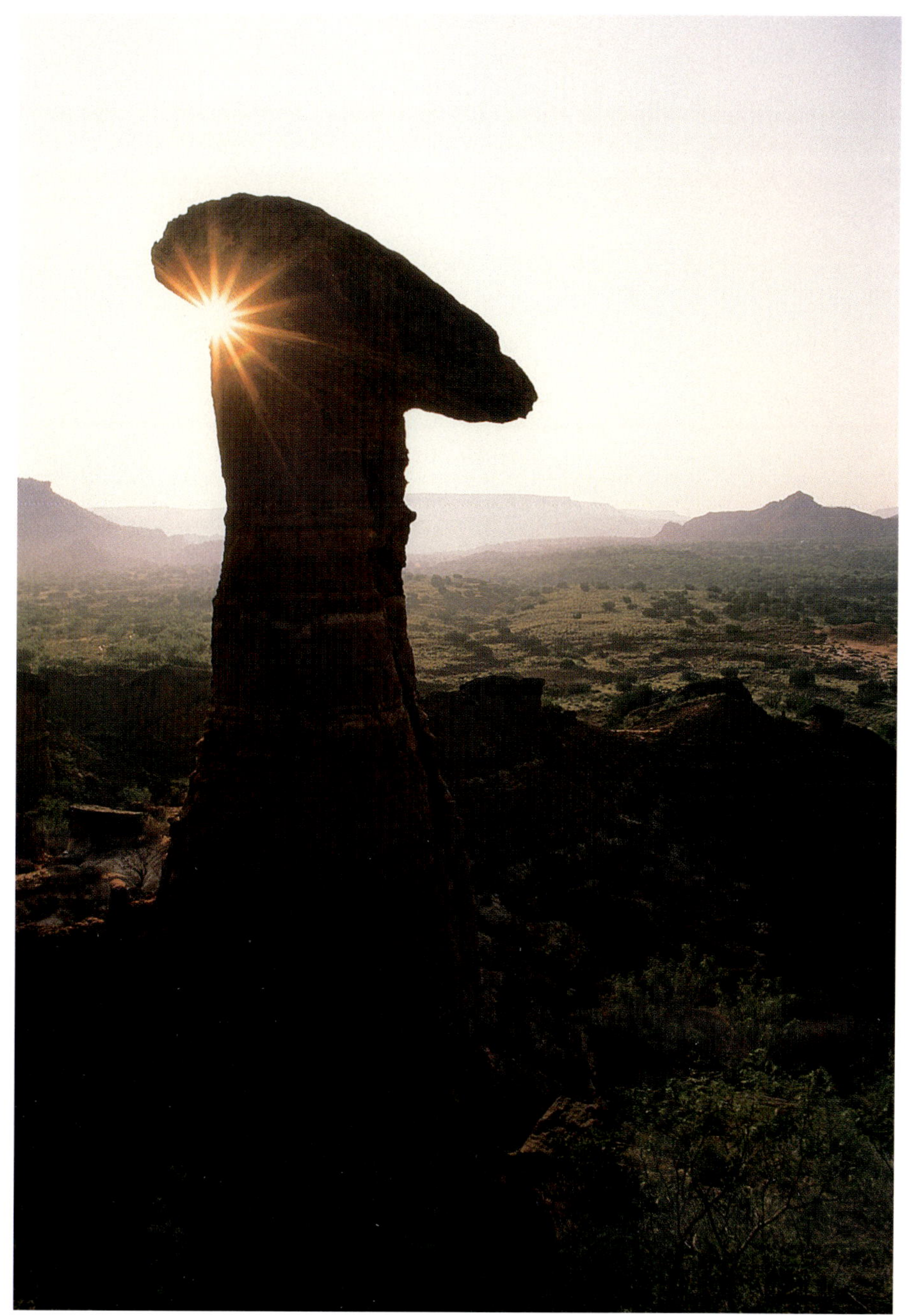

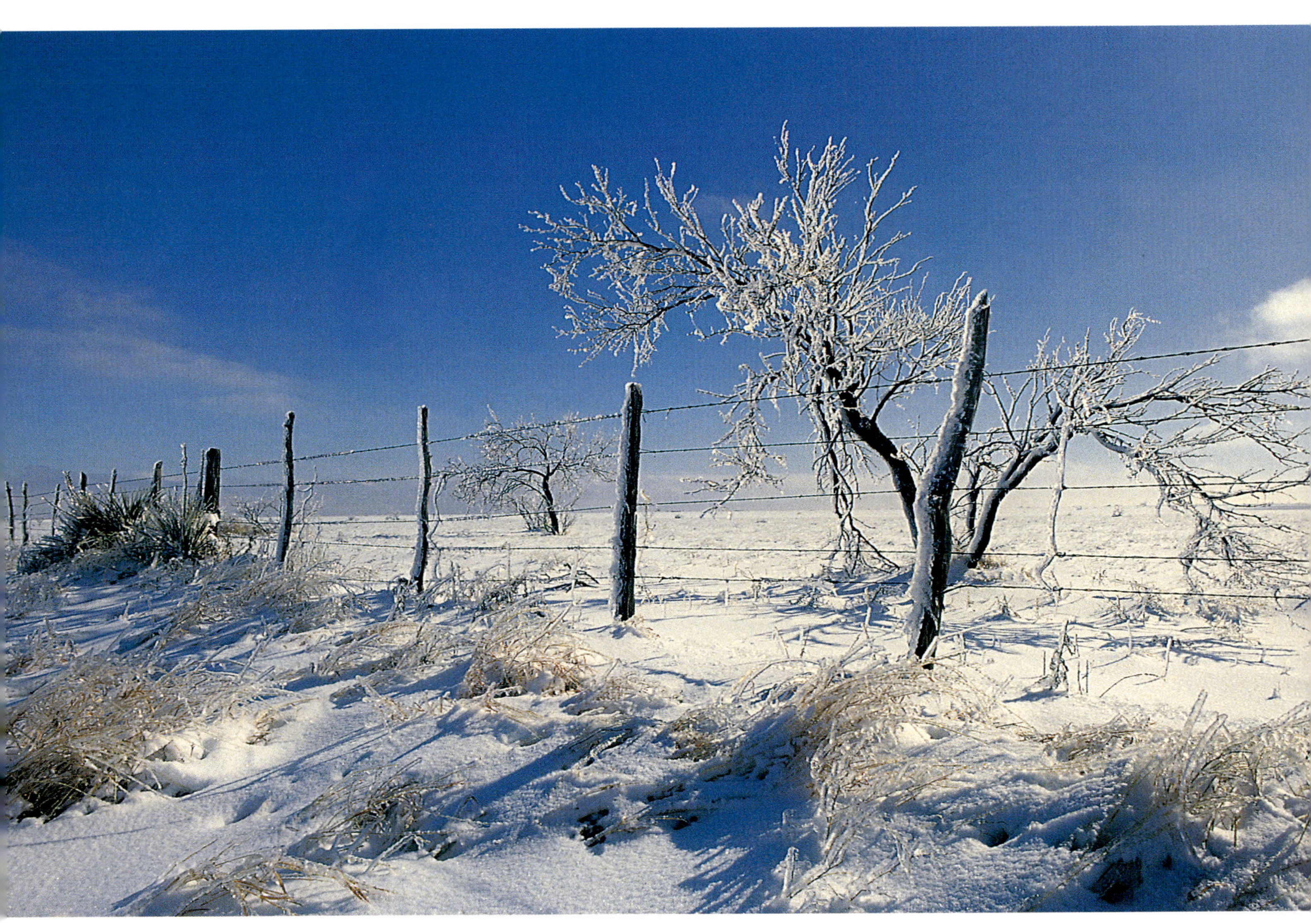

COOL WATER GUSHING FROM THE EARTH

Drifts of snow at barbed-wire posts
make starving coyotes ours. We hear them at night
in pastures they swear to the moon they own,

leaving paw prints as warrants. They prowl
under stars they also claim, plunging through drifts
by the barn, tracking our mice and rabbits.

These fields are not our fields, though we own
padlocks on a house and stalls. Our horses
dream of oats, not worried who owns them.

We lie with curtains wide and watch the ranch
fill up with snow. The Plains are flat to wide horizons,
to any town. This was the world we wanted,

no debts, wide skies to stun us. Years ago
in mountains, we raised babies like vacations,
doubting dowsers like ourselves could be at peace

without them. Now, our children have gone,
and rocky fields are home. By cactus parched
like salt blocks, we reined and dismounted,

no town, no houses anywhere. In a year of drought,
we hired a drilling rig and unloaded. Our fists
learned quickly how to witch, ears tingling

with the clang and crash of steel, shouting advice,
calling each other for help in sudden wells,
cool water gushing from the earth. Tonight

under a roof of snow, we flounce a blanket
and let it fall, crawl under and fold each other
close with all the heat we own.

IN SPRING, THE CEDAR WAXWINGS

Often, when I travel to auctions
or haul cattle to market,
my wife stays home to paint
or write the grandkids, water jays
and cardinals and in spring,

the cedar waxwings. Every day's a gift,
even at our age. Even a day's too long
to be away. I miss the crinkle of her lips,
the wrinkled suntan of her hands.
Life is grass, stunningly brief,

but abundant in so many ways.
Only yesterday in high school,
I said *I'm gonna marry that girl.*
Suddenly, seven grandkids later,
I still don't see how a man could be

this lucky, even though the moon is up
and rushing. Something's always
prowling around at night—
coyotes, rattlesnakes, owls.
We like to sit outside and rock

in darkness, even though we're out there
where it happens. We listen
to the splash and battle of bass
in the lake, the squeal of a mouse
when an owl grabs it and flaps away.

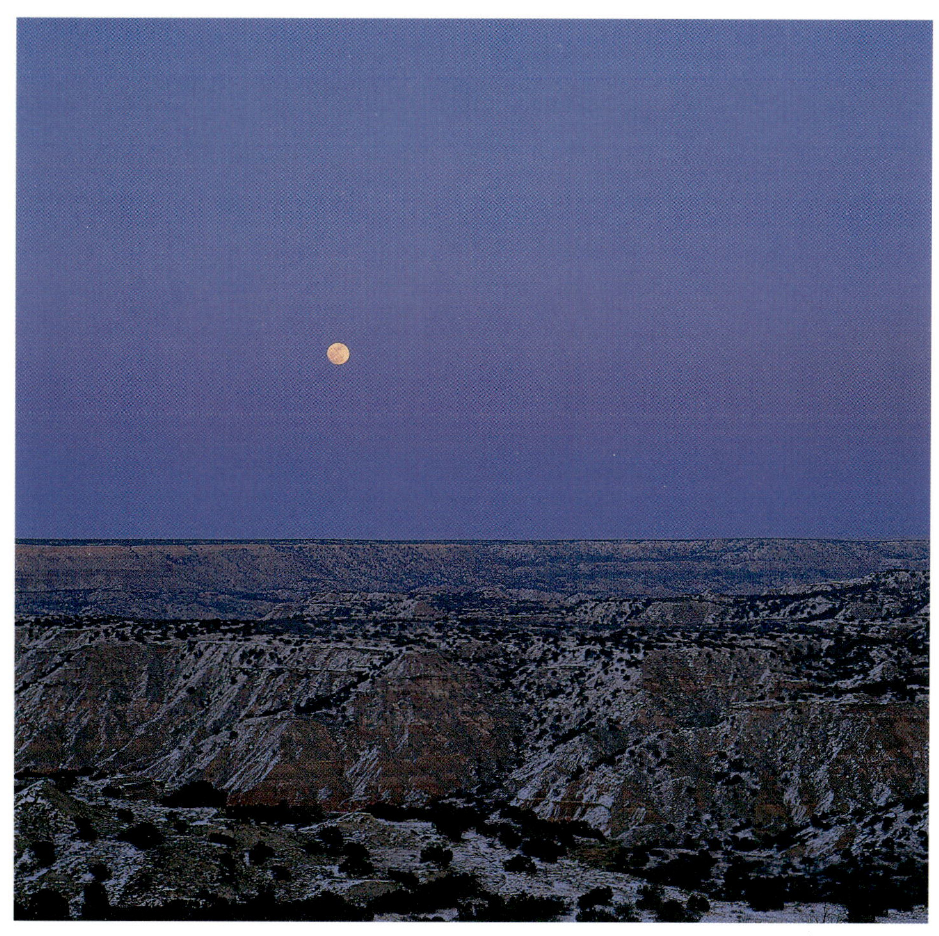

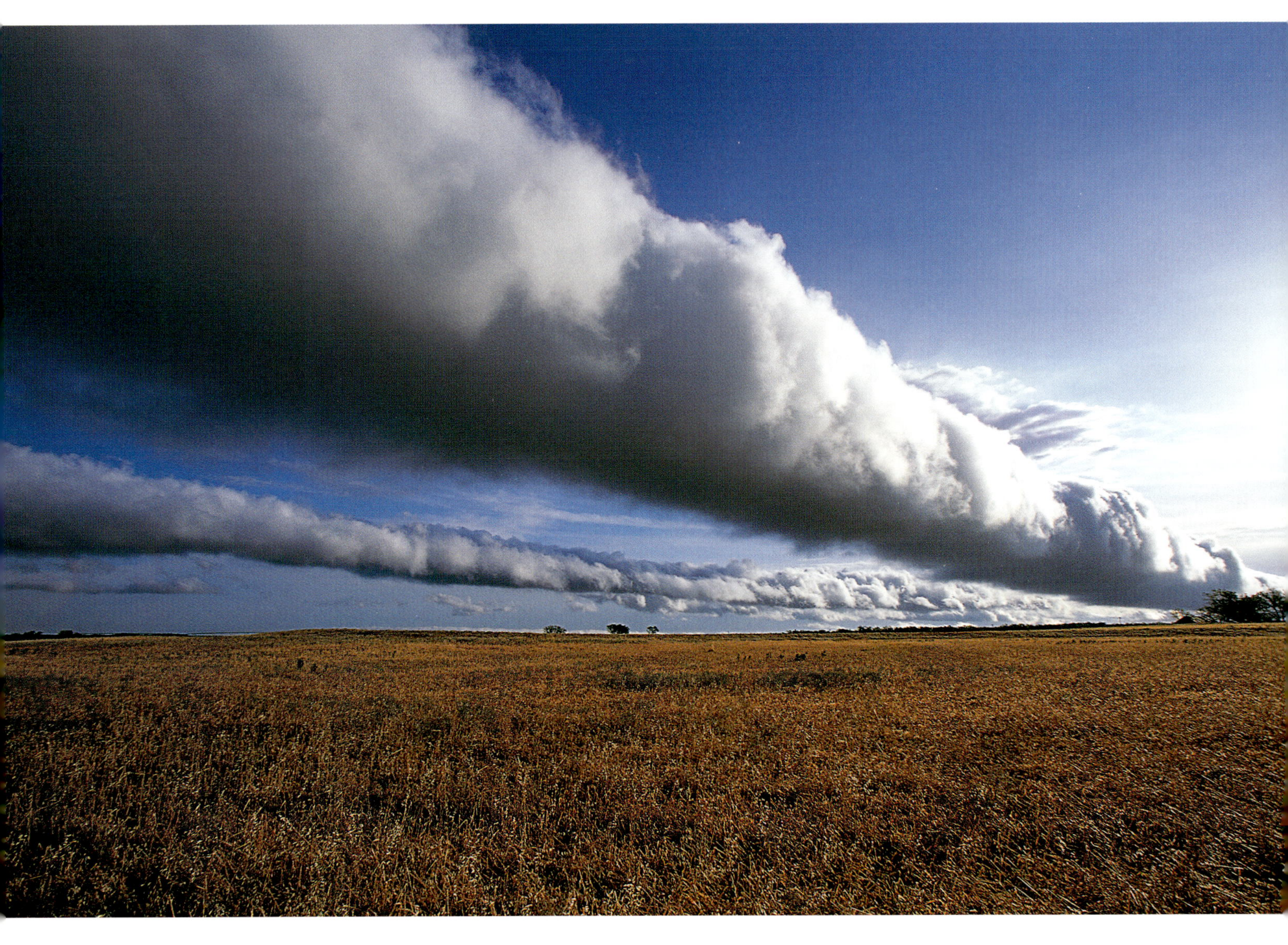

LEAVING SIXTY

Riding flat, hardscrabble plains,
we hold the reins of geldings
with fingers stiff in leather gloves.
The sun burns mirages blue as oceans:
Shanghaied, we're trapped in a fleet
of boats, these creaky bones.

Charming Columbus, his scrolls
rolled into a globe, his tales of gold
and spice enticing. Look ahoy,
they're dropping off the horizon,
old friends once young as Columbus.
The world is flat: Isabella's fool

proved that by dying, leaving a skull,
the only gold of a dunce.
Columbus found the edge of the earth
years later, and no charts
or spinning globe could save him.
Only his nurse saw the old man vanish.

Far from port, my wife and I
wave semaphores of love
like *Santa Maria* scrolls:
We're headed west, loaded with gold
and spice, stiff riggings locked,
no way to shift the sails.

CROSSING THE ROAD

What's a boy to do, both shoes caught in the tar,
the road past our house turning to street,
and me, a chicken trying to reach the other side.
Men burly as uncles swore and shook their shovels,
laughing. My mother waited on the porch,

drying her hands in her apron. My big sister teased,
her gawky girlfriends howled, and someone screamed
Tar baby! I swear I tugged, cursing the only words
I had learned, squashed down in July asphalt
like a bug, like Captain Marvel in the comics

turned into a tree, unable to budge. And of all days,
on my birthday. Carl would see me soon, and Mary Jane,
all kids I knew pointing on the curb and dancing.
Like a god roaring up on his motorcycle, my brother
dismounted and stared. Tucking a Camel in his lips,

he lit and flipped the match away, came strolling down,
fists doubled, snorting smoke, not smiling.
Massive, towering above me, he jerked me up
without my shoes and hauled me like a sack of oats
back to the grass, his own boots ruined.

I remember him that way, almost my age, not the telegram
in World War II, not the box of belongings
they sent from Okinawa, not the flag Mother hung
in the window for all cars to see speeding past
the four-lane street, pounding my sneakers down.

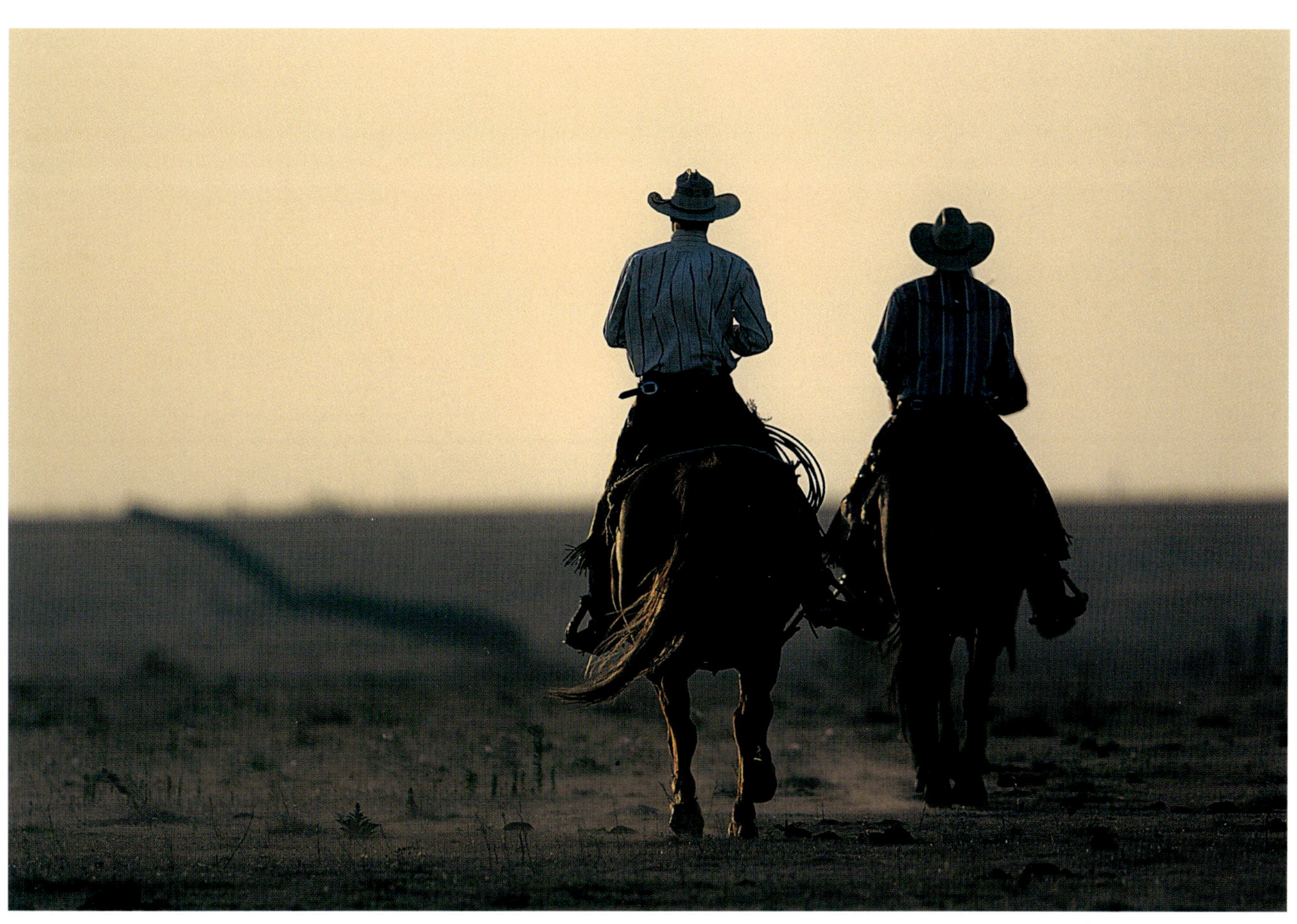

2

PRAYING FOR RAIN ON THE PLAINS

HARDSCRABBLE JUNE

I miss the dull routine of rain,
corn bogged in fields around a town
in Iowa. Here, rattlesnakes

hear the skin of cactus stretch
and squeak like leather. No wonder
rattlers love drought that boils

the odor of mice. Months without clouds,
the ranch is awash in mirage,
a rich man's tongue in torment,

horses I'd trade for camels.
Plunder is what bobcats
and starving coyotes do to barns

and chicken coops. Roosters,
watch out: they know who rules the roost,
and you're dead meat if caught asleep,

your hens dragged off to pups
or dusty caves for kits with wide
wet eyes and teeth already sharp.

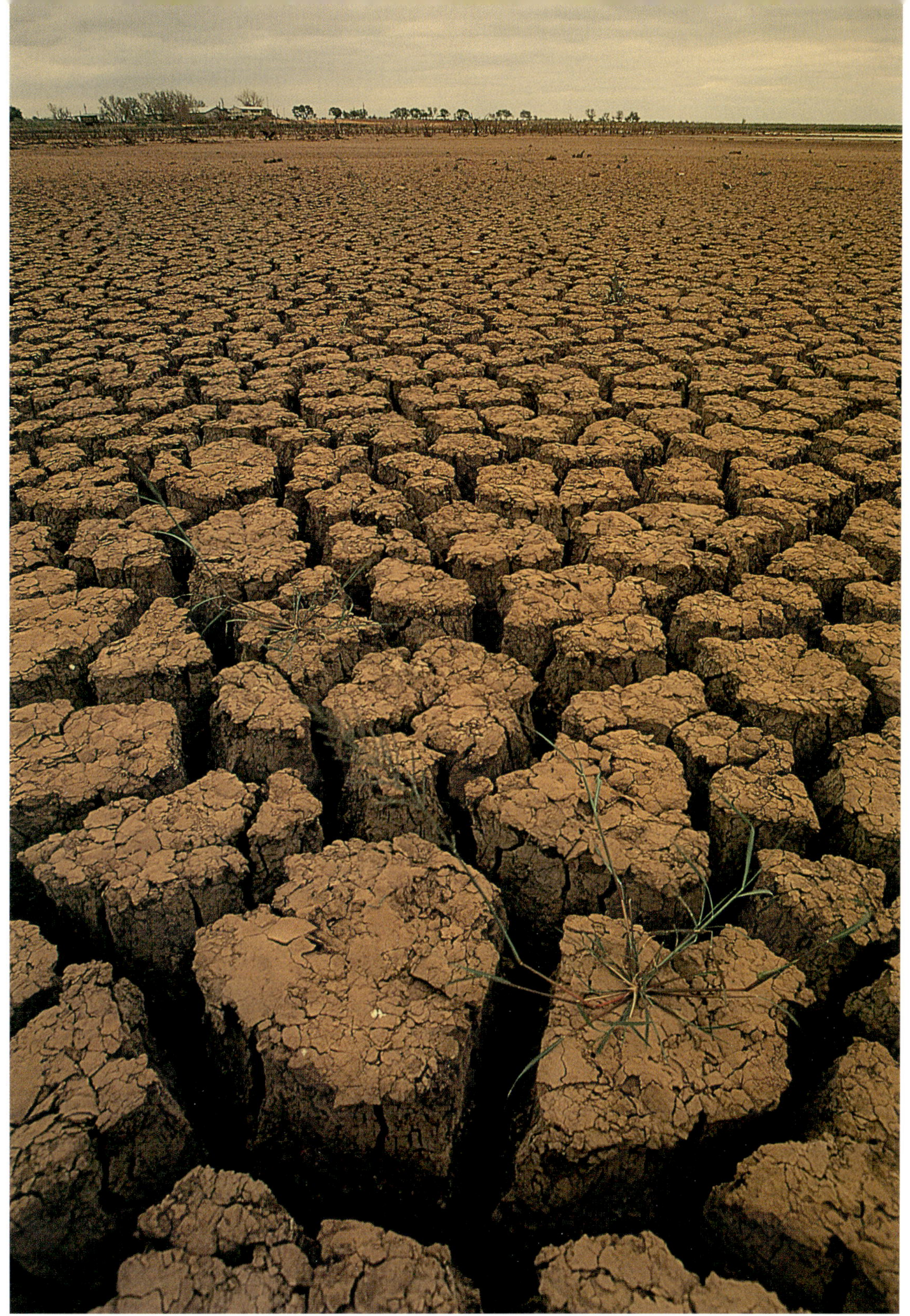

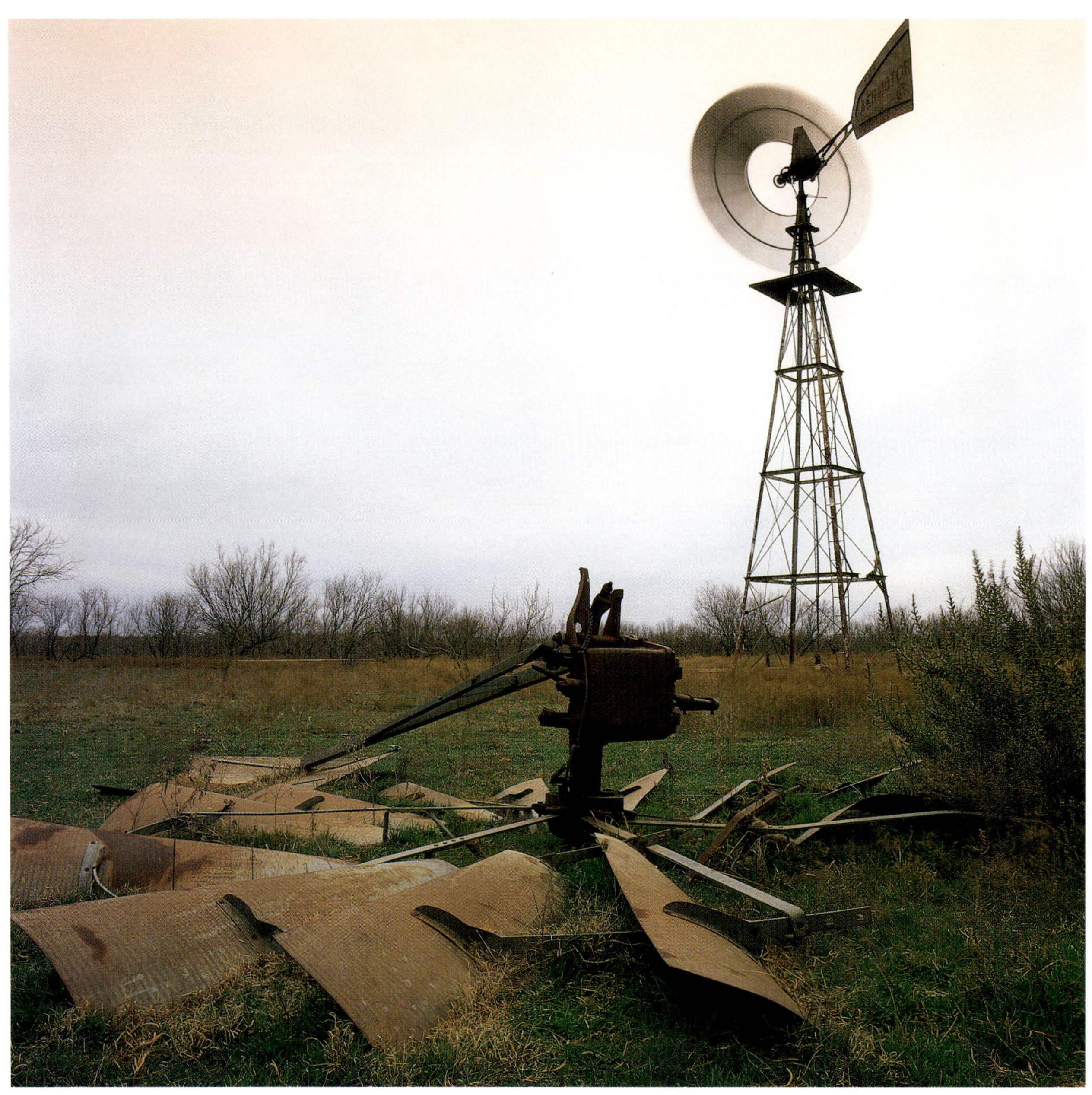

WISHING FOR MORE THAN THUNDER

Mirages hover like angels fanning the fields.
We see them in summer, a shimmer of wings.
Our stubborn steers ignore them, wading dry acres.
They hook their horns in invisible robes,

shaking their heads to graze. For them
the sky is falling, the grass is manna.
Having lost all hope when they entered
the round corral as calves, they stuff themselves

even in drought, as if all pastures
on the Plains are theirs. They never wonder
if God's in His heaven. Stubble is fodder enough,
alfalfa paradise. Watching steers graze

in a lake of shimmering light, seeing angels
fanning themselves, we wonder if even they
could make it rain, how many spin on a windmill,
how many squeezed would make a decent cloud.

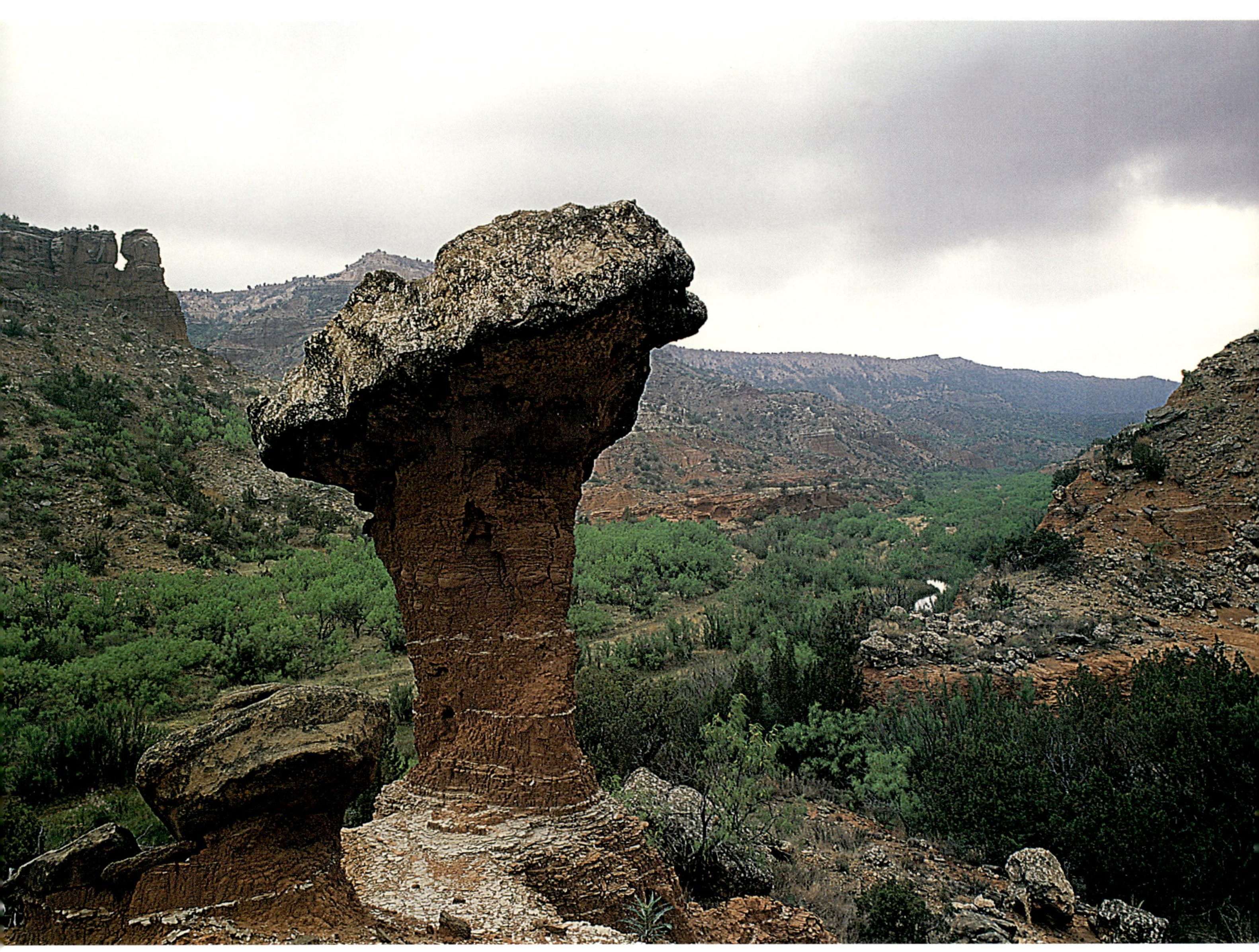

ON A SATURDAY AFTERNOON IN THE COUNTRY

Not once in the canyon west of here
had we ever killed a thing. And so
the afternoon we saw the buzzards
swirling like a whirlwind,
we knew they had found what they needed

without us. We sat on the screened-in porch
picking them off with our fingers,
eyes squinted against the sun
they soared across, dull black against
the light, the blackest we'd ever seen,

and on a day when nothing
was happening to us, rocking,
one of us thinking of something
to say to break the silence,
shelling our black-eyed peas for supper,

when down in the canyon something
came to our minds, something still
and final, teeth bared and grinning,
something that made it that far
up the canyon, this time.

WHEN THE CHILDREN HAVE GONE

What could we say, for they heard rumors:
something was out there that shouldn't be,
futures only they must own.

They rose on silver wings and disappeared,
far from summer sun on prairies.
Driving back after a week with grandkids,

we pass the asphalt hours by naming pelts
of flattened rattlers, coyotes,
crushed armadillos. What needs a meal

clacks its beak and staggers oddly off
into the sun, fat belly sagging, black wings
flapping a tight possessive spiral back to bones

belly up under the thump of tires
with nothing better to do than swerve.
Back home, we listen to coyotes howling

songs they've sung for years. My wife believes
in the peace of dark, the burning stars.
I watch light shimmer on her face,

her flashing eyes. Now it begins,
the gold and purple of the Plains. Blink
and miss it, like flecks of silver in her hair.

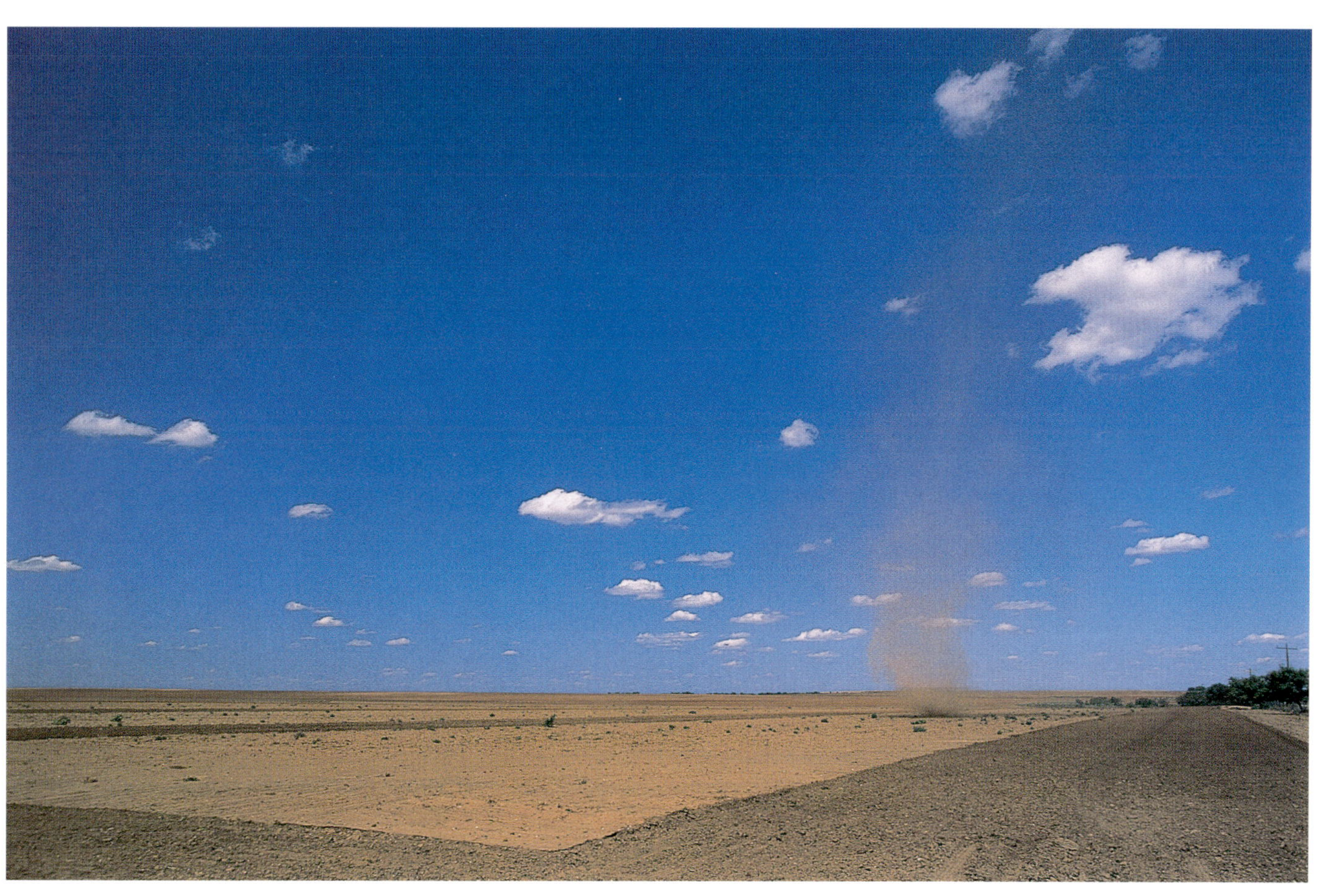

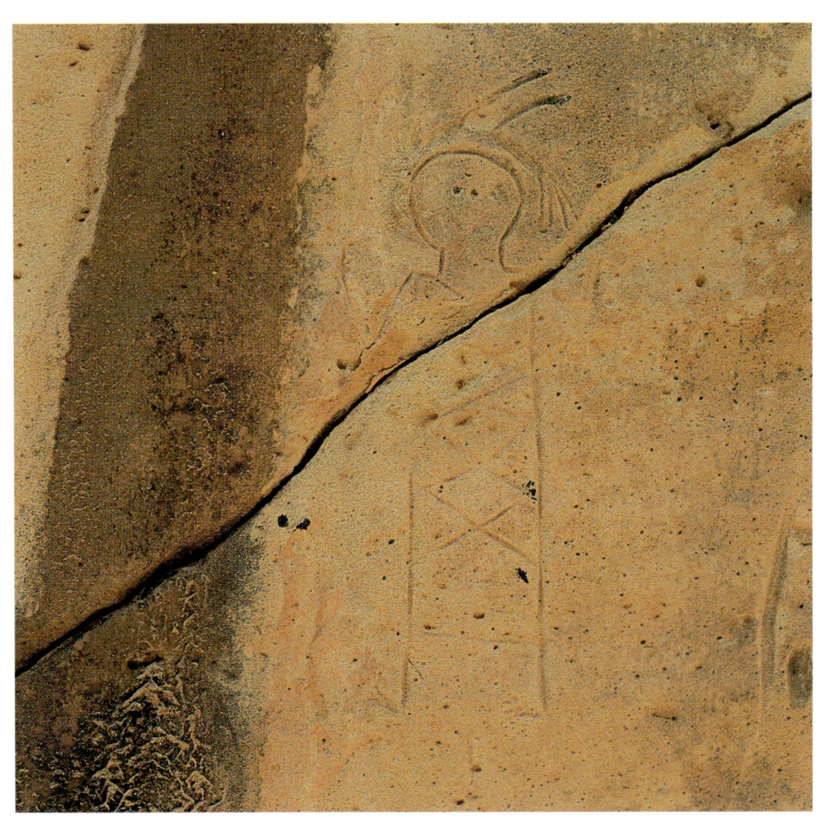

REMBRANDT AND THE ART OF MERCY

They say the luster of gold addicted him
to fat, round guilders' purses.
They claim his florid nose exposed
a painter's lust, that even the scent of stiff,
splayed bristles glazed with oils aroused him,

and skin like honey on the tongue
provoked him, made him pose models sweating
till they wept. They claim he painted haunted faces,
that nothing glistens but their hats and helmets.
Yes, what he loved and pitied most was flesh

that's caught but never saved by canvas. Consider
his florid elders astounded by Susanna bathing,
his naked Danaë with her god of gold. Behold
the fragile, eggshell flesh of sad Bathsheba,
her toes and thighs scrubbed slowly

for a king. If only he could capture those
in ocher, rub her troubled eyes so they could see.
Notice the gold, pig-bristle swirls that touched
his dying Saskia's neck, her honey lobes,
the sweaty radiance of her breasts.

THE WINTER DADDY DIED

I propped the rifle by the hearth
and pulled my wet boots off.
Mother slit and ripped the hide
like skinning a chicken. If rabbits bother you,

she'd say, don't bring the dead things back.
I washed my hands, the fur, the sticky blood.
Water already boiled, the big vat
spattering, potatoes and carrots chopped.

Rabbit stew and aroma of bread
woke Daddy up, in spite of cattle snowbound
last night, his beard frozen when he stomped
and came inside at dawn. Mother whispered

Go back to sleep. She closed the door
that creaked, turned down the stove
and poured the buttermilk, broke bread
and melted cheese. My brother shivered

until she lifted him to her lap,
and we sat eating by the fire. Flames
turned to sparks, the snow-wet pine logs
popped, steam hissing from pockets of trapped sap.

My brother reached up and touched her hair.
She raised his cup and let him sip.
Wind made the chimney moan,
the orange flames flick. Broth bubbled

behind us, and Mother hummed,
carrots and onions and wild meat.
Daddy had split enough logs until summer,
stacked high against the house.

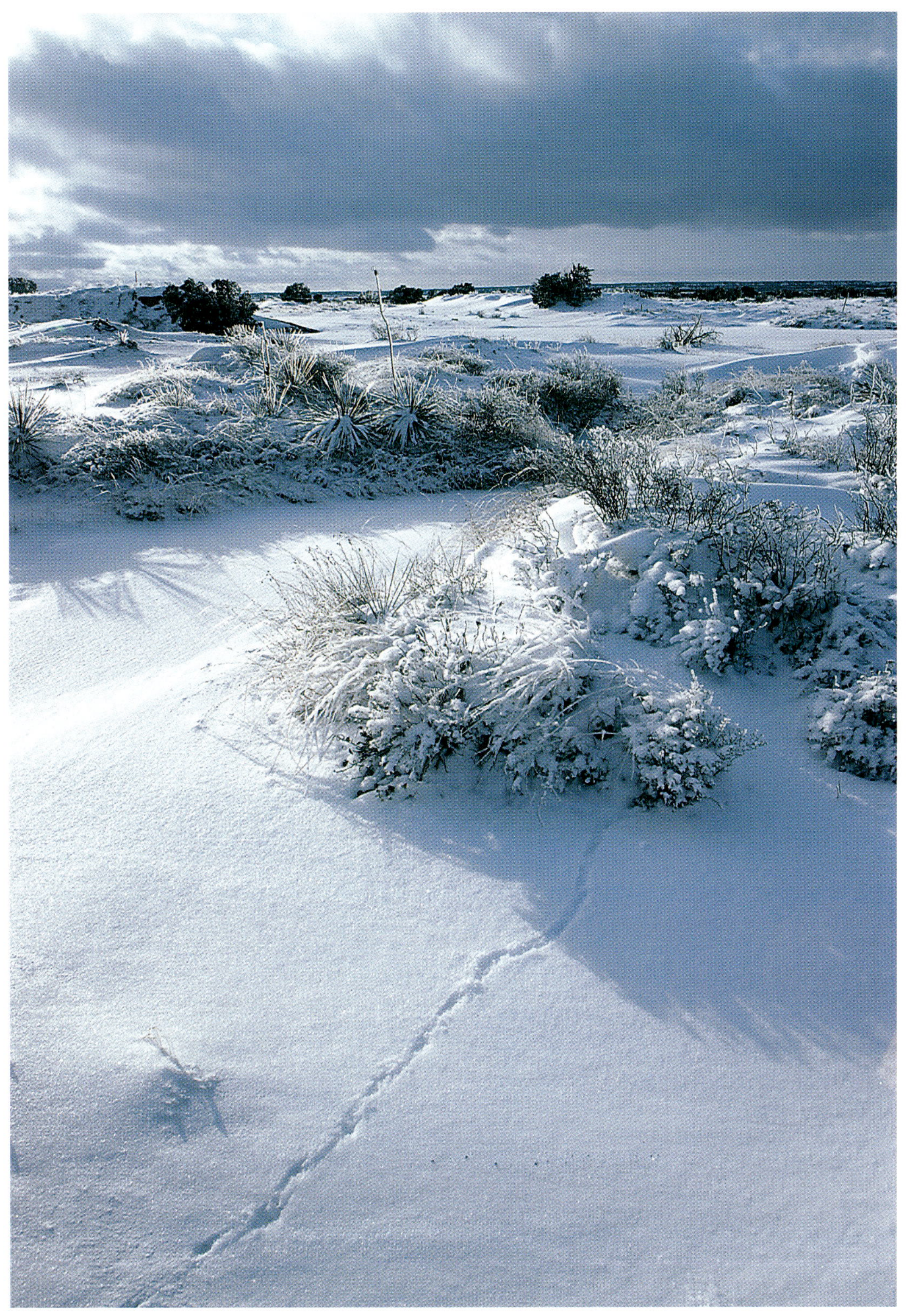

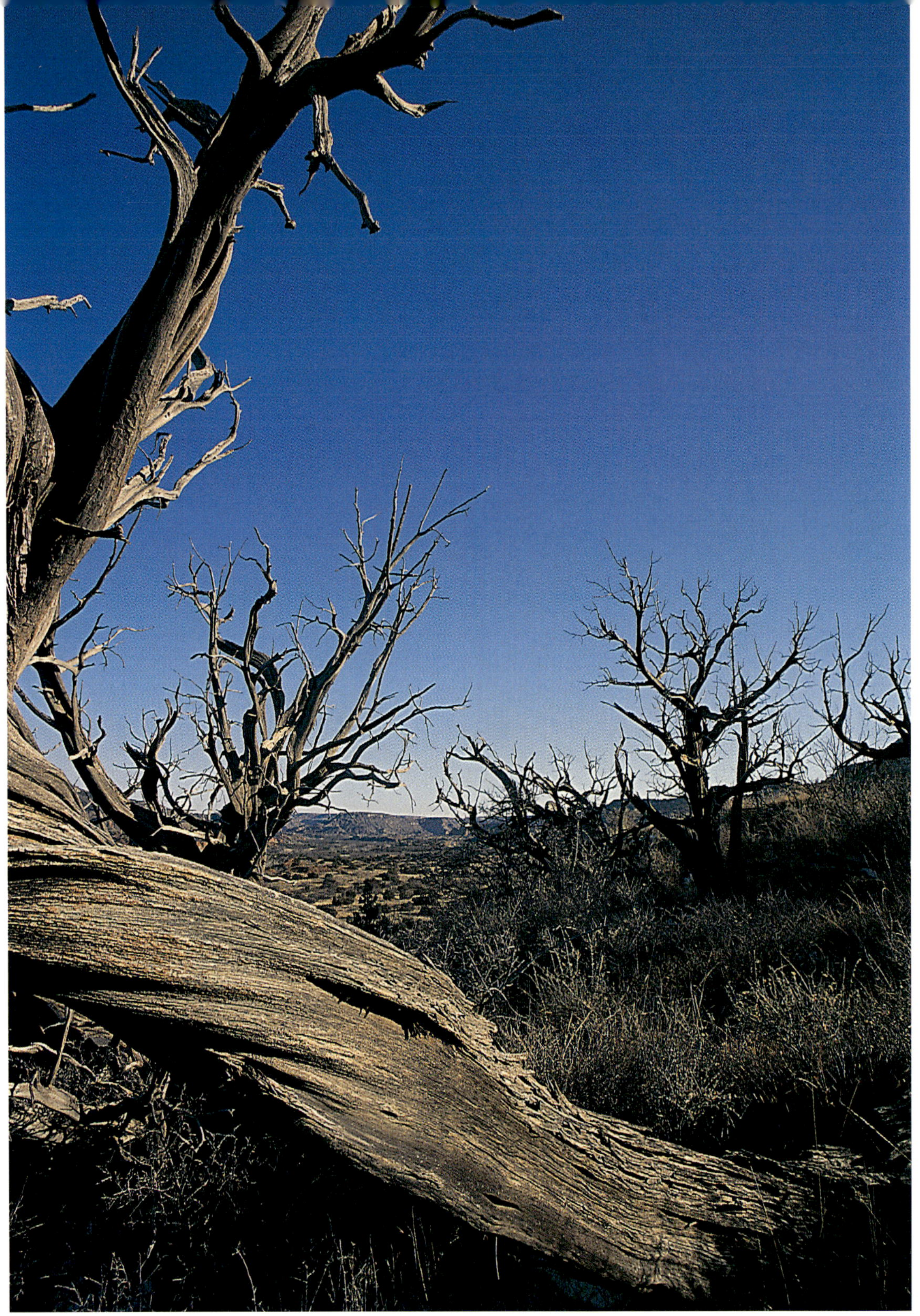

BLACK WINGS WHEELING

I've seen her lift a calf
half-starved, lost in a thicket,
carry it twisting between mesquites
from cow to cow until one
full-uddered and lazy
would take it. She believes

nothing should be alone for long.
Every drought, we find buzzards
stacked in a spiraling cylinder,
red heads and fanned black wings,
tip feathers pronged like knives,
coasting, waiting for something to lie down

under a black circling mobile
and close its eyes. Grass-stubble
clings to caliche, crackles when anything
tries to run silently away—
lizards with slit mouths, lost dogs,
does with wild eyes and rapidly beating hearts.

IN GUSTY WINDS THIS WILD

Hawks don't hunker down in burrows
when it blows. Their claws dig hard
on posts against stiff wind.
Sand gashes the skin like glass.
People pop their contacts out
and weep the scratches clean.

Hawks on barbed wires bob
and ride it out, beaks to the wind,
wings tight as if diving. In April,
wind pounds daily from the west.
Nothing flies in gusty winds this wild,
not even hawks. Like that one

across the road, caught
near our mailbox. Here,
squeeze the binoculars
and watch those feathers flounce.
Watch the claws, that splendid head.
His eyes don't even blink.

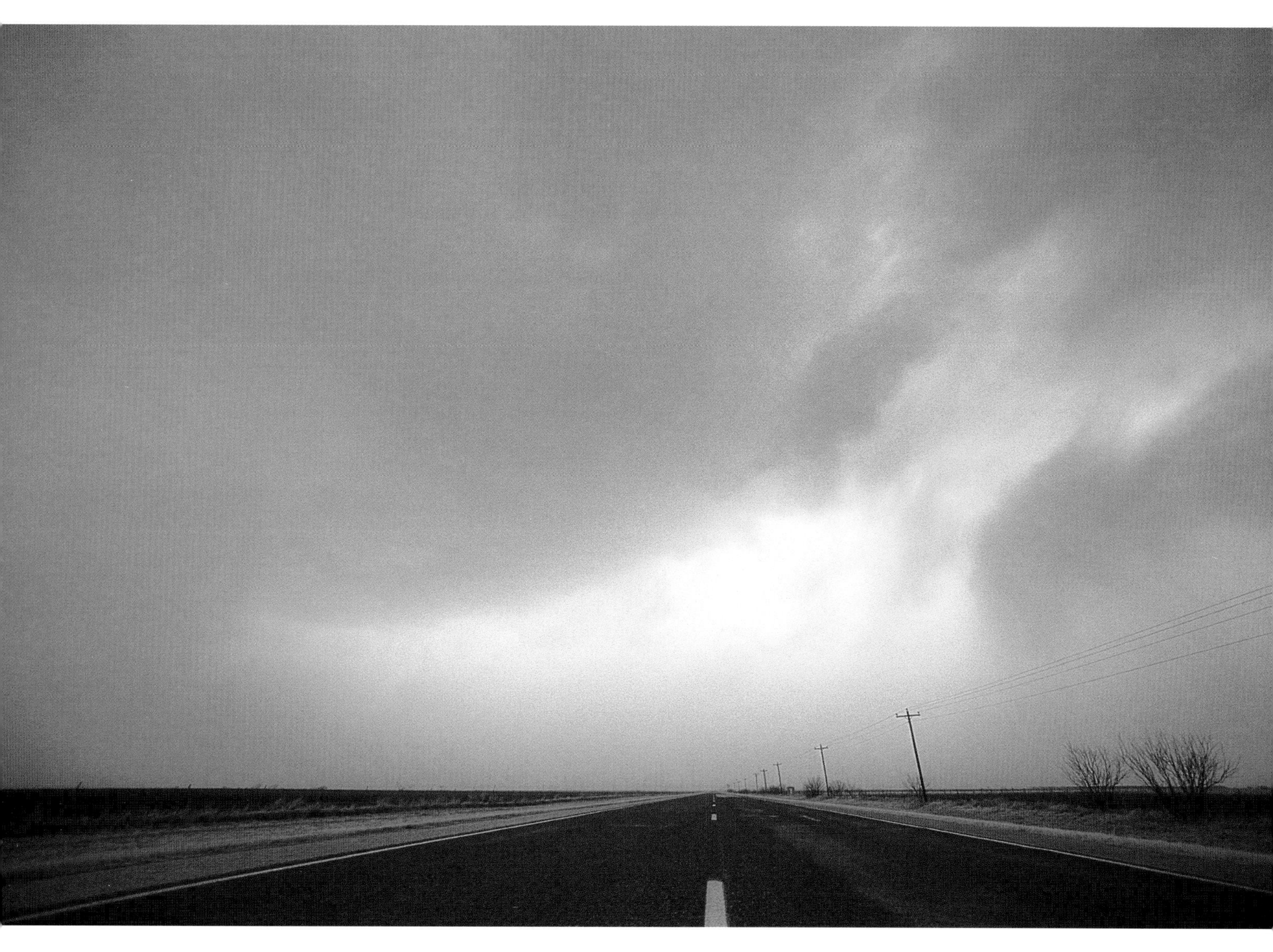

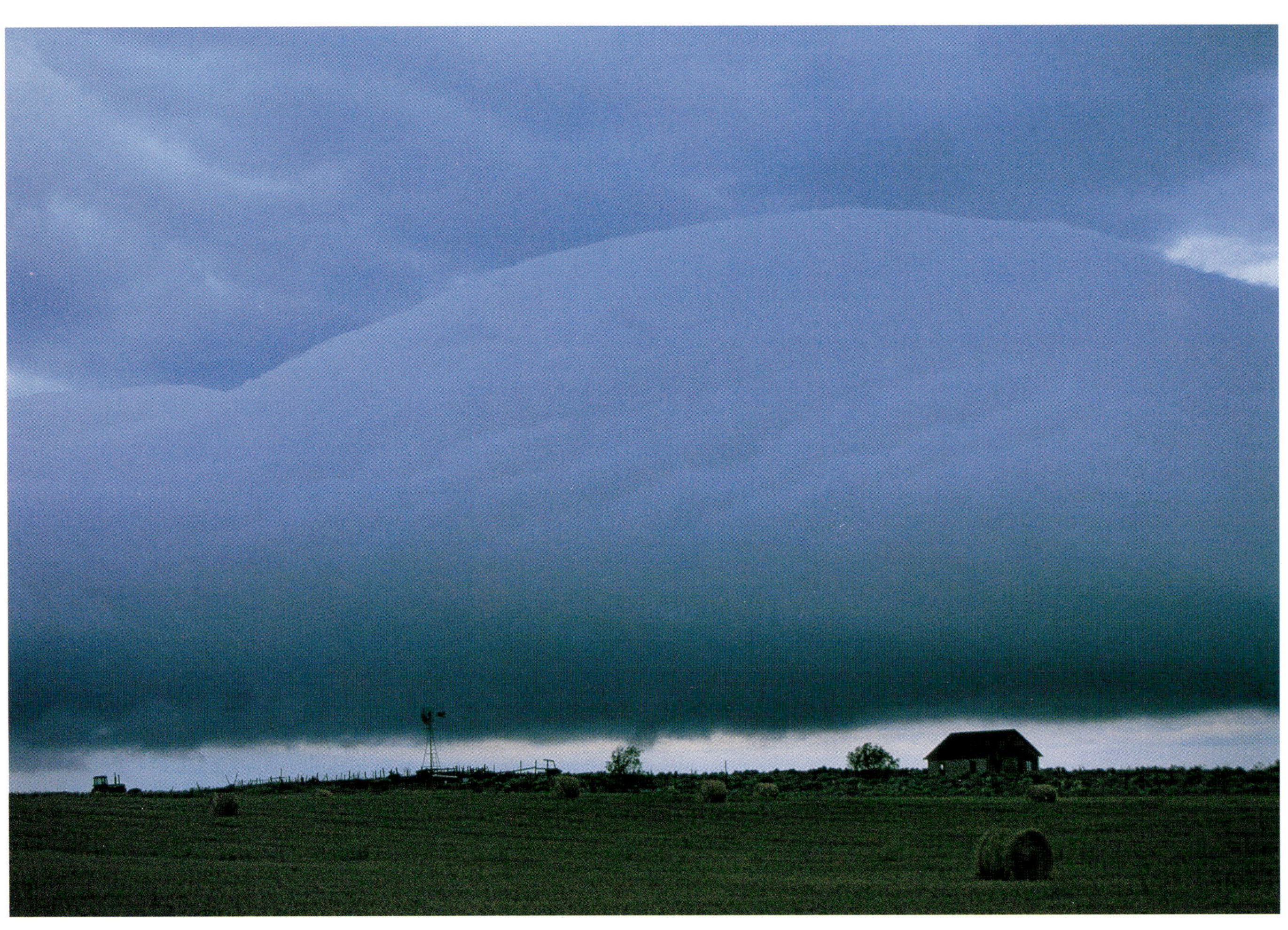

PRAYING FOR RAIN ON THE PLAINS

If it comes,
let tractors stall hub-deep.
Pull off your boots and walk without socks,
squeeze globs of what you are. Feel mud like Vaseline,
the crushed and processed ferns and dinosaurs.
In a million years we'll ooze from vaults
and metal caskets, back in the mud where we belong.
Even West Texas dirt grows beans and cotton,
peppers that make us weep. Let rain come
by the bucket, let prices soar after floods,
let it hail. Pastors throughout the Plains have prayed.
Farmers who sulk at home and tinker with plows
while their wives drive pickups to church,
even burned, skin-cancer atheists
stare at flat horizons without a cloud
and blink.

LET THUNDER RATTLE THE GLASS

At last, loud thunder's ours,
cloudbursts and hail. Pastures
and coyotes claim the rain
we prayed for. Call the bank,
even that cautious banker's awake,
enough rain to plant sorghum.

Fill up the mugs and come to bed,
let thunder rattle the glass,
bashing us both to silence
beside the blinds raised high.
I'll raise the windows and let rain
splash the screens. Lean back

and sip hot coffee till it's gone.
Lightning gashes the night
like lake ice shattered. Come,
rock softly in the dark
and hold me, woman,
this storm won't last for long.

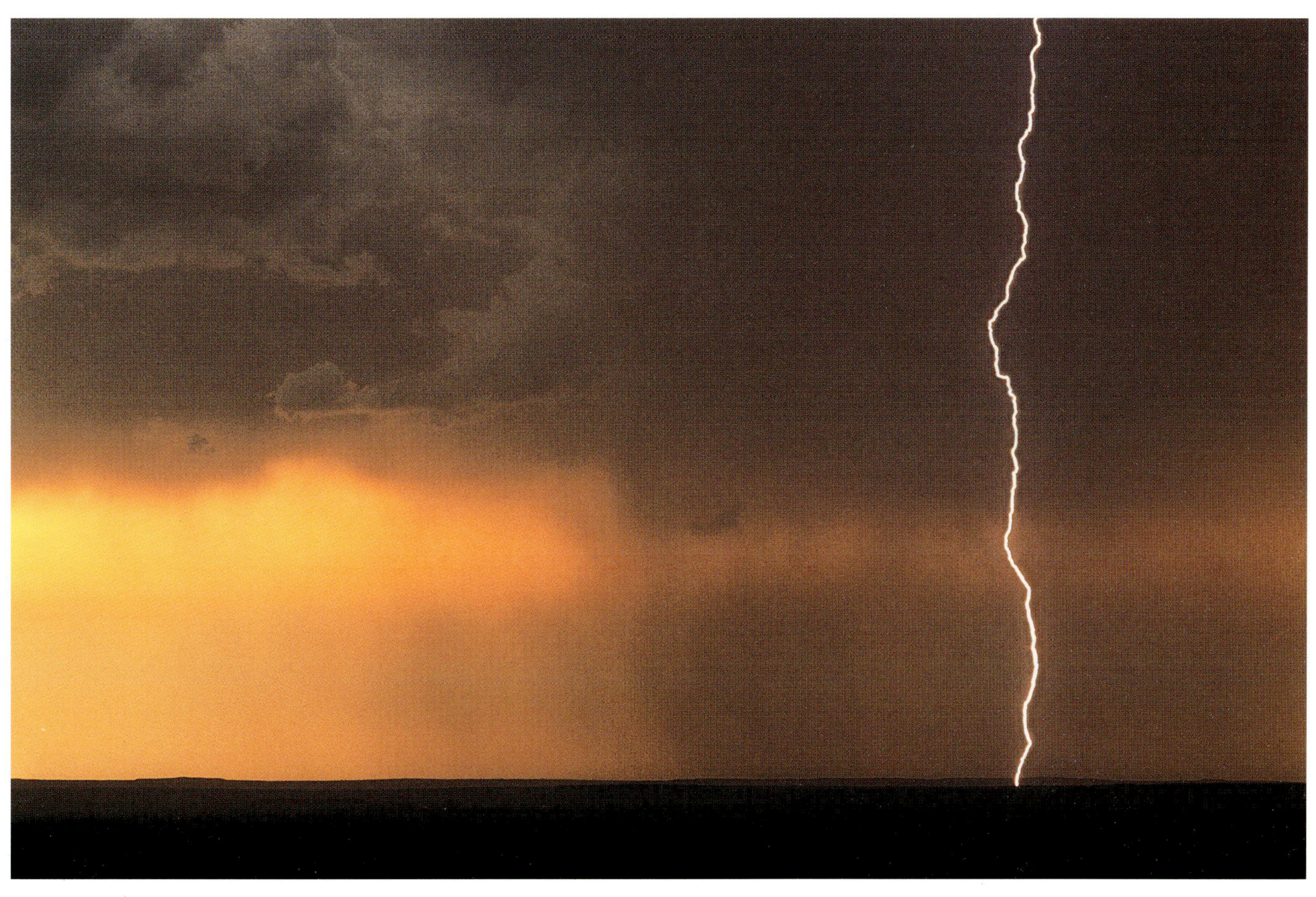

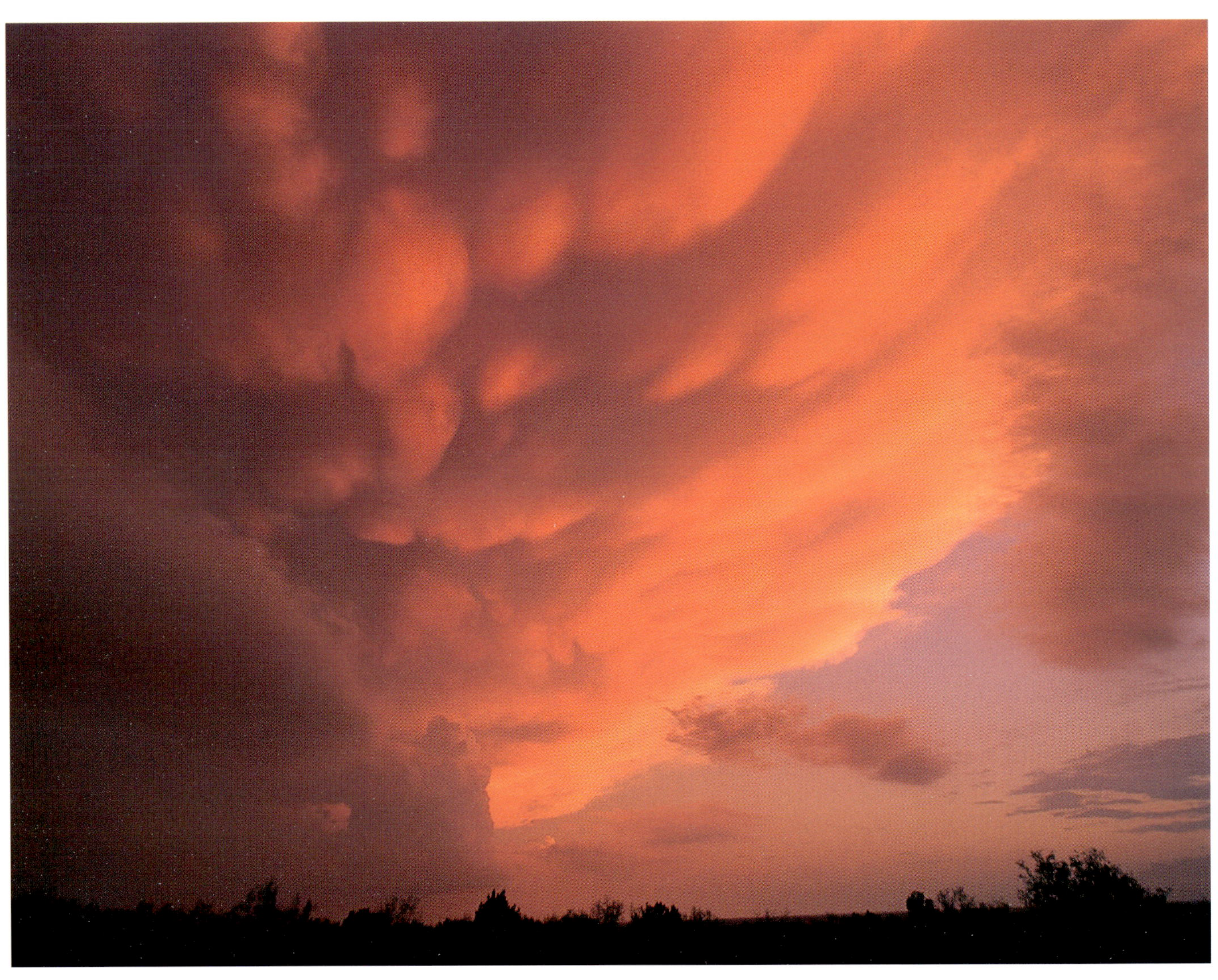

WHAT PLUMP MISS PRITCHERT TAUGHT

In training class, Miss Pritchert whispered
Rain in drought is hallelujah baptism,
a Jacob's ladder we could climb. Showers
are heaven's answer to prayers, any storm

the promise of bowls overflowing.
But old Deacon Howard found the devil
in details, boys bored in Sunday School.
Follow a rain drop fast as it falls, *plop!*

it's gone. *That's us,* Deacon Howard howled,
slapping us silly with nonsense. *Right, rain drops,*
Earl scribbled on a Bible's flyleaf and winked,
head cocked, a pound of brown hair in his eyes.

If rain is your way to heaven, Howard shouted,
the rope's undone, pitched overboard and tumbling
like a waterfall, an avalanche of trite petitions
dying as they fall. Dogs and cattle drown,

snakes wash away down arroyos. Oak trees
float in the Brazos after storms, old cars
bob along like trash from the trailer park.
Thunder cracked, and Deacon Howard hushed.

But oh, those saucy girls between training class
and church, giggles in the hall like sleet,
teasing us along as they pranced, almost dancing,
some girls with bulges in their hips and bras.

We shouted above hard rain and shoved,
hoping they'd turn, wait up, pass notes
back to us, secrets plump Miss Pritchert taught
them alone, maybe drawings of what boys want

and girls shouldn't do, what happened to wives
not sung about in Psalms, why Jezebel went bad,
what Eve dreamed about, what luscious Delilah
did to Samson, and how many times.

HOME ON THE RANGE

We coiled barbed wires under thunder,
oak posts so old they were pulp
tumbled by cavorting calves, time to drag
posts back to the barn to burn.

Whoever built that fence went broke,
four times too many nails, posts split
and wound with bailing wire. Rain
turns the plains to muck that stalls pickups

and hobbles mules. Only a mile to go,
so my sons and I kept ripping off wires
and winding, heaving stiff bundles to the truck
up to the hubs in weeds. Rain made barbed wires

shine, great lonely places of the Plains.
All that, decades ago, today only a shower
and rainbow. Our children rose and flew away
to Tahiti, Dallas, Spain, and now we're alone

with our thirtieth herd, another barbed-wire fence.
Nights on the swing we're surrounded by pasture,
fat cattle safe, four dogs that startle coyotes
from lakes a mile away. Rocking, I watch

the moonlight in her eyes, the haze
of silver in her hair. Windmills whir the same
old songs, roar of tires on the highway,
headlights of neighbors coming home.

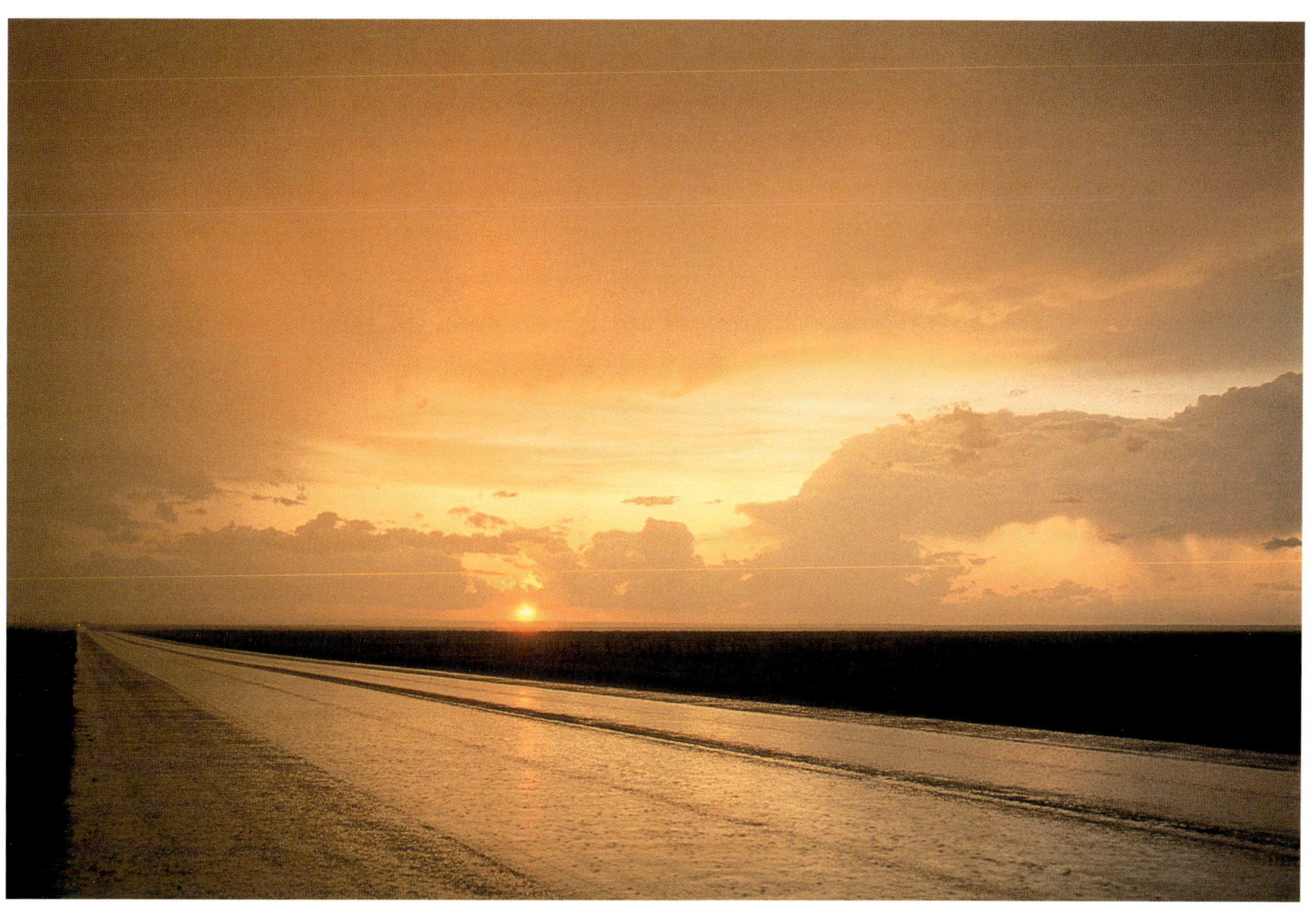

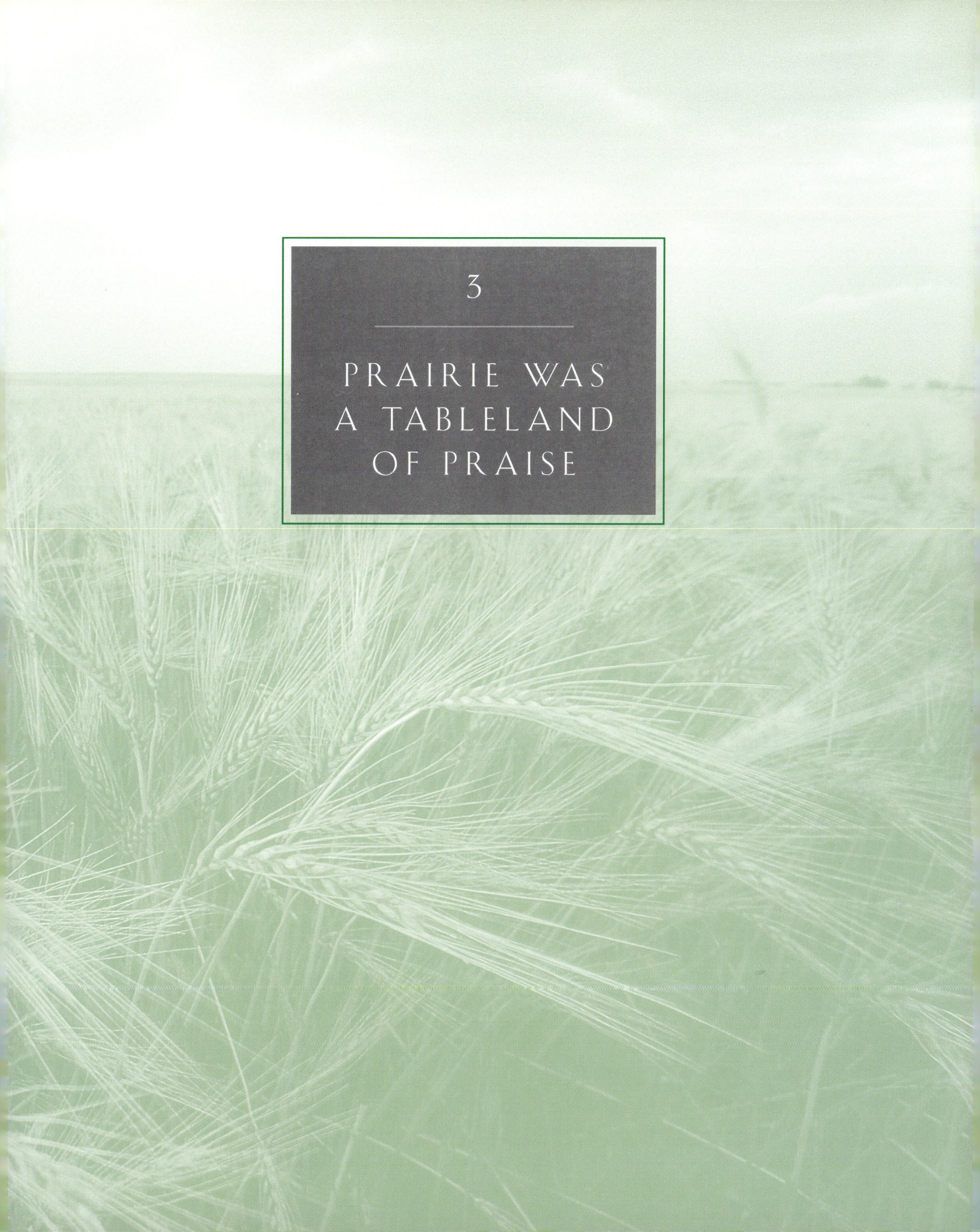

3

PRAIRIE WAS A TABLELAND OF PRAISE

FINDING MY FATHER'S HANDS IN MIDLIFE

What enters my hand is stiff
and cold, like old leather,
rough like the hide of a bull.

So this is the fist
of my father, the fist
he fed me with, the claw

my hand turns into. Even the nails
are his, brittle and thick, beveled
when I hold them under light.

Broad fingers, puffed at the joints,
knuckles of both fists buckled,
crisscrossed with lines like scars.

I see his blood in veins here
and here, like dry Texas streams
that flow and disappear in limestone.

When I make a fist, I see his
half-moon thumb fold over four
tight fingers, a picture of family,

that big thigh-muscle shank
of his thumb something we closed on,
muscle we loved.

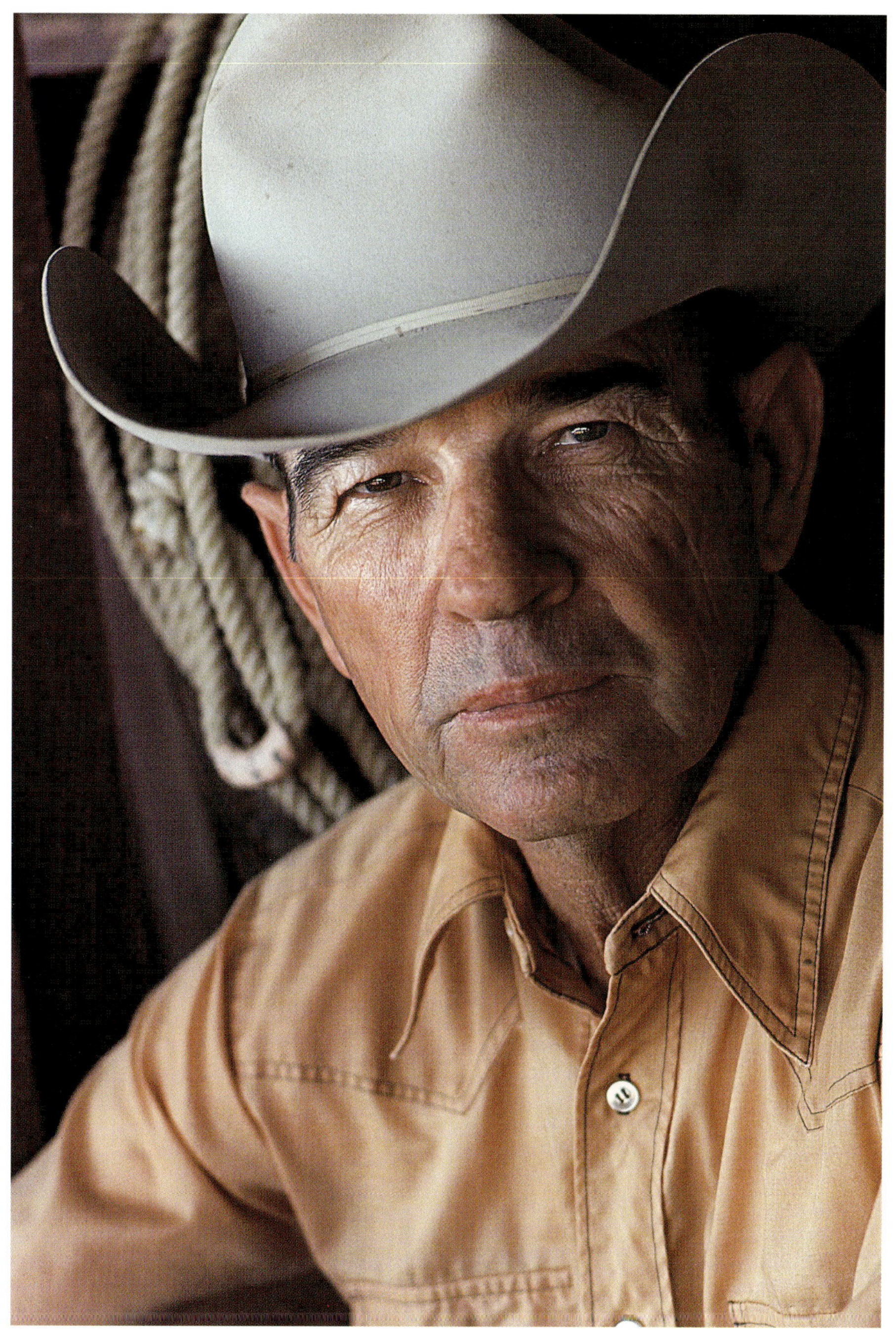

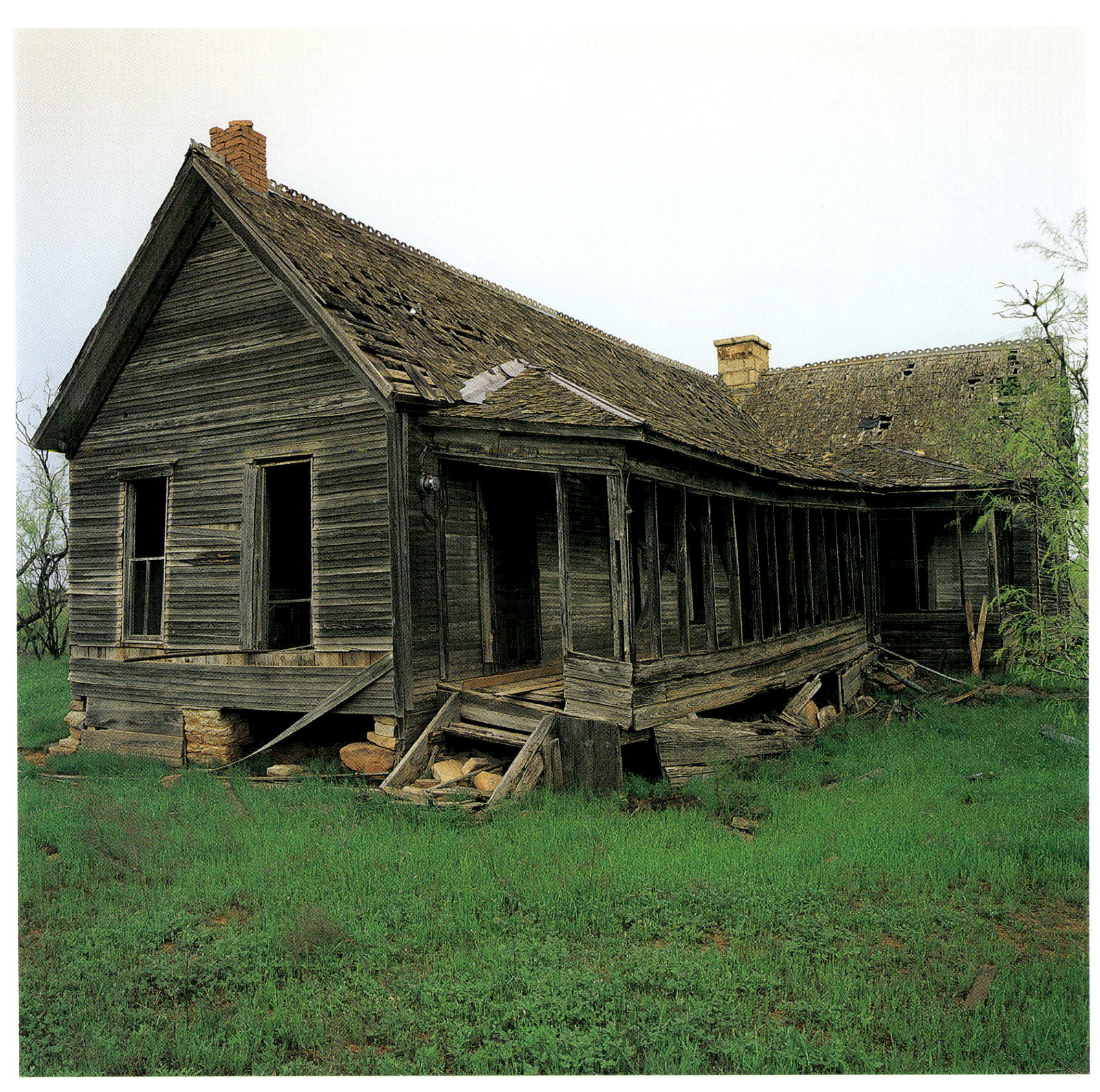

PRAIRIE WAS A TABLELAND OF PRAISE

Unlatch the table leaf, cracked piece of Ohio craft,
and fold it down. Quakers who knew how far,
how close to the heart God was, my great-greats
came to the plains when a river crossing took faith

in God's rod to part water. Mahogany that dark
fed them quail and leavened bread over trails
to this rattlesnake prairie, their wagon wobbly all day,
the bull-necked oxen hot. Each night, they jerked

this table out of the wagon and lifted the leaf to eat,
daily ark of their covenant to praise whatever bread
remained. All winter, until their first box house and harvest,
they slept in a scorpion dugout, raised the leaf each meal

to feed eight shivering children, then lowered it
for feather bedrolls. Let it down, that leaf of a keepsake,
gently, leave it here, even scarred, in the entry,
history we pass in our hallway to the hearth.

NIGHTS ON THE BRAZOS

We waded the North Fork in moonlight,
bumping into logs, slowly stepping over,
testing the rocks and moss like soldiers.
Billy Ray and I joked about snakes,

too young to worry about war.
Big Joe Bubba owned the lantern,
flashed it from shore to shore,
exposing a thousand eyes.

He reached to touch us, so close
we could hear him wheeze.
What we needed waited after dark
to crawl openly on shore,

mud turtles drawn by the moon.
Slowly, we stalked them all
through one warm foot of water.
Each one we saw, Joe Bubba

stabbed with a wavering lantern,
kept it away from the Brazos
while we flipped it on its back.
Mosquitoes sang and bled us,

owls stuttered and dived away.
Swifts skimmed the stream,
feeding. Our soaked gunny sacks
dragged like tails. Suddenly,

a scream like a bobcat, on our side
of the canyon. We froze—nothing
our BB guns could wound—first sign
of a world we couldn't control.

We waded shallows while brothers
fought Pacific battles, owls
and bats darting by to scare us,
as safe that year as we'd ever be.

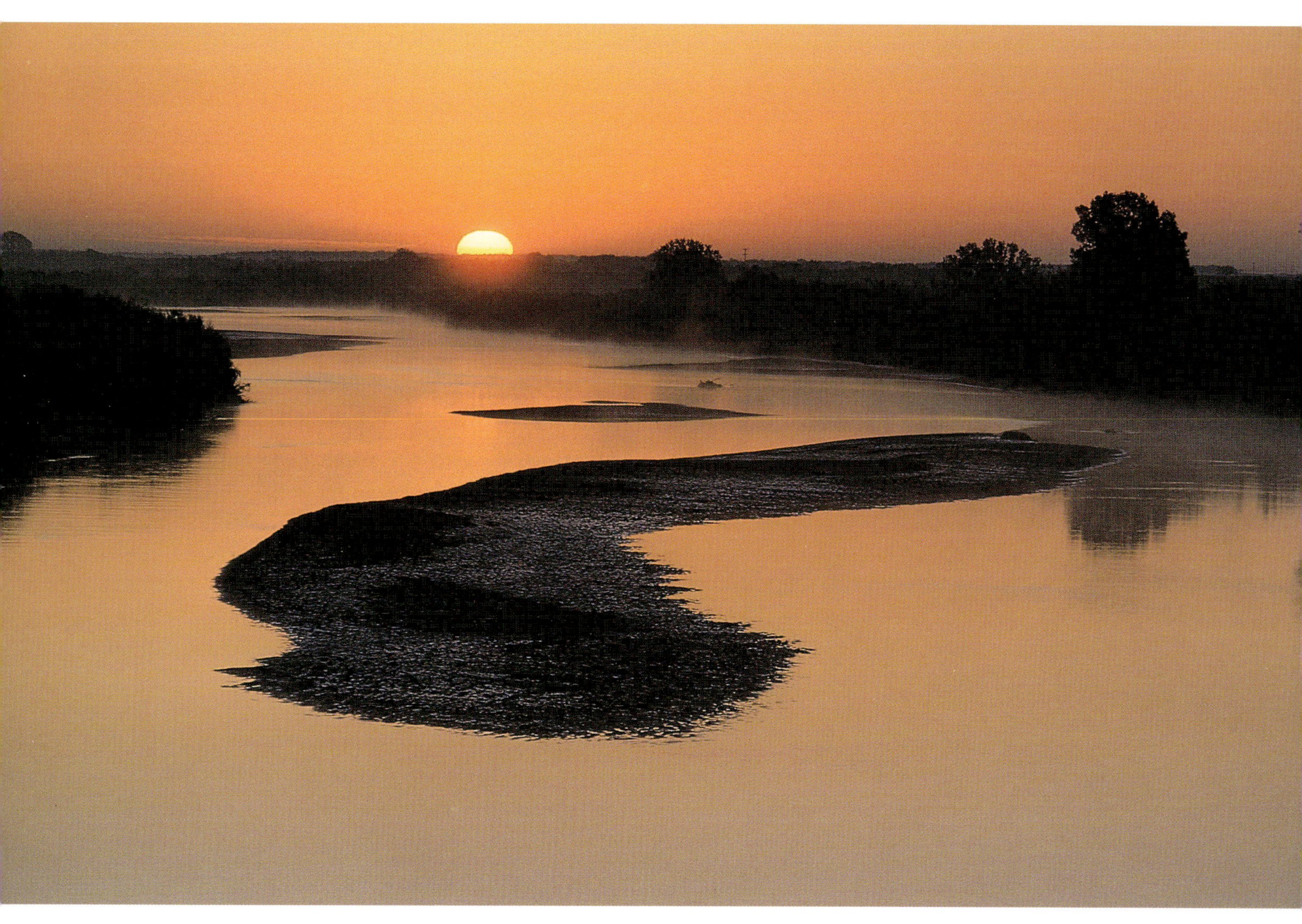

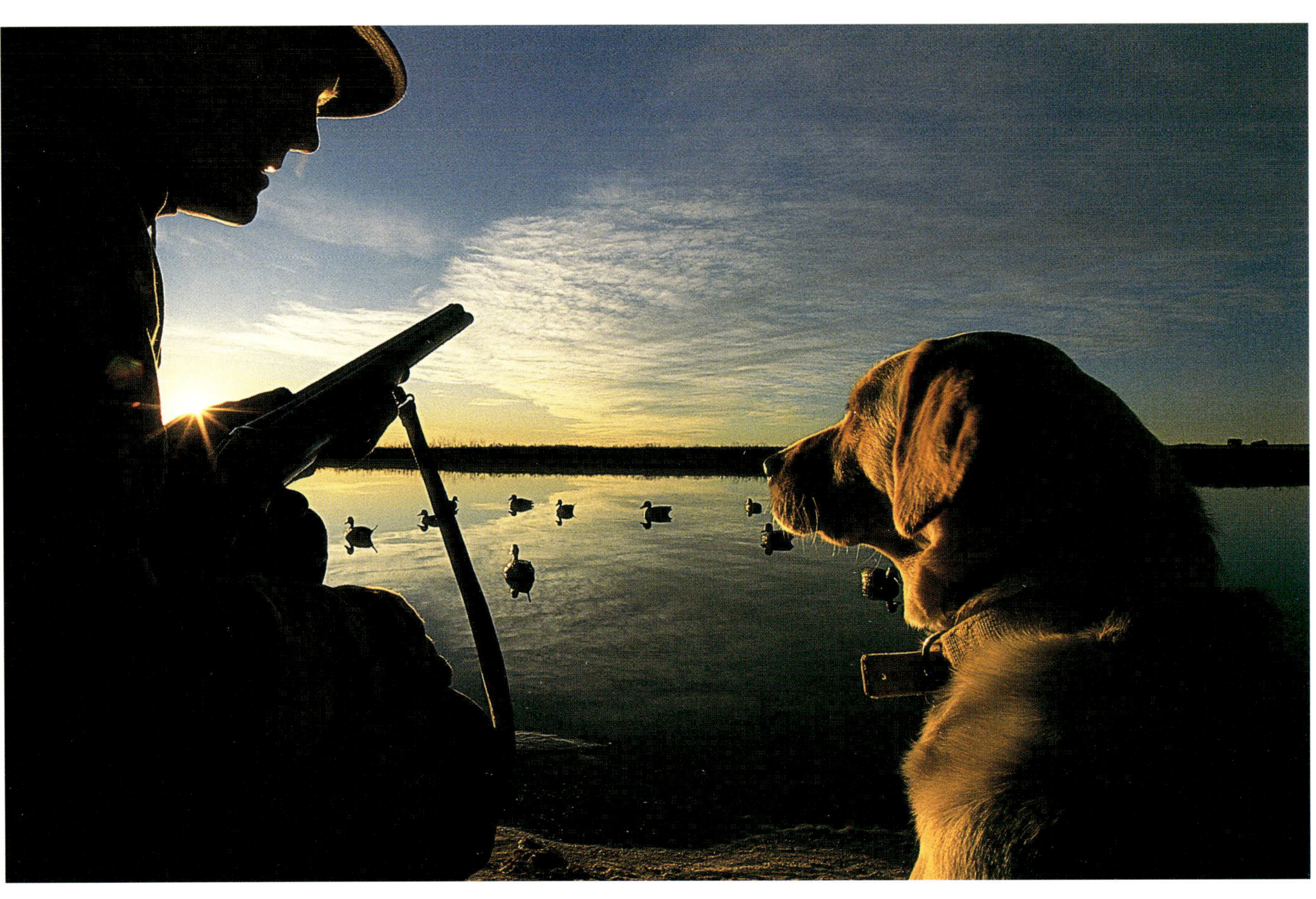

BIG DOGS AFTER WAR

Decades of dogs jumped over his tailgate
to sniff the news from pickups around the ranch
and down state roads. Balanced,
unbalanced in turns and stops,

they watched my uncle inside the cab,
doing magic with wind flapping their lips.
Troll was the first after World War II,
a fluffy St. Bernard that shoved

and made that pickup rock. Back from war,
Uncle Bob had faith in dogs, the only pets
he trusted. I worked his ranch in summers,
learned how to cuss when anything

went wrong, heard nightmares
that waked me down the hall, shouts
only Aunt Kay could stand. Often,
I found him in the barn at dawn

with coffee, alone with that pre-war pickup
he polished like a toy. Years swift as crops slid by,
a long, fast litany of dogs big as horses. Attila,
Goat Boy, Little Caesar learned that amazing trick

to please him, legs shoving gravity away
and soaring over the tailgate,
the whole world swaying, drooled on,
pounded with massive, wagging tails.

THIS COULD BE EDEN

It could be smoke, clouds without a breeze at dawn.
The earth stands still, no cars or trucks,
no sirens or banging of dumpsters,

no slamming doors. I believe Palo Duro's here,
canyon tops lopped off by haze layers pale as sky.
Two hawks glide down the mile-wide valley.

A jay plops on the feeder and pecks,
pecks, the eyes a black thin bandit mask.
He sees me inside and stares, and flicks more seeds

and flies. No other sound, my wife asleep
on the cot. No one within a mile of our tent,
or if others are here, they're afoot, in sneakers,

toting an old-fashioned tripod and camera,
wondering where to set up, how to capture the hour,
this silence deep in the canyon,

someway to show their children in distant cities
that this, this is where time stood still,
Eden in the blink of an eye.

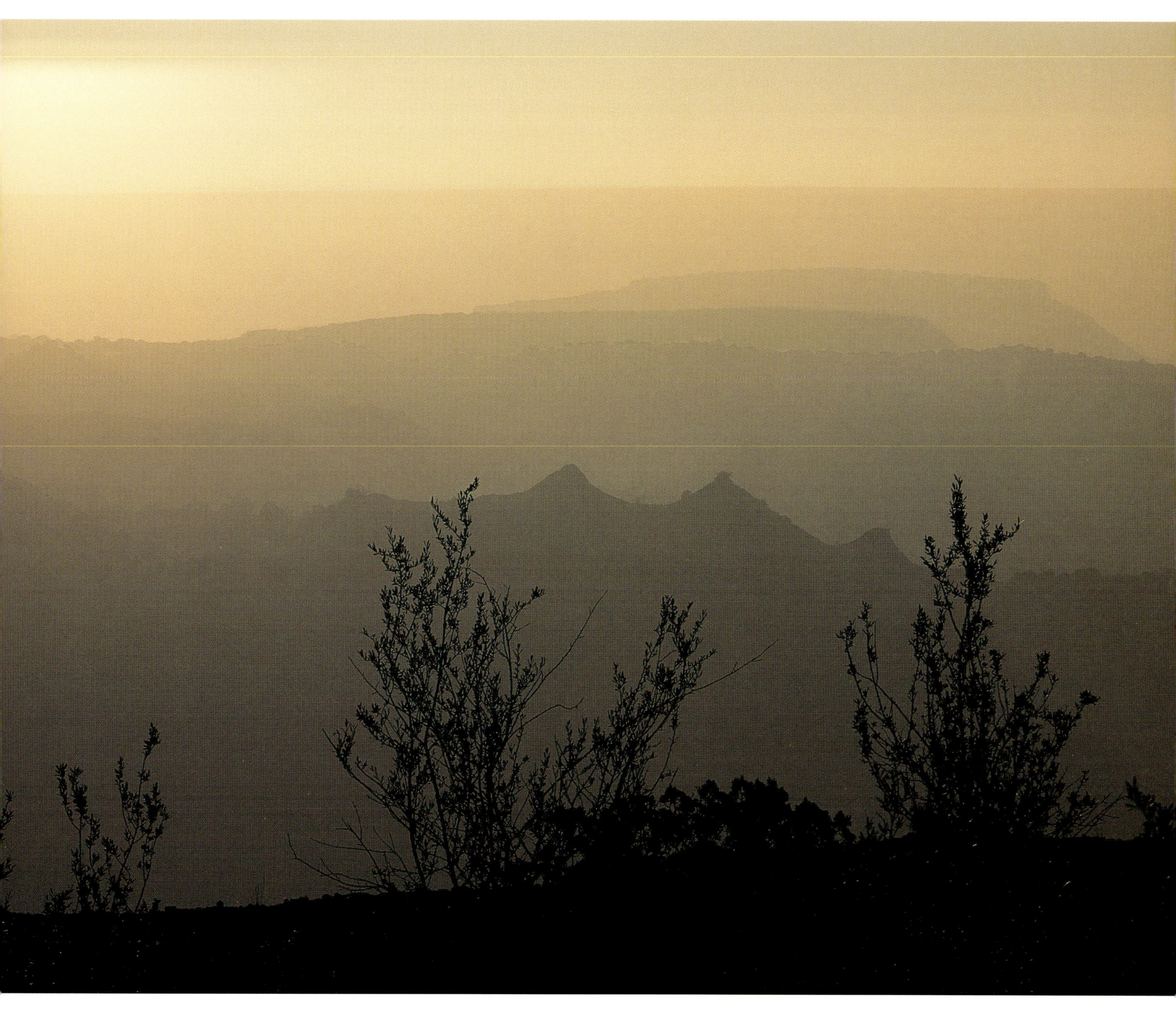

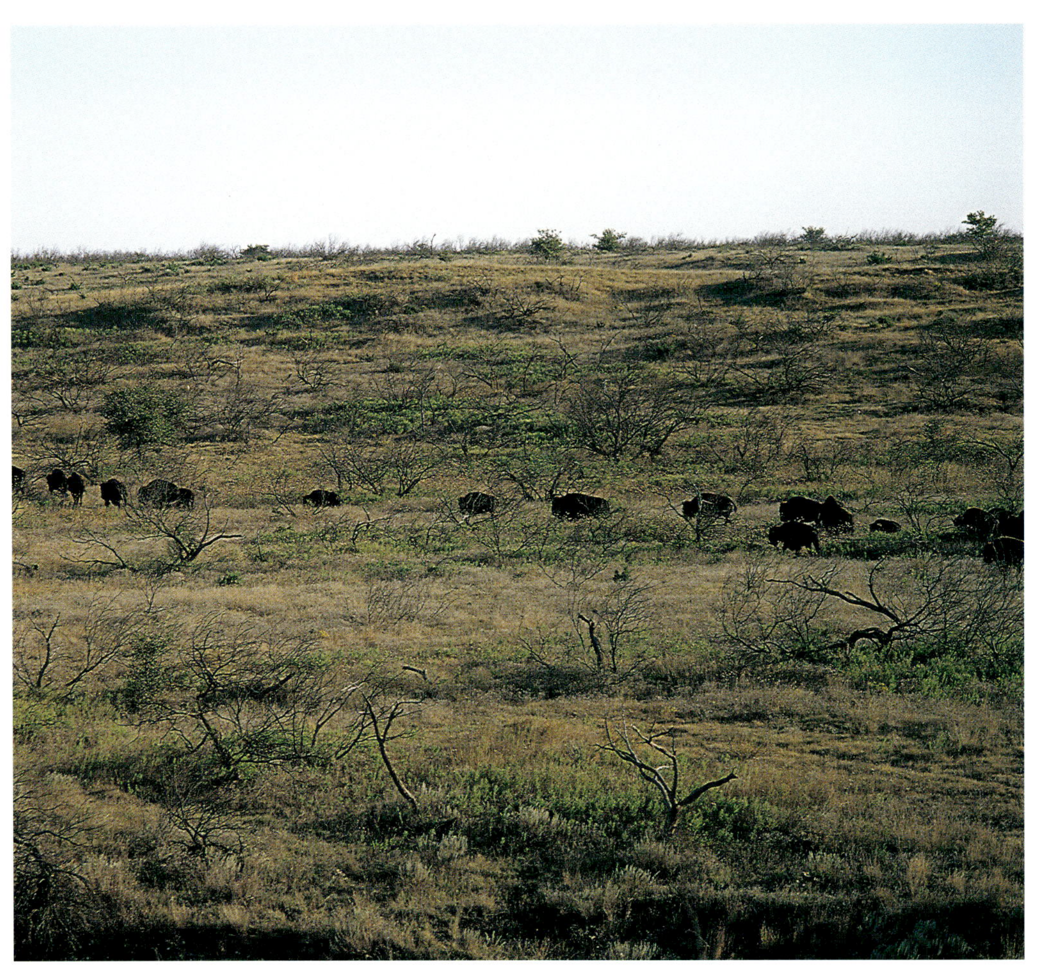

AUNT FLORENCE AND THE KALAHARI

Swarms kept Uncle Bob's boarders in honey,
hives he learned how to smoke in Africa
the month he took Aunt Florence to convalesce.
After her second mastectomy, Aunt Florence
had bathrooms built and carpets, a bed and breakfast
halfway to Amarillo. Bob traded cattle for gazelles

and Kalahari zebras, a prairie sanctuary licensed
for lookers, not one to be shot without a warden
flown up from Houston. Tourists from forty states
stayed with them over those four years, a waiting list
months long. Picnickers paid eighty dollars a day.
Uncle Bob's cowboys drove dozens out in Land Rovers

equipped with biscuits and little tubs of honey and tea,
binoculars with pliable steel cables at every seat,
giraffes and wildebeest near enough to whistle over
and feed, in spite of rules. When Florence died,
my cousins flew back for a teary weekend and left,
not one to carry on the herd. The bees were the first

to go, hauled off by a converted bus like a dump truck.
Nine cars from the train ten miles away loaded
African livestock like an ark for a ranch in Arkansas
licensed for exotics. Uncle Bob wouldn't watch the auction,
safari furniture Aunt Florence picked out in Dallas,
the wicker trays. Sweaty, he helped load the emus

and buffalo, even the vultures in cages.
Before he moved to the mountains, he gave his gelding
and saddle to me, his summer nephew, whatever I found
in the tack room. He sold the bony longhorn steers
to the packing plant at a stockyard, mainly for their horns
and hide, trophies for hoods of Cadillacs and walls.

THE PERKS OF BEING A GREENHORN

The foreman smoked a cigar and drove a Jeep,
not the trail boss I bargained for.
The horse I drew from the remuda

was a gelding, not the palomino stallion
I'd fancied since first grade. Each time
I took the bridle and saddle horn and yanked,

his withers trembled. I wondered if he was ashamed
of being a gelding and fat, or of me,
the greenhorn. All summer, I rode alone,

the new guy banished to the far arroyos,
the haunt of buzzards and the dumbest strays.
I mended fence and hauled the lost calves back,

turned around and found my place,
a bedroll under stars. That fall, high school
was all I thought it would be and more,

girls in bikinis at the beach on weekends,
dreamy with lipstick in chemistry,
bending to Bunsen burners in tight skirts

and cardigans, the equestrian club
over-enrolled with girls in love with horses
and cowboys, any tall kid who could ride.

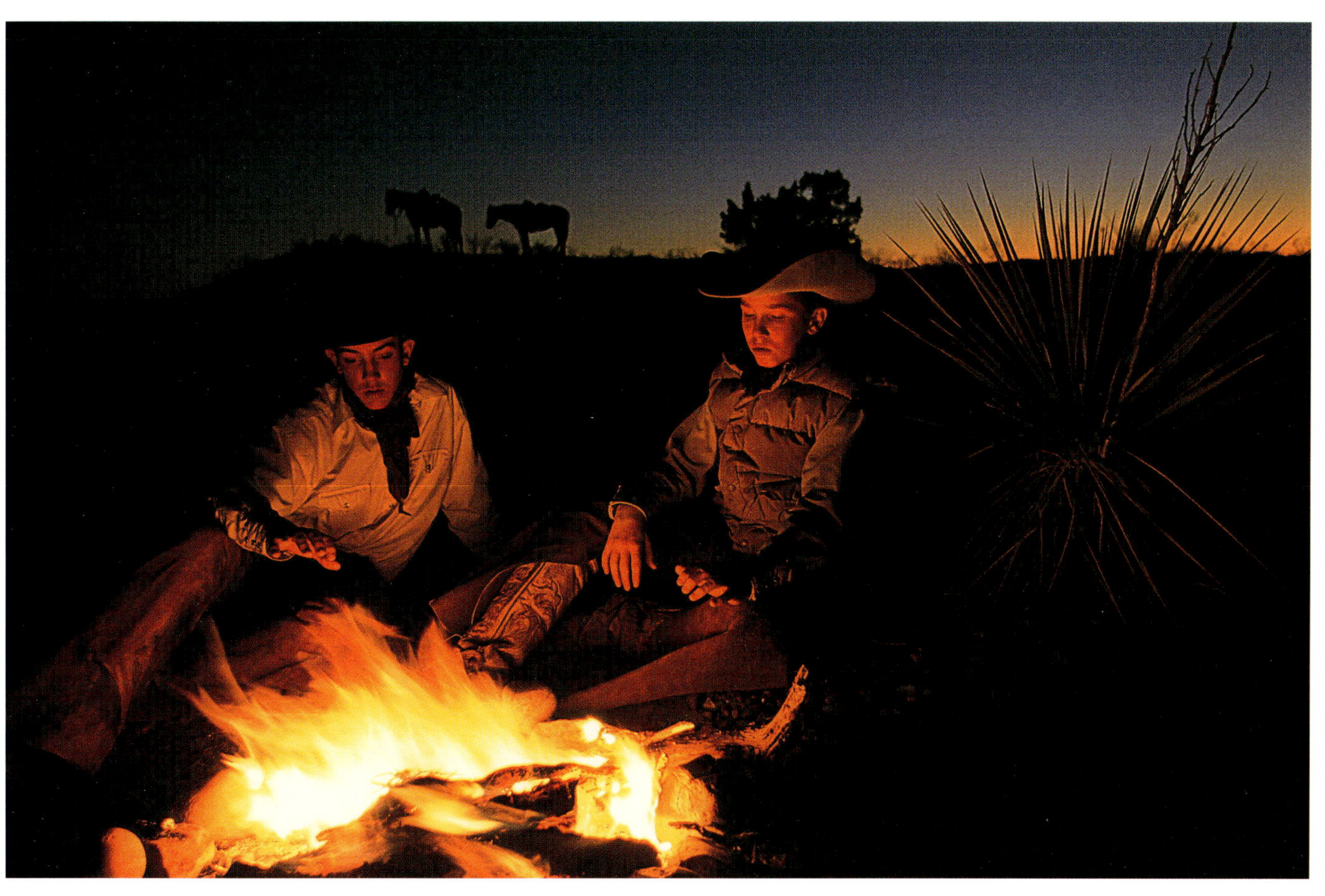

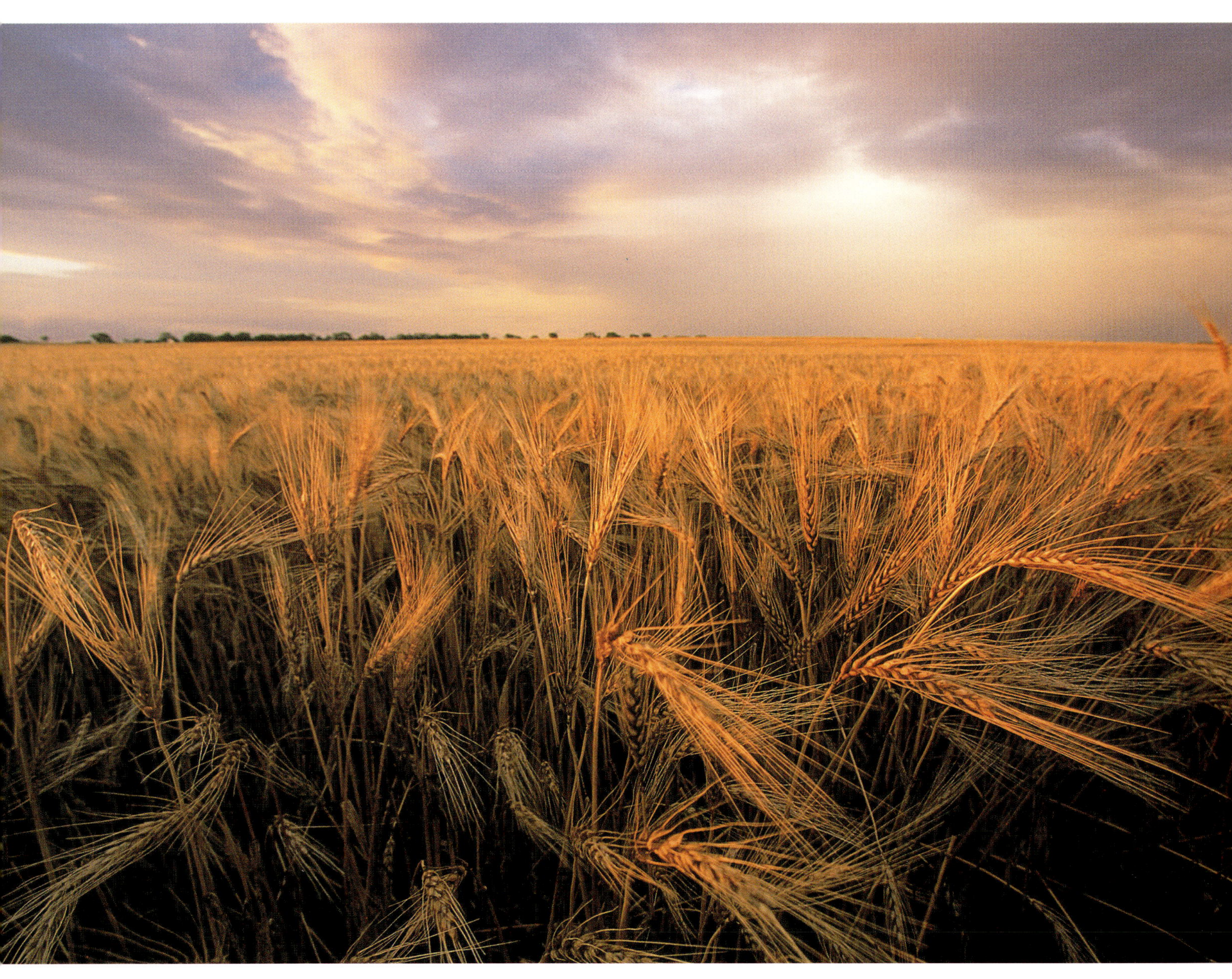

GRANDMOTHER'S WAGON TRAIL DIARY

Grandmother packed her diary away
or burned it, months after reaching the Plains.
I've searched the attic and basement,
through all we own that was theirs.
Weeks out of Ohio, their covered wagon

was sand and smelly underwear,
the last clean stream days back.
She believed the small, still voice of God,
the hope Friends wrote about prairie,
like pastures of heaven when it rained.

I need that voice of a woman
alone with a man and a pencil,
following oxen without a trail into Texas,
December when they reached
the Red River, about to freeze.

Did she doubt they'd find it, the promised land
not a crescent of milk and honey, but flat
and vulnerable to drought?
She helped Grandfather stack a sod house,
draped canvas to make two rooms.

They hunted, they burned dry buffalo dung
for firewood. They raised three babies
and buried four. Misery must be
losing a child, no matter when
or where it dies, loving their brief life

and bowing, suffering both beauty
and blizzards, abiding the boredom
and horror, the splendor of it all.
The diary's missing, the canvas door,
the wagon nowhere to be found.

CLOUDS DRIFTING THIN AROUND US

Bring back the days of waves slapping the shore,
gulls and rowboats bobbing on the bay.
Rocking at dawn, we talk, amazed
we're this old, clouds drifting thin around us,
barometer falling. Wherever we go
on the deck, we're home under canyon walls
crumbling red as dust. We go away
by strumming Spanish love songs
and touching. Coronado crossed these plains
out of breath, coughing, his polished armor
strapped to horses, offering crosses for grain,
hoping to reach the Gulf before he starved.
His soldiers threatened the natives for rain,
for gold. What if he didn't return to Mexico
broke, but found the gold and sailed to Spain,
loaded with spice and bracelets? How long
would he curse his luck and sulk, how old
before these distant rocky plains
were what he missed, these dusty fields we own,
swapping Spain for armor rusting in the hall
and a galleon anchored in the bay?

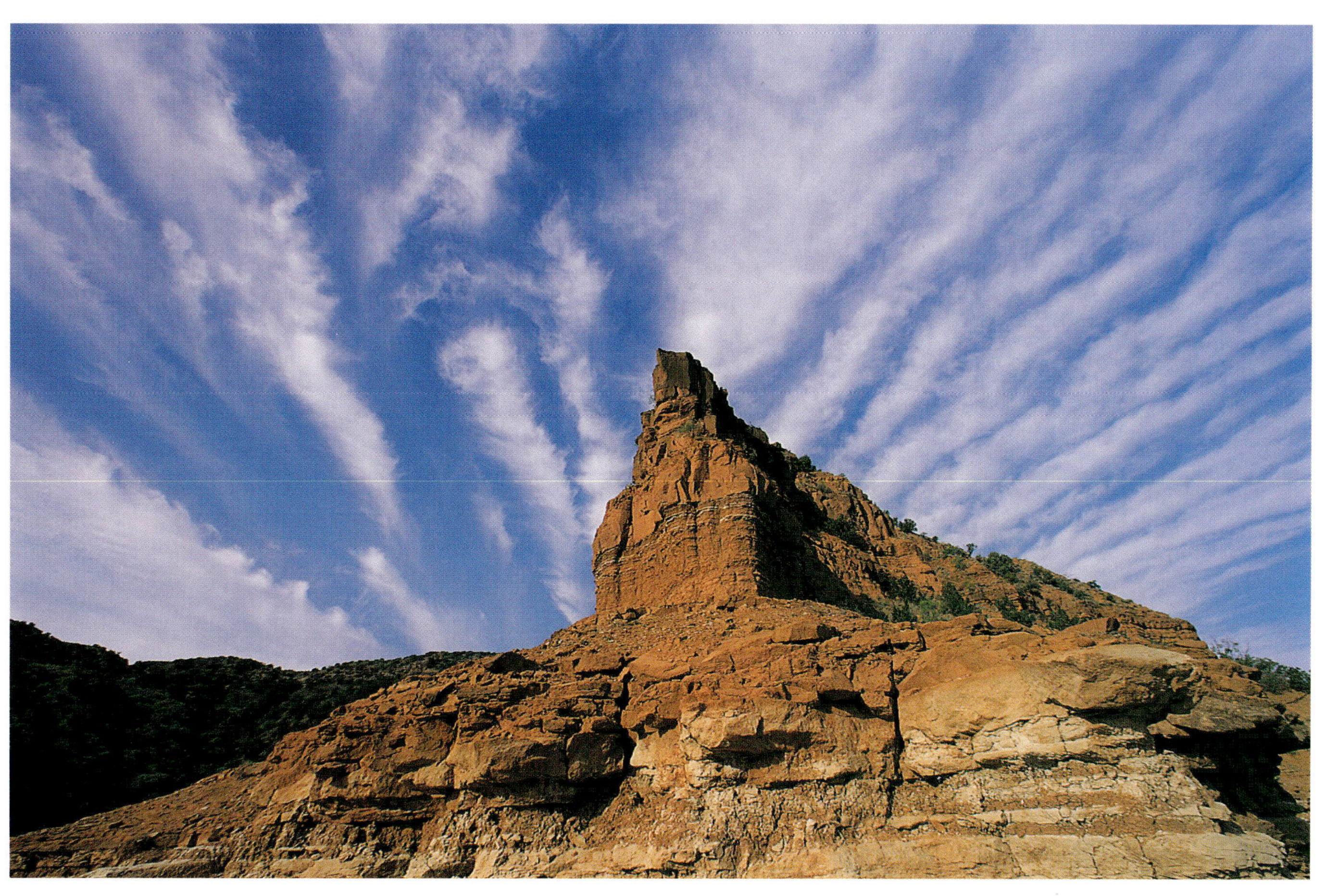

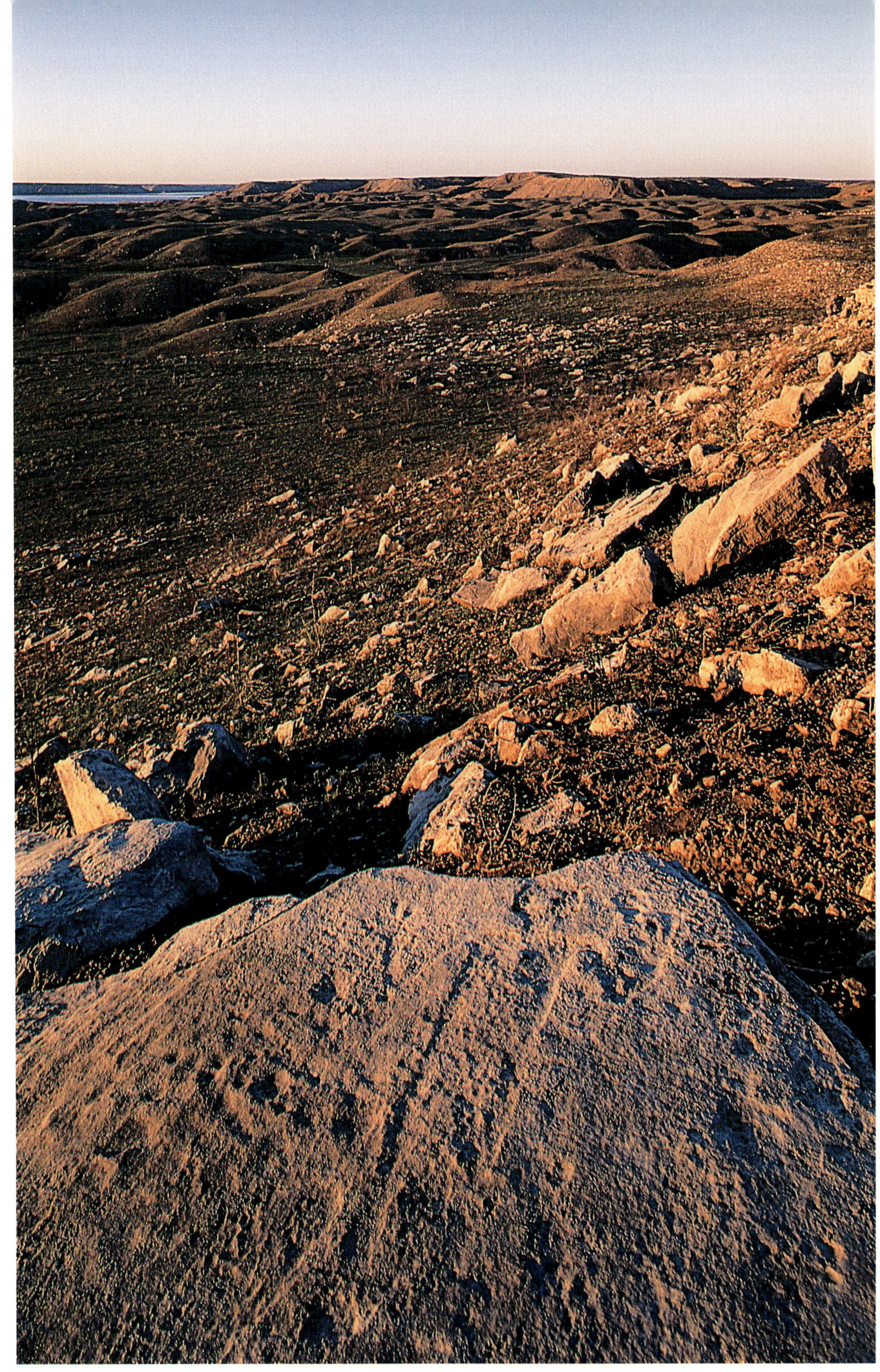

ALL THAT ACHES AND BLESSES

All that aches and blesses lives in the skin,
the thinnest organ, that turtle shell we scrub
and rub the wrong way daily like brass lamps
no genies rise from to save our bones
and ashes. We wade uncovered into guilt like ice
and curse the towels that leave the same thick
hide as always. We envy snakes that shed
their skins, chameleons that translate
themselves in colorful languages.
More than the heart, we give ourselves away
in skin, the blessing over all we are.
We feel the deepest loss of fathers
not in our bones, but skin they'll never touch.

GRANDDAUGHTERS OF THE PLAINS

Old women in buckskins posed, cutting up
like Annie Oakley, bifocals off and bold
as Calamity Jane, tongues out.
They poked each other and laughed,

proud they survived sandstorms.
Some came to the Plains in wagons,
bouncing babies in more than name.
Some grandparents were Quakers from Ohio;

some, mule skinners, cowboys
who married schoolmarms
and broke the plains with plows.
Some drilled for water, struck oil,

and left flat ranches to children.
A Hundred Wonders, they called themselves
when the club formed forty years ago.
Now, only twenty *Granddaughters of the Plains*

remain. They changed the name
after too many died. For years,
they counted down, *The Ninety-Nine Wonders,*
Ninety-Five, not funny by eighty-one,

brittle as beer bottles on the wall,
but like it or not, old grannies,
tough as sand. Some come in wheelchairs
or walkers, better to laugh

about themselves than sit home
watching re-runs of Lucy and Guy Lombardo
on New Year's. They could always cajole
some grandson to drop by with his wife

and camera between parties, good sports
who didn't mind confetti
and a live band strumming cowboy songs
and old gals shouting loud.

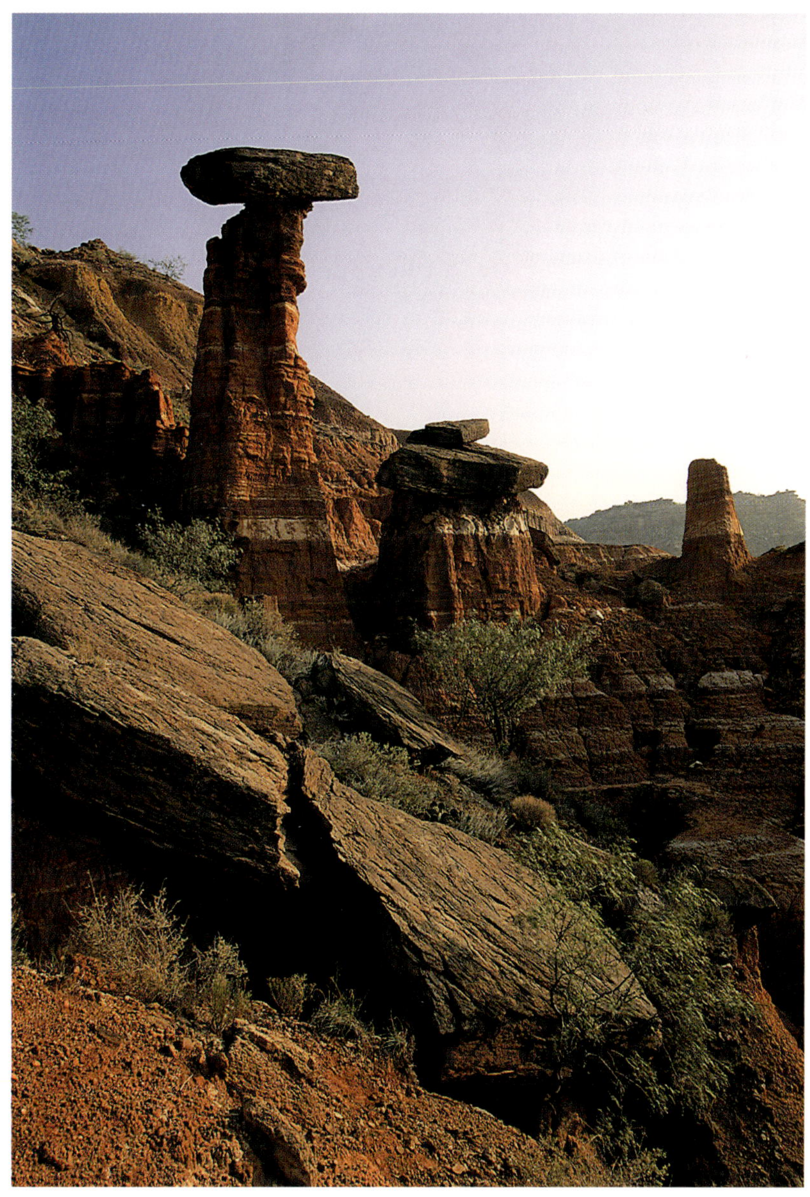

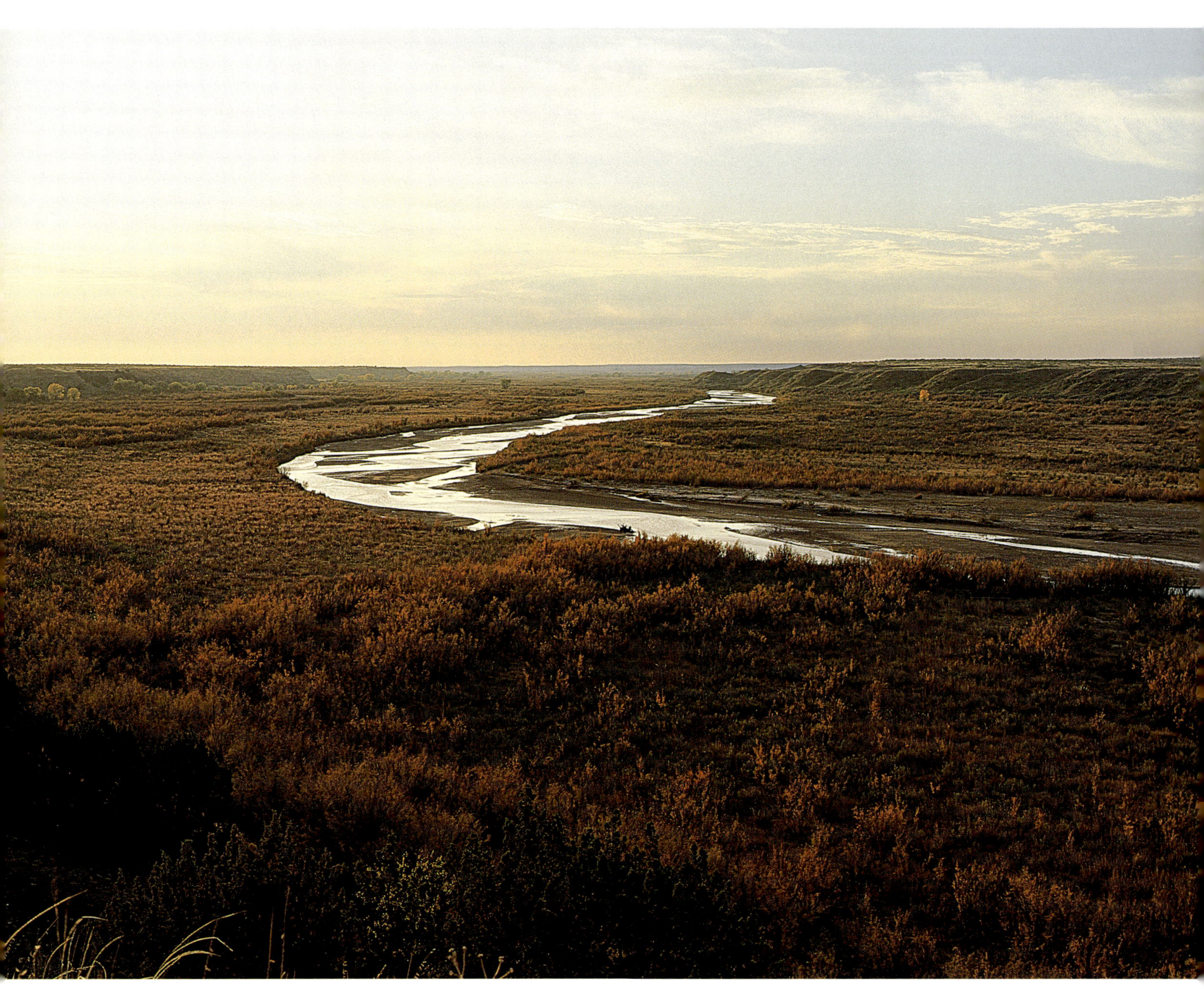

PATTING EACH OTHER'S HANDS

She's learning to cope with dust I track back
bearing letters stamped upside down by grandkids,
smudged, sometimes the nose of a Crayola clown

our preschool ballerina drew. So this is the way
we grow old, absentminded clown tracking mud
and woman picking up needles from haystacks of our lives,

ignoring stiff knuckles, stitching Raggedy Ann and Andy
out of scraps. She crochets clothes for dolls
and wanders through the house, staring at the phone,

the walls, knitting shawls for widows she inherits,
her mother's aunts and in-laws. I've seen her rub
and rub her knees when she thought I nodded off.

Sometimes I feel it, too, out in the shop, carving,
trying to make a block of oak say hawk or robin.
Our children far away are older than we were

when we drove here and unloaded, propped up
a sagging barn and planted oats and alfalfa,
dug post holes deep enough to hold a herd,

patting each other's hands till midnight by the fire,
our children bathed and put to bed upstairs,
winter storms far off, that first drought easy to ignore.

JOGGING AT SUNDOWN

Jogging means time leaps forward
an hour, and dusk begins.
Fast spins the minute hand,

a wheel of chance, and what it brings
nobody knows, or when it stops. God,
who melts the snow without a clock,

whose rocks and boulders
tumble down ravines, have mercy
on grandbabies, on us all,

for we are brief as vapors,
bone built, soap-bubble bodies,
and you are master mild as snow

but full of force as winter falls,
massive, patient as glaciers,
and father strong and fond.

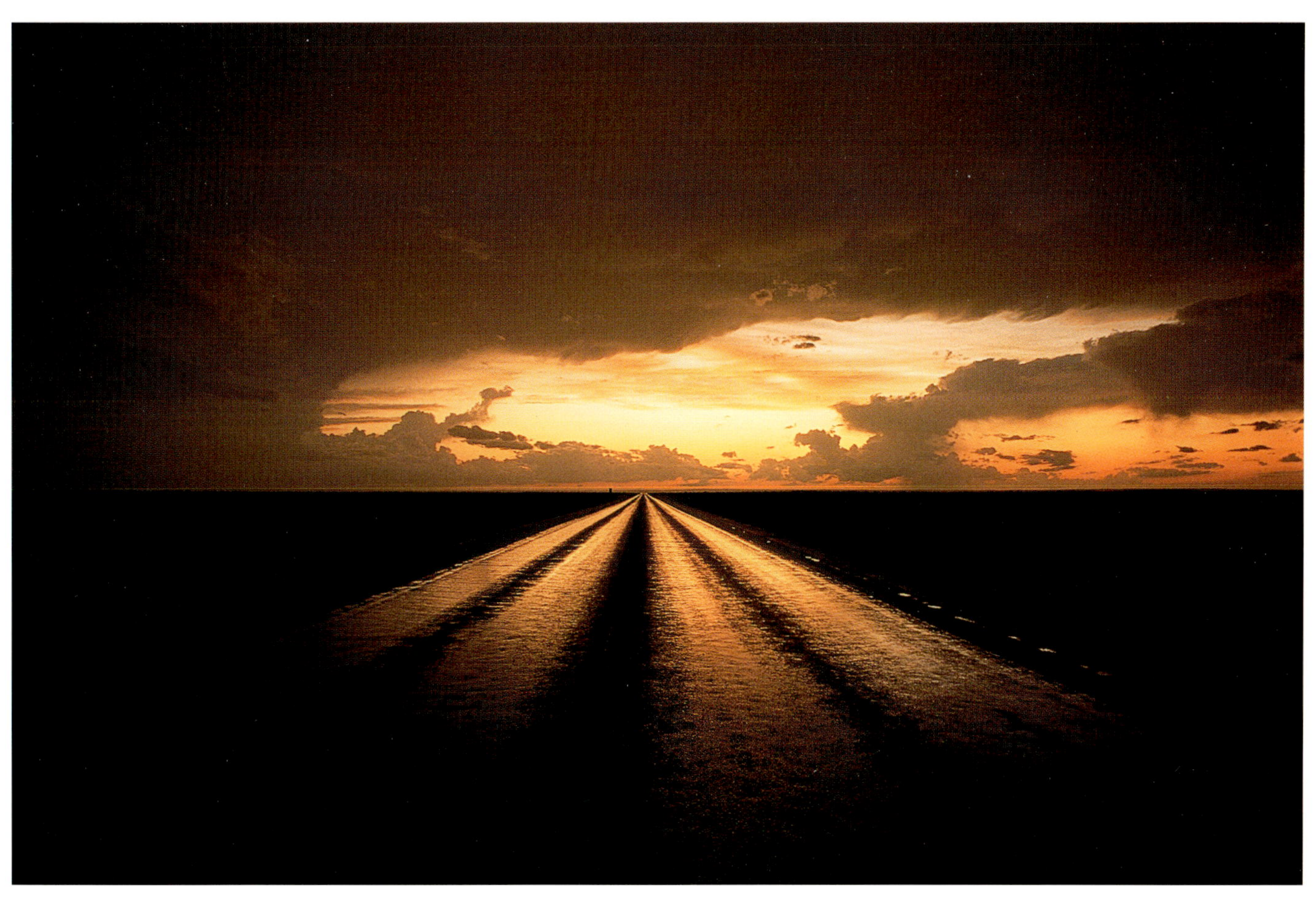

4

WINDMILLS LIKE CATHEDRAL WINDOWS

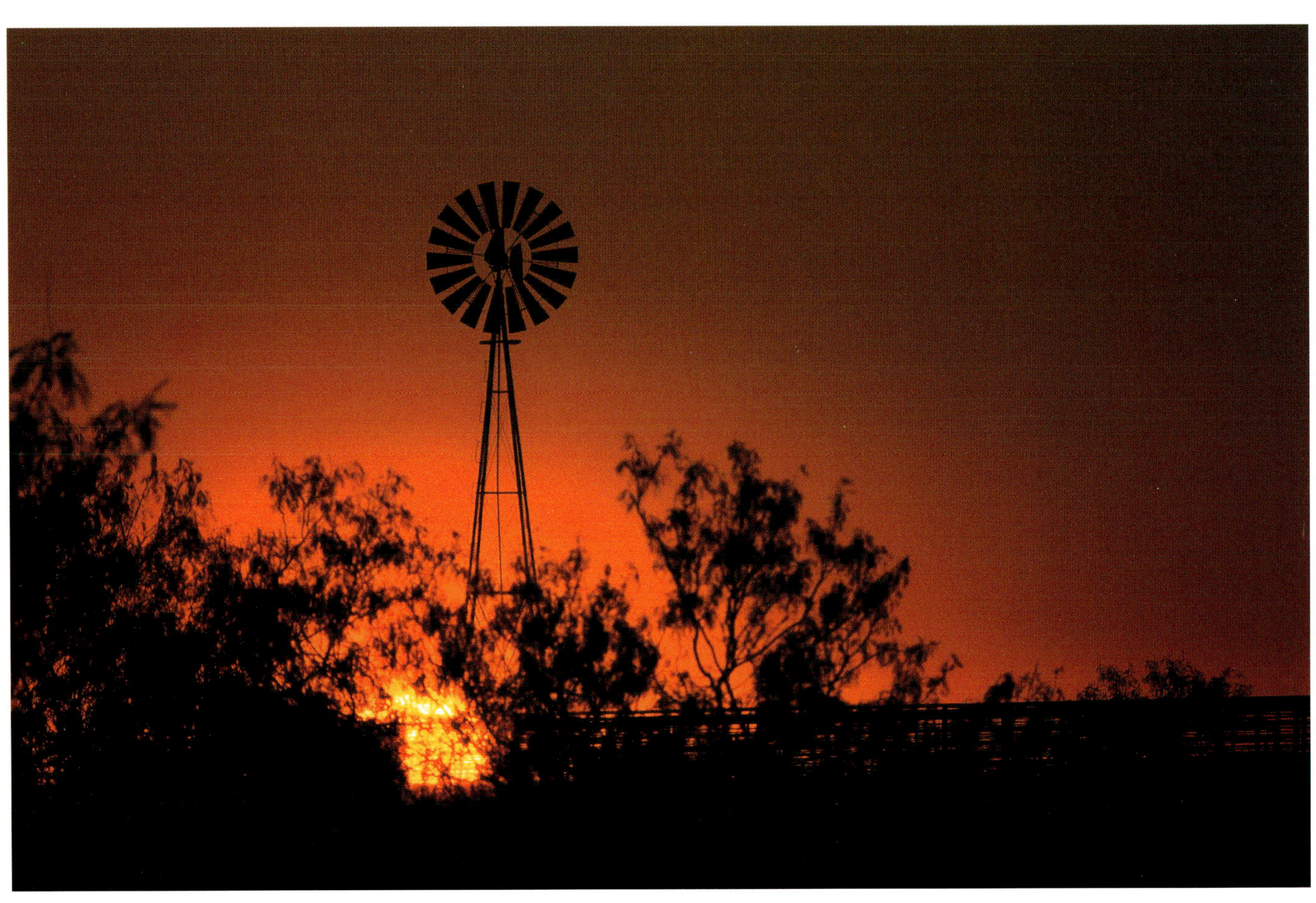

WINDMILLS LIKE CATHEDRAL WINDOWS

Uncle Oscar built them
but wind set them spinning
wide as cathedral windows.
Platforms a man could stand on

to oil without tumbling,
tighten bolts big as fists.
He dug the holes, angled deep
in the earth toward God,

center where blades could spin.
A windmill lifts all water
Moses could ask for.
Aunt Martha bathed nine babies

in the tank. Their house rambled,
one story flat as a nomad's tent,
always towels and soap for one more.
Who needs the north star

on a ranch? Wherever we are,
we're home. Barbed wires
mark borders for a man,
needing no compass, no sextant

to find his way back,
driving calves that wandered
down arroyos and almost starved.
Uncle Oscar rode five miles

in any direction and saw
the top of the world, windmills
spinning on massive posts,
foursquare gospel of water power

bolted to hold the blades
and rudders, to aim the ranch
toward God's almighty gales,
to face whatever blows.

MY FATHER ON HIS SHIELD

Shiny as wax, the cracked veneer Scotch-taped
and brittle. I can't bring my father back.
Legs crossed, he sits there brash

with a private's stripe, a world away
from the war they would ship him to
within days. Cannons flank his face

and banners above him like the flag
my mother kept on the mantel, folded tight,
white stars sharp-pointed on a field of blue.

I remember his fists, the iron he pounded,
five-pound hammer ringing steel,
the frame he made for a sled that winter

before the war. I remember the rope in his fist
around my chest, his other fist
shoving the snow, and downhill we dived,

his boots by my boots on the tongue,
pines whishing by, ice in my eyes, blinking
and squealing. I remember the troop train,

steam billowing like a smoke screen.
I remember wrecking the sled weeks later
and pounding to beat the iron flat,

but it stayed there bent
and stacked in the barn by the anvil,
and I can't bring him back.

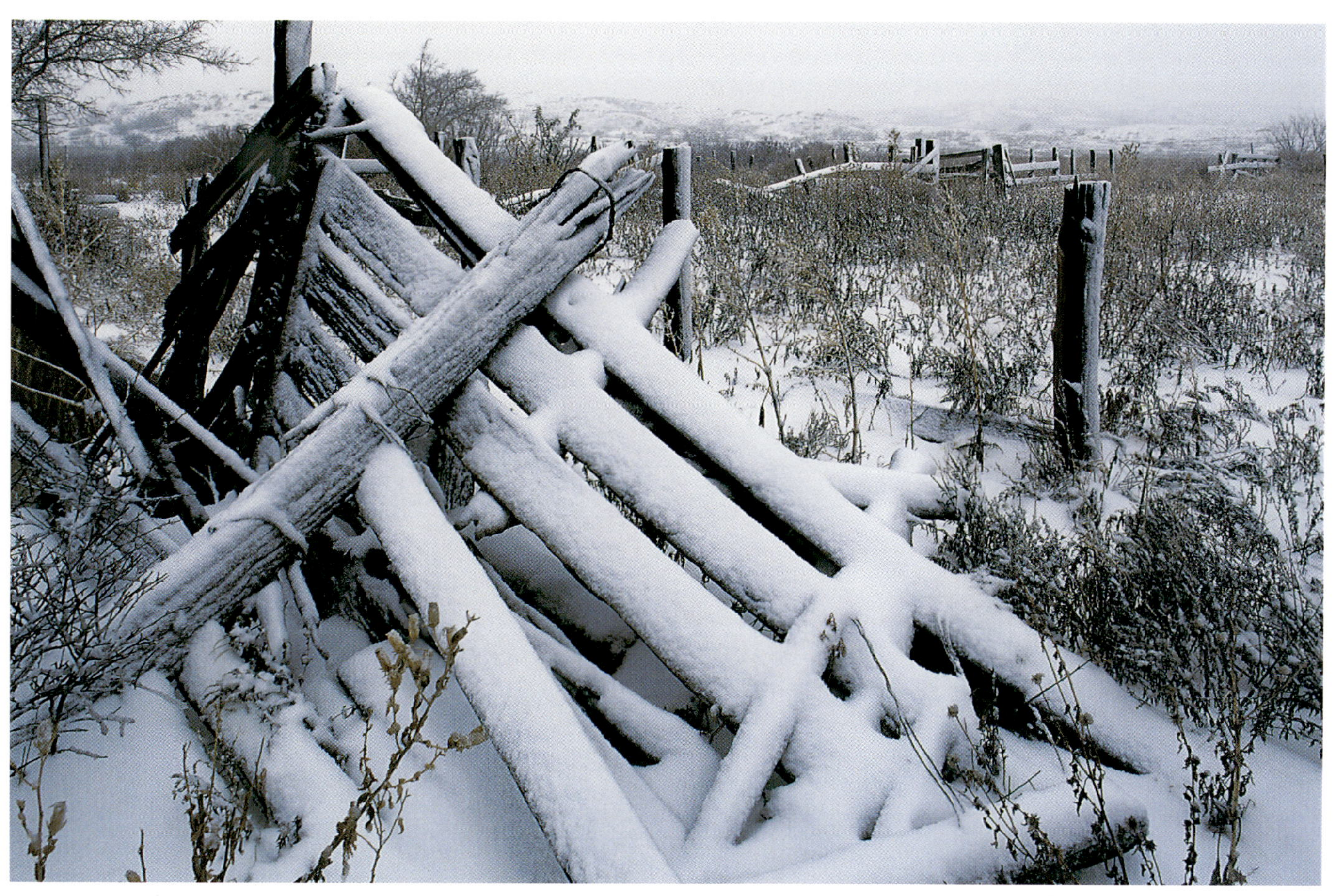

WHATEVER OLD COWBOYS TELL US, THEY'VE ALREADY DONE

Hobbling along from Dallas condos to ranches,
Cadillac cowboys grow glossy as leather, old boots
and saddles with silver-inlaid initials,
even their nicknames—Tall Boy, Curly, Stud.

Old shoulders slump as if Neiman Marcus blazers,
heavy and western tweed, are mail. Old Uncle Roy
caught horses by walking slow, bowleggéd, head down
and one gloved hand held out. Now, he can't stand up

without shuffling, rocks and rocks up out of the car.
The driver catches his elbow, and Uncle Roy tries
to cock his head to thank him. He's skin and bones
with a Stetson and black bolo tie the color of his shirt.

I'm here with cousins because he's here,
about to be cheered and crowned king of the cowmen
for a year, the town's roundup. After western bands
and announcements, after a dozen other awards,

we wake him up, chin on his fists and elbows.
Grinning and groggy eyed, he's ready as he'll ever be
when his name is called, the whole hall rising to applaud,
whistling and shouting. Bobby and I take his arms,

and he's up and shuffling up steps to the podium,
black Stetson back so he can see old friends in the crowd,
waving as if he's wearing gloves again and spurs,
mounting the rodeo gate, ready for the bull.

LOADING THE SUMMER CATTLE

They are coming from the summer range,
wading deep lakes of mirage. The men on horses
are patient, Stetsons low over bandannas

worn to keep from choking. I lean on the gate,
smoking, humming some country and western tune
that keeps on whirling through my mind,

the same old words that make us human,
doomed to know we'll love and lose sweet darlin'
before it happens. August cattle are slow

at sundown, not even bawling. If they know
those trucks come from the slaughterhouse,
thirst muzzles them. They know bales of hay

were here all winter, and so they trudge
obediently out of the last mirage
over pasture of a hundred roundups.

Squinting, I take out the last
half-inch of cigarette and flip it,
climb down and swing the iron gates wide.

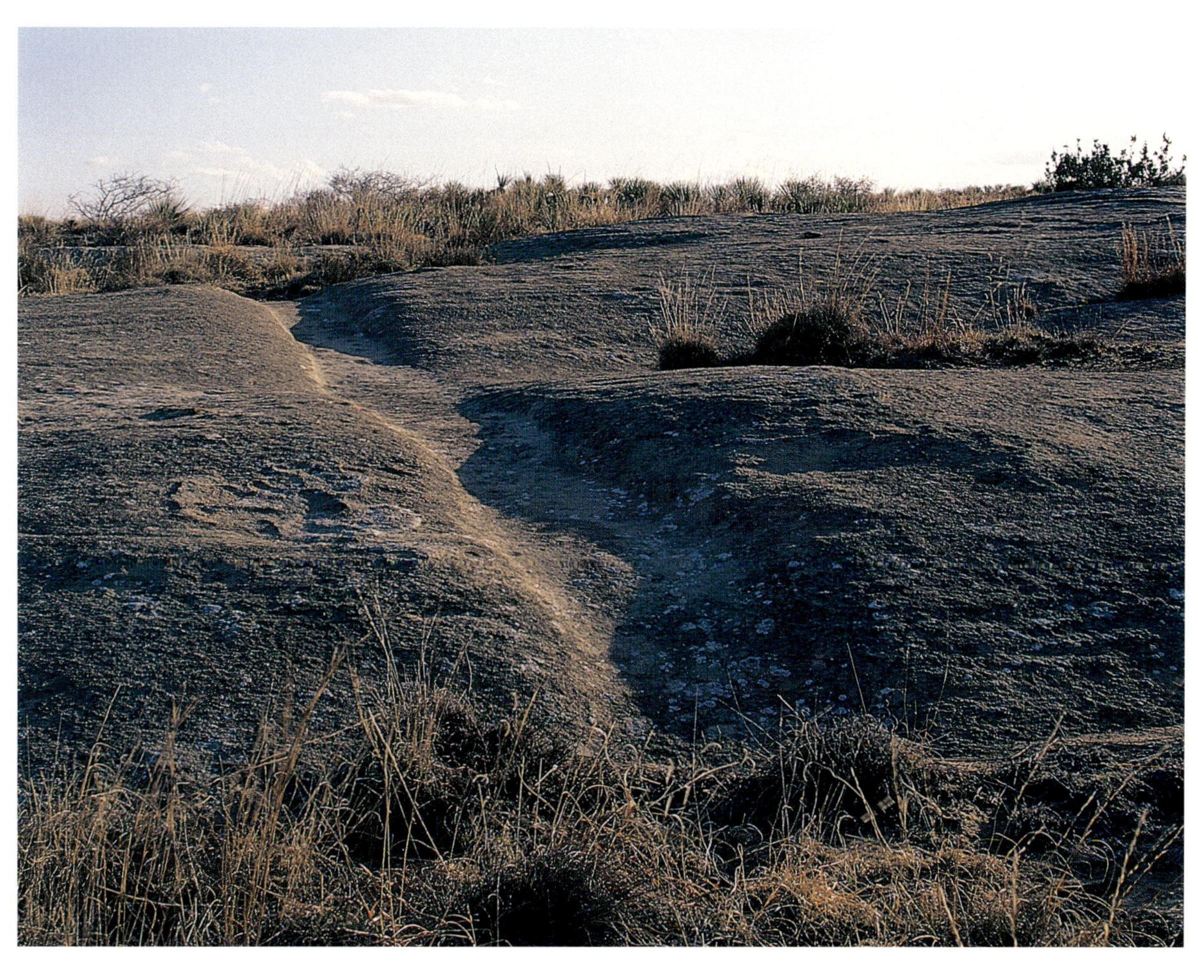

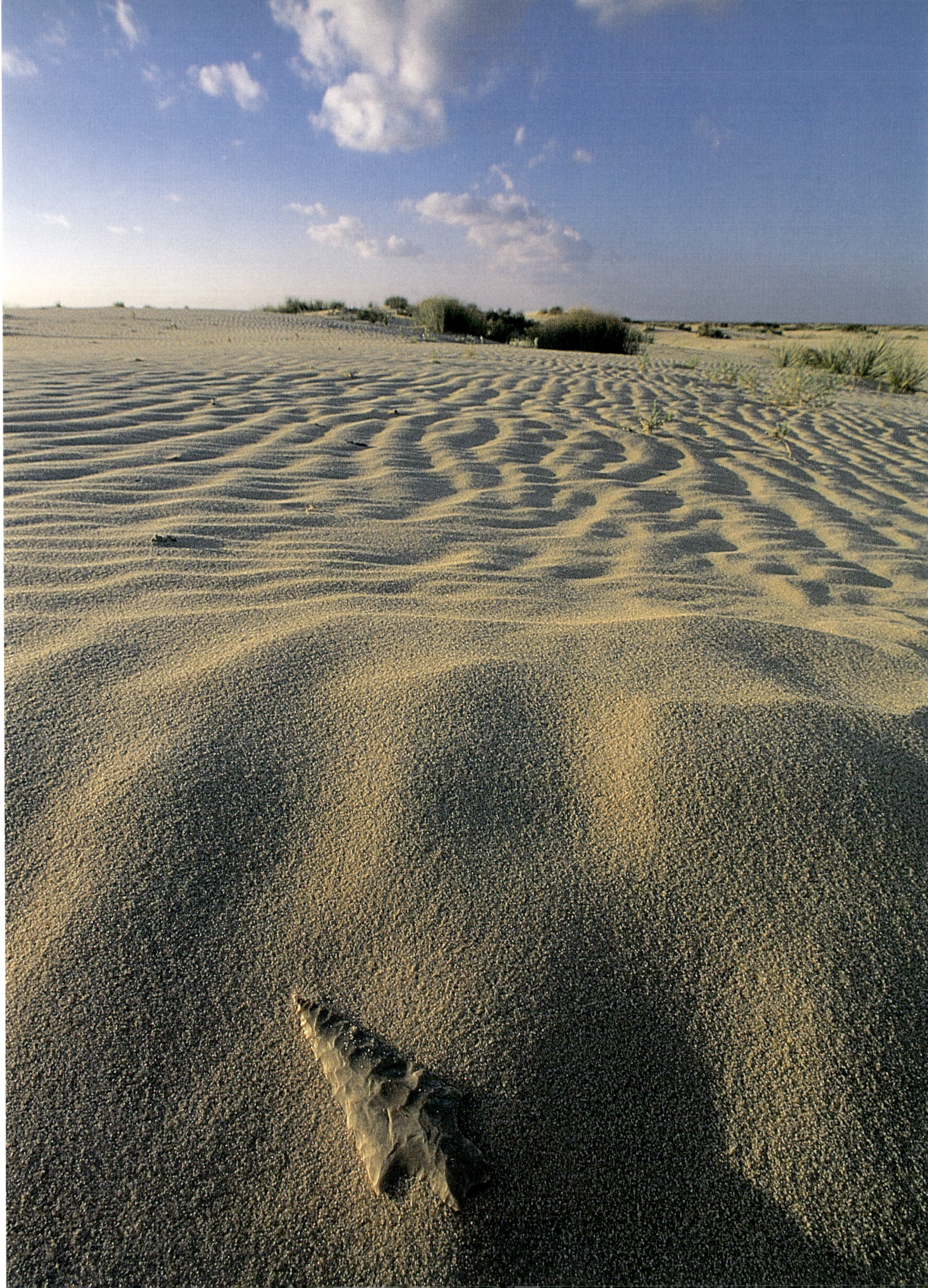

TAKING CHARGE

Brushed out of sand and cactus,
this field's a canvas of coyotes.
They howl to the moon as if they own it,
fearing we'll evict them. They've seen us
dragging maps like sextants.

Weekends, we drive out from town
and kill the engine, easy to coast
on land flat as the moon. We pitch a tent
and open lawn chairs quietly.
Grandfather plowed these fields for decades,

hoping for oil, for cotton. He left us sand
blowing back to plains, and mineral rights
not worth the taxes. After rain, wild geese,
a thousand pheasants. Someday,
we'll bulldoze a dozen acres for oats,

rent an auger and drill for water
and buy some rutting goats.
At night we'll listen to owls
and watch the billies in moonlight
whetting their horns on barbed wires.

We'll pull the old barn down
and build a porch with a swing, a chimney.
We'll add troughs and a barn
for the goats, and dogs to keep them safe
from coyotes starving in the dark.

UNCLE OSCAR AND THE ART OF CARVING

Uncle Oscar shaved away old age
with each flick of his wrist.
If wood was a duck, it floated;
if he whittled a flute, anyone's fingers
could play it. Under courthouse oaks,
old men owned benches like pews,

an amen corner of sinners, their quarrels
the bawdy stories we wanted.
We shoved each other for dimes
the old men flipped to us all like fortunes.
We raced to buy their peanuts and Cokes,
blessed if they slipped us cigarettes

but enough to sit at their feet and listen.
Curls of wood piled up like wool,
lies going up in smoke and shavings.
Forests disappeared in their fists,
blocks of wood into toothpicks.
Some only whittled, drawing slow blades

like breaths, their hollow eyes far off.
Others tried what Uncle Oscar carved,
their clumsy ducks like otters,
gnarled flutes like ocarinas. For years
he taught them all he knew about dying,
and one by one they learned.

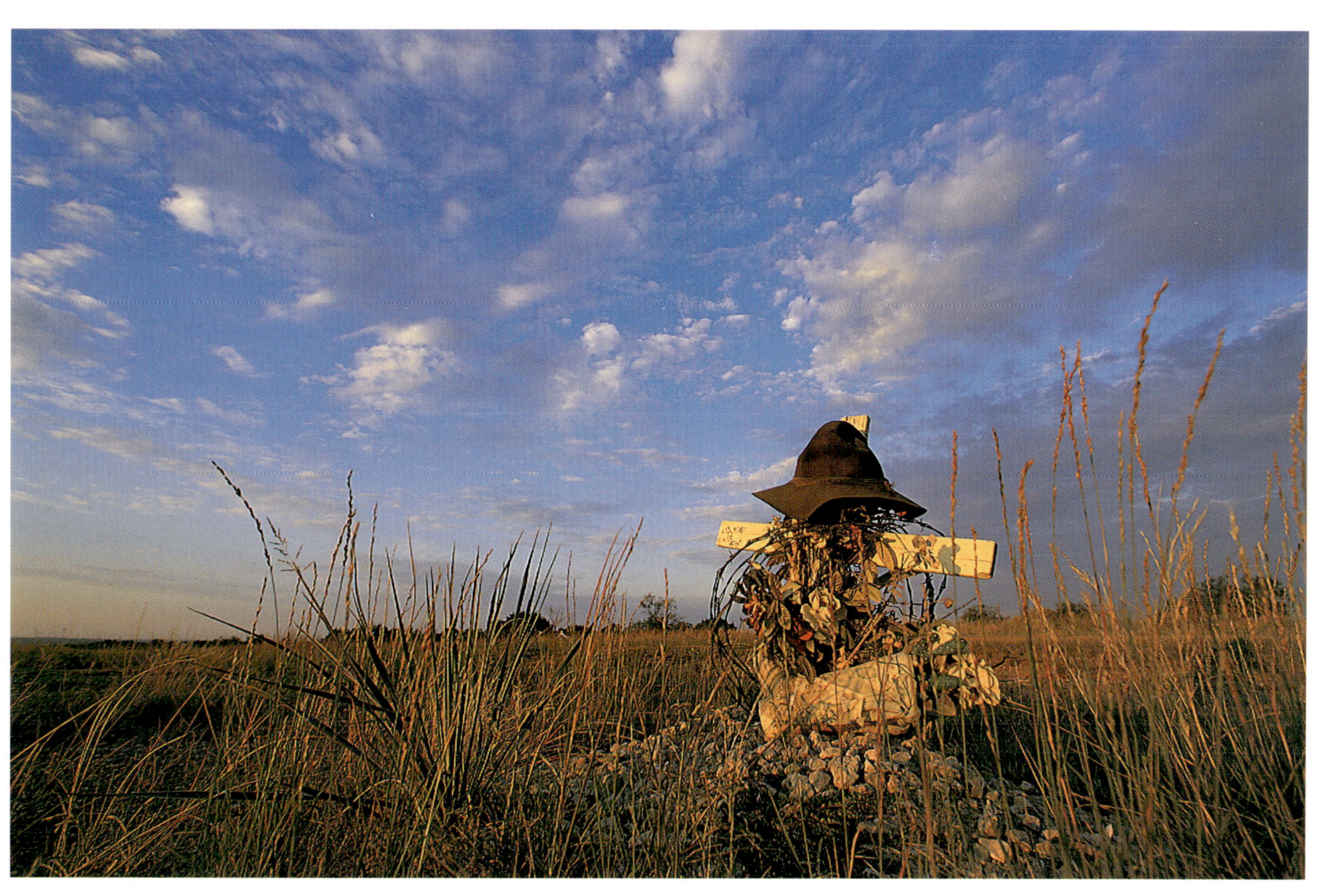

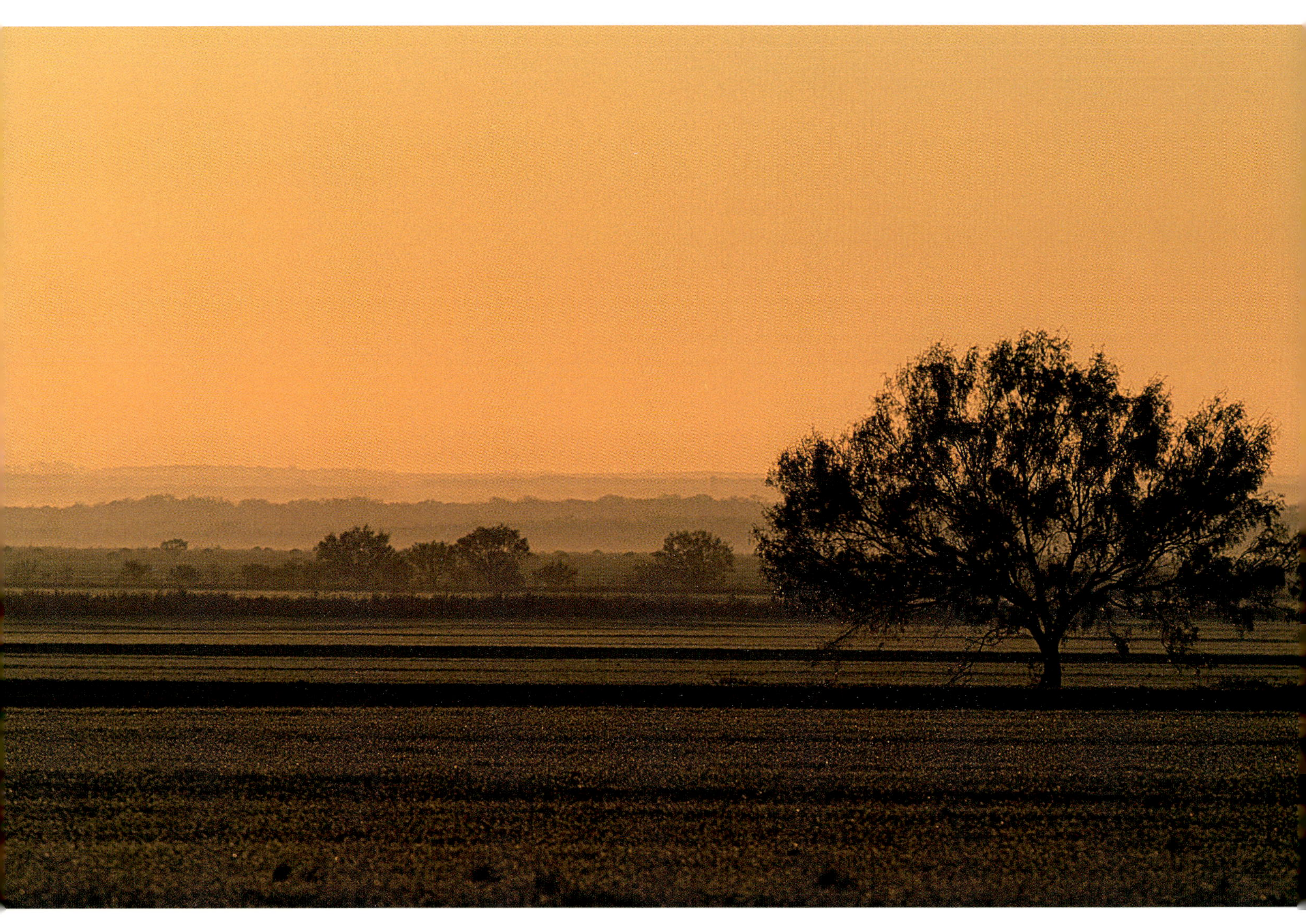

FROGS CROAKING THEIR LOVE SONGS

At dusk we visit neighbors we've ignored.
We miss good folks who've moved away.
Let wishes keep all friends alive. Hold on,
we call, we're coming. The sun comes up

and nothing's changed. Our hands were made
for teats and milk cans, daily rations for cows
lined up and bawling. Cows waddle off
to graze, to dream of bulls. I slam the gate

and latch it, stomping my boots to clean them.
We tell a prairie all we hope it means,
inventing corrals and barns. Each year,
we bulldoze tons of weedy mesquites

and stack the roots, another acre for pasture.
All day, we whisper nothing. The loudest shouts
are lost on steers and goats that ignore us.
We hold communion with wheat and oats,

no end to feeding. We watch dark wings
forever gliding, skies never at a loss for hawks
no wiser for watching the world from above,
no safer than rabbits balled up in burrows,

not knowing when to run. For solace, explorers
called this Brazos River the arms of God, *Río*
de los Brazos de Dios. We invent rich sounds
wise as well as ancient and give those names

to landscapes—*cholla, horizon, stone.*
We've hurled the fear in ourselves to the moon,
our longing for peace into sunsets. At night,
we listen to far-off barks of dogs, frogs croaking

their love songs, millions of stars lighting their leaps
to each other. At dawn, we sit outside
and watch the stars go under, each blink of our eyes
erasing thousands, the sun slower than us but coming.

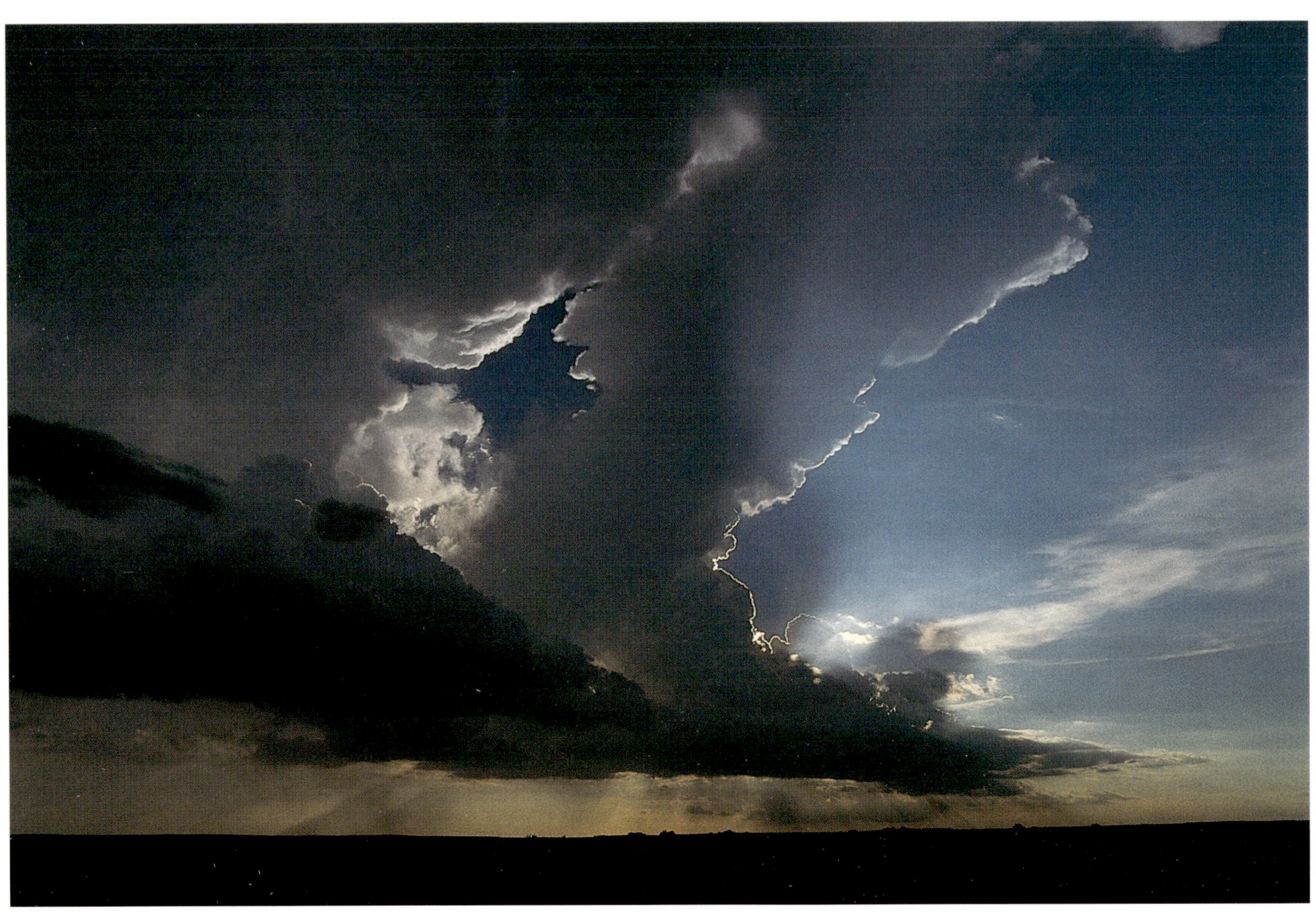

LUCK OF THE DRAW

Witching on dry land is prophecy,
and drilling a well, creation.
Pipes of our neighbors' wells dry up,
and they auction all they own.
We seed each angry cloud
and dance each dance with weather.

When it's time to irrigate dry crops,
we crank an old Ford engine
and pump the purest water
up from nothing we've ever seen,
pouring our luck over pastures
flat as the moon.

The Ogallala aquifer drops
three feet each season,
and nothing we know brings water
out of stone. Home is a casino
of chance and choice,
four arms that hold each other.

MOTHER'S CHIHUAHUAS

Wind chimes dangled from hooks, five lazy cats
half asleep, sprawled on the welcome mat or curled
by Mother's rocker. She taught my brother and me
to leap across, to follow her saucy Chihuahuas that waddled,
pointy tails jiggling, tongues dripping and pink.

Mother taught her dogs to bark at shadows of wings
to keep them lean, running and stumbling, clumsy
as twins in a playpen. Her yard was a garden of pets
and ponds, shaded by tall pecans. She fenced a vineyard,
penned goats and horses beyond the barn. Her face

was leather, sun-burned but soft as a Chihuahua's tongue,
flushed from stooping long in her garden without a hat
but laughing, snapping green beans in her rocker.
That woman loved her dogs and chuckled at cat tails
inches away from her chair, flicking like the tick of a clock.

Each time we caught a tail and stretched it there,
Mother stopped, her fingers snapping the beans with pops,
leaning back and rocking only when the cat flipped
its lucky tail away. Dogs knew if they were ignored
and knocked us over, licking until we grabbed and rolled them

in the grass. I remember our grandmother's last good month,
coughing but laughing at my brother with a cream cone
on his head, a unicorn, and Mother holding her hand for weeks
in the hospital. I remember our mother's fat, lazy dogs
that whined when my brother and I swung the gate

to feed them, leaping, lapping our eyes, breaking away
and yapping, little bellies dragging the grass.
I remember the Siamese trotting out and blinking,
hungry and sullen, the Chihuahuas bumping and nipping,
nudging us all to play, to chase the birds away.

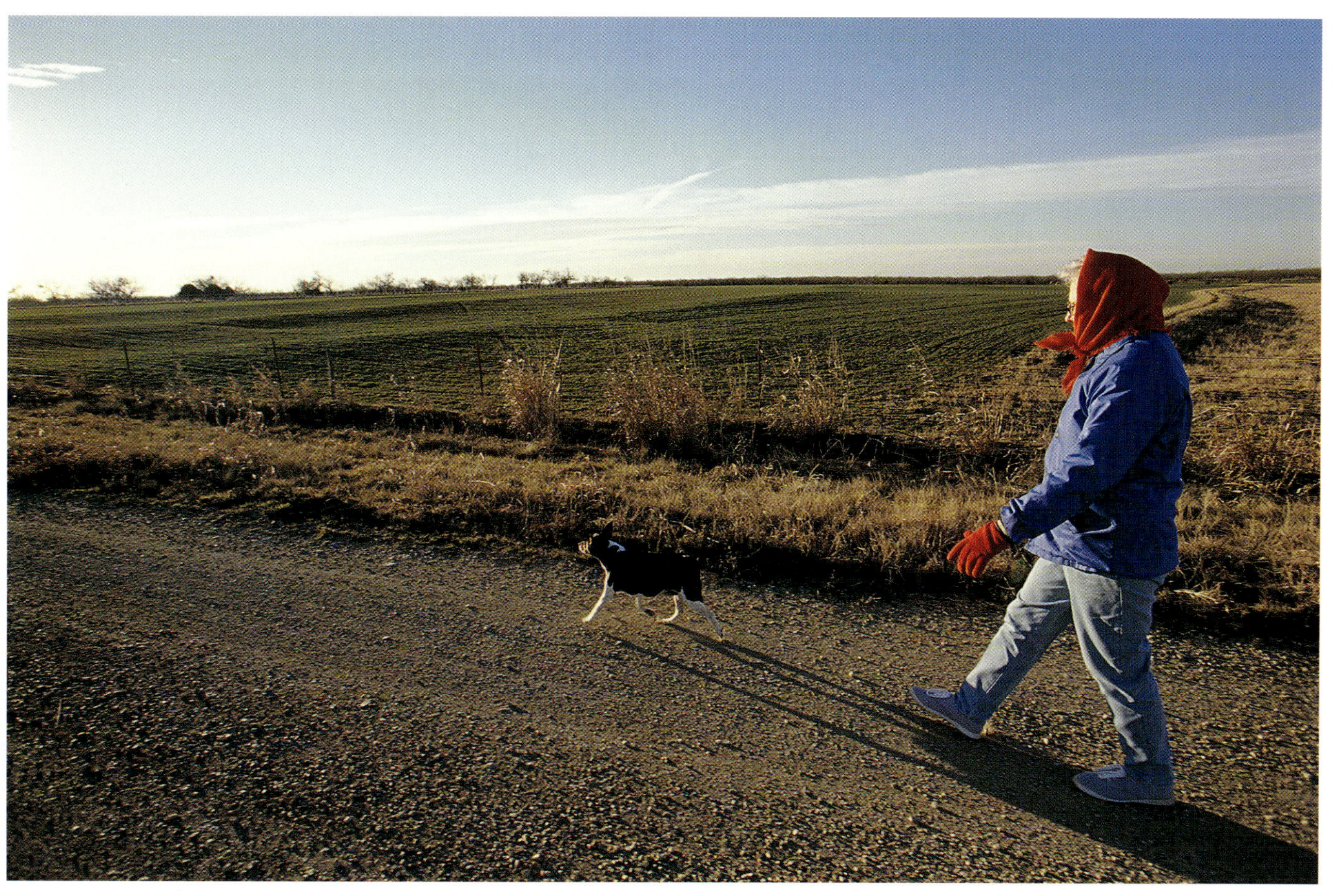

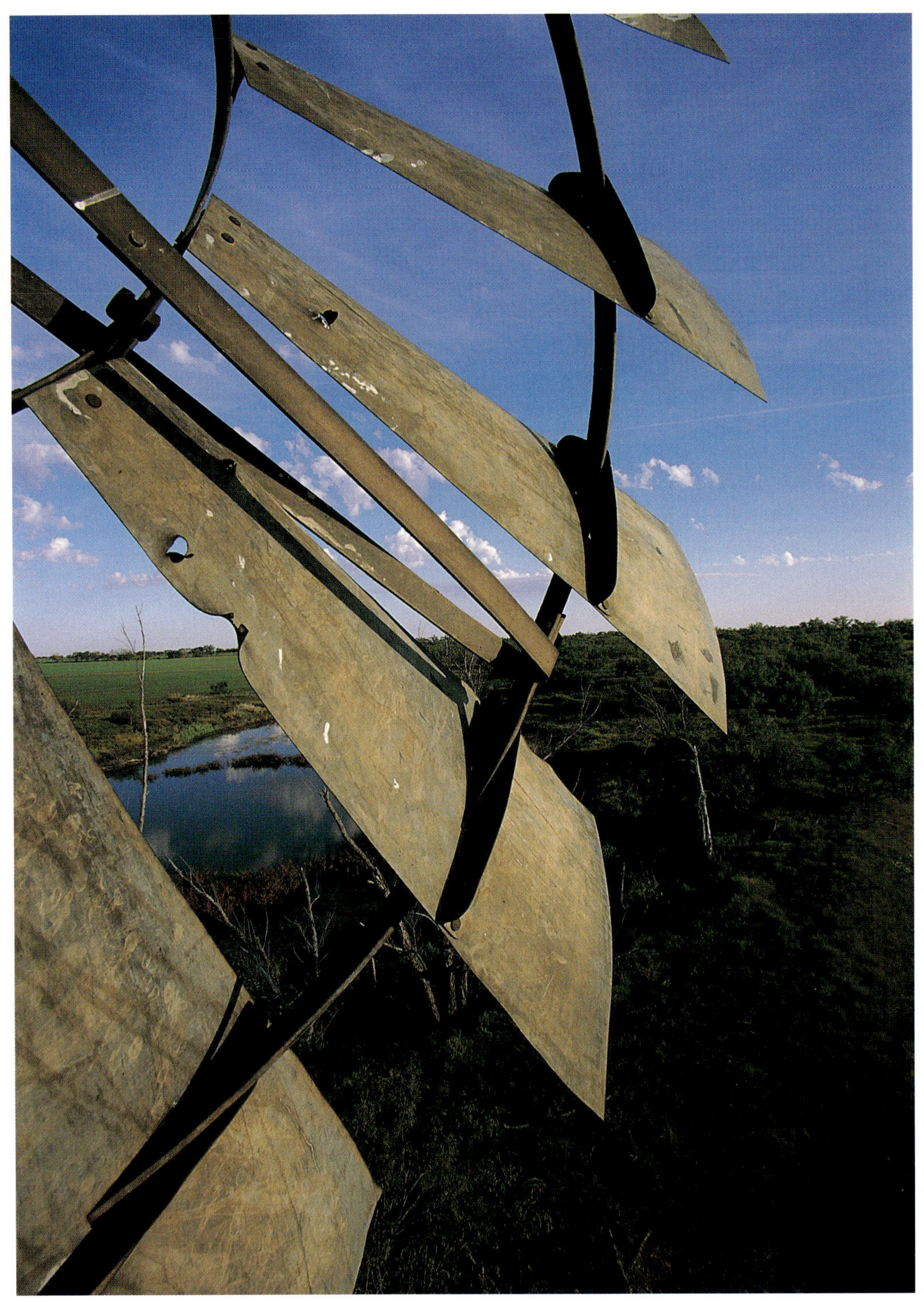

OUT IN THE PASTURE AT DUSK

We leave the windows wide for owls
and ignore coyotes that woo the moon,
complaining they own the ranch. Skunks waddle by,
sniffing for traps. Granddaddy taught me

north and south through his pastures,
past bulls to windmills and muddy ponds.
He slapped a dime-store compass in my hand,
turtle with a tin head wobbling on a pin.

Miles from his barn, I climbed crossbeams
and saw the plains through spinning blades,
a round horizon without a town. Buzzards patrolled
in slow whirlpools, and coyotes loped away.

I thought I'd never be lost on a gelding
trotting home. In jungles outside Saigon,
even a compass lied, no directions out.
Now, after that war a world away,

the ranch is mine, no trains on tracks
laid out by crews long dead. I swore
I'd ride the range and never look back
in spite of friends missing in action.

Goats claim the ranch, butting each other off
as if they own the troughs. At dusk, we stare
at plains we'll harvest tomorrow. Heads bowed,
the goats lie down, worshipping only now.

My wife's brown eyes know dark from dawn
and lead me always home. Nights,
I feel the needle wobbling like an old man
on a high wire, but pointing north.

BUYING THE LAST HALF SECTION BACK

Layers of weeds can't hold bad lumber up.
Anarchy of rot draws us to the barn,
bare walls collapsed, the steep loft cracked.
Our neighbor's plows and hay rakes rust,

vines of morning glory tangled with bindweed.
Wind drags cardinals and jays like a magnet,
tumbleweeds stacked like concertina wire
against the door, the whole barn bowed,

about to burst. Nothing of his herd is here.
He hammered nails to last, caught boards
somebody handed up, maybe Grandfather, held tin
into place and pounded a roof down tight.

The bank hauled the cattle off, when the ranch failed.
Oaks he planted for shade are stumps.
The windmill beams are pulp. On flat plains
far from forests, he hauled them all

and turned a prairie into wind and water
and called it home. Look at that, a horseshoe
over the door, the nails still snug, a roof
he built for love and called it luck.

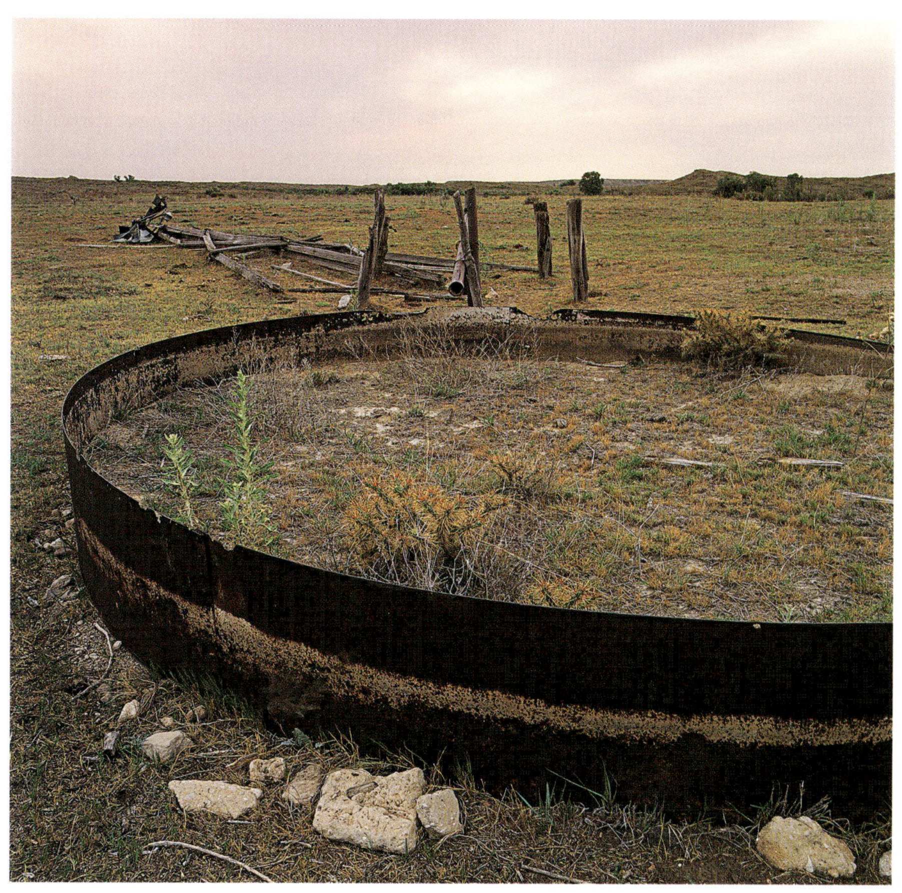

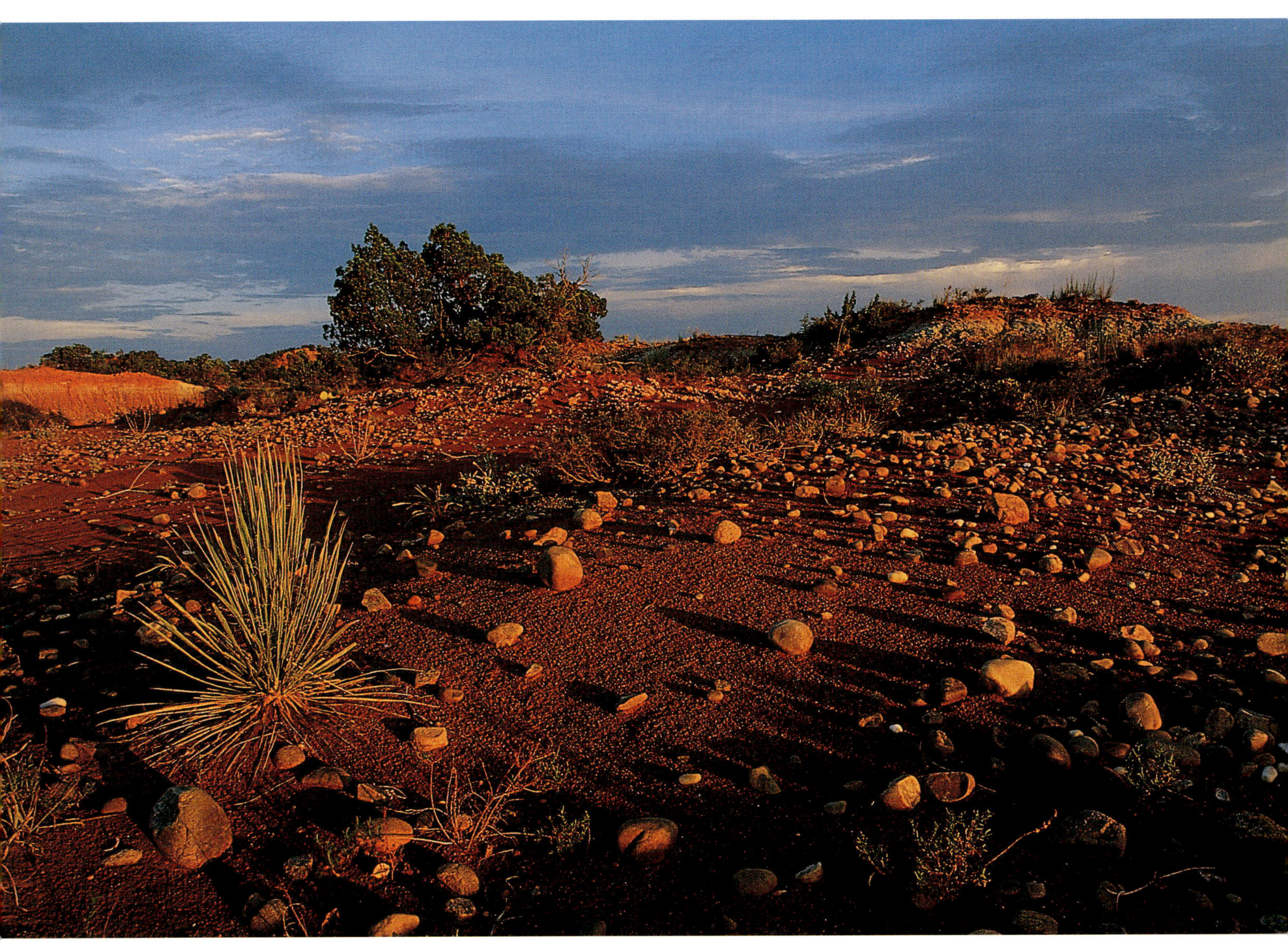

IN FIELDS OF RATTLESNAKES

I watched it writhe away,
dragging a tattoo of diamonds,
and wondered how many fangs
in a field, how many snakes
to an acre? I can't kill them all,

so why bother? Some other year
we'll meet, alone and on its terms
or mine, stick with a loop
for its head, or me without boots,
jogging in dry July,

blinded by backache and sweat,
old age a decade away,
passing cactus it hides in
waiting for mice. I'm no St. Patrick,
so snakes will stay on these flat acres

longer than goats we feed.
Goats graze and butt each other,
strutting, afraid of nothing,
stomping on snakes by the barn,
their bony legs like spikes.

DIAMONDS IN THE CARNEGIE MUSEUM

Our guide was blind and kind, chatting about diamonds
we half circled like a wagon train in a box canyon,
no way out but united for the night,
bound for Montana. She was thirty-five or forty,
without a ring. Her dazzling eyes rolled back

and blinked. She was singing, prattling
about diamond mines and dreams, but singing,
her voice charming us to look. She loved those halls
she never saw, loved all of us she had touched
in the lobby, touched each one only once

but knew us, or made us believe she did.
I wondered what marvels she could sing about
or show. She turned and tapped her way
with a penlight-thin retractable pole,
turned to the bulletproof transparent glass

and sighed. She was a bride among diamonds
and we mere cousins in from the cold, lucky to share
what she held at arm's length every day,
too precious to wear, crushed coal and fire
in the heart of earth too radiant to see.

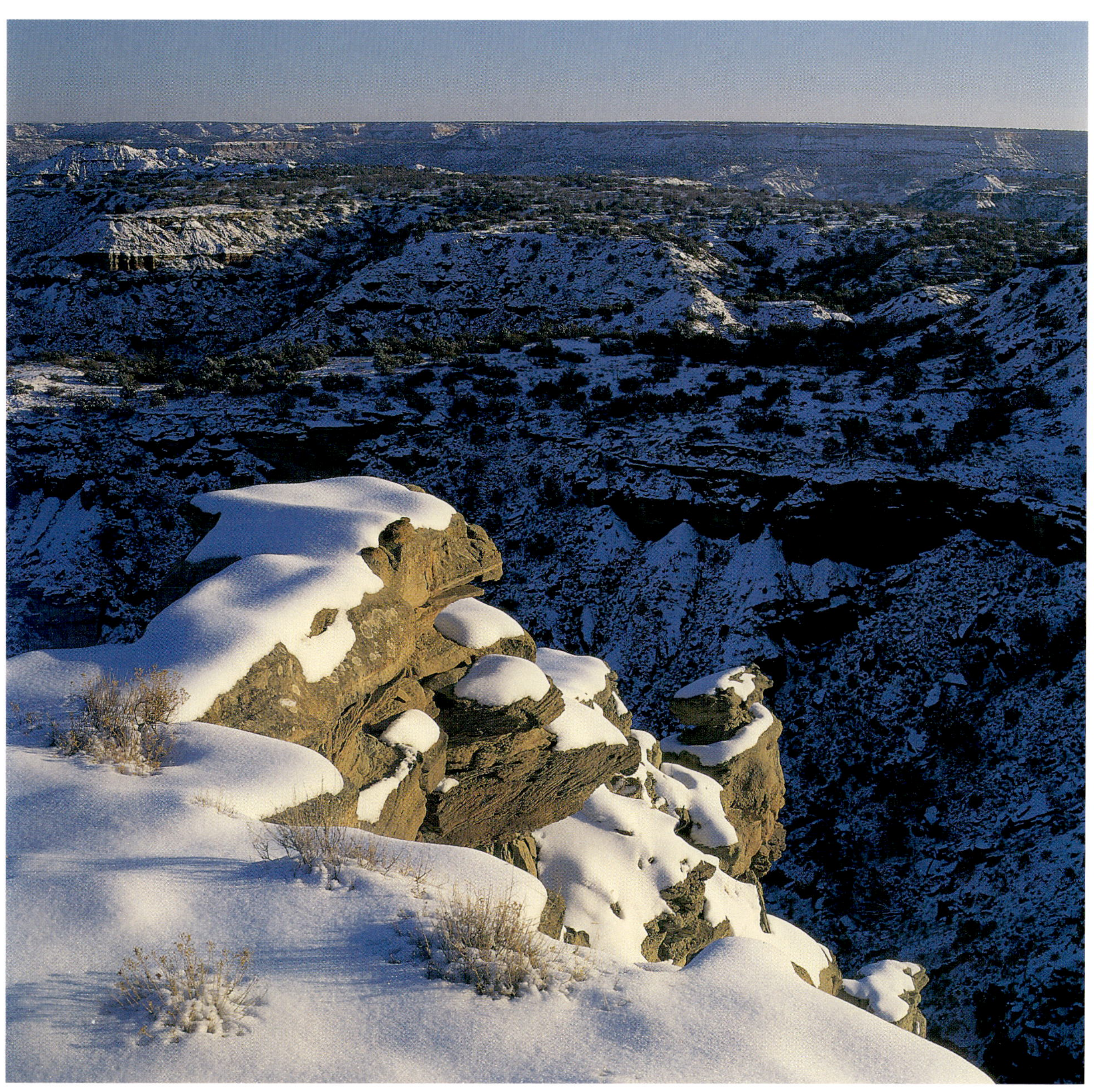

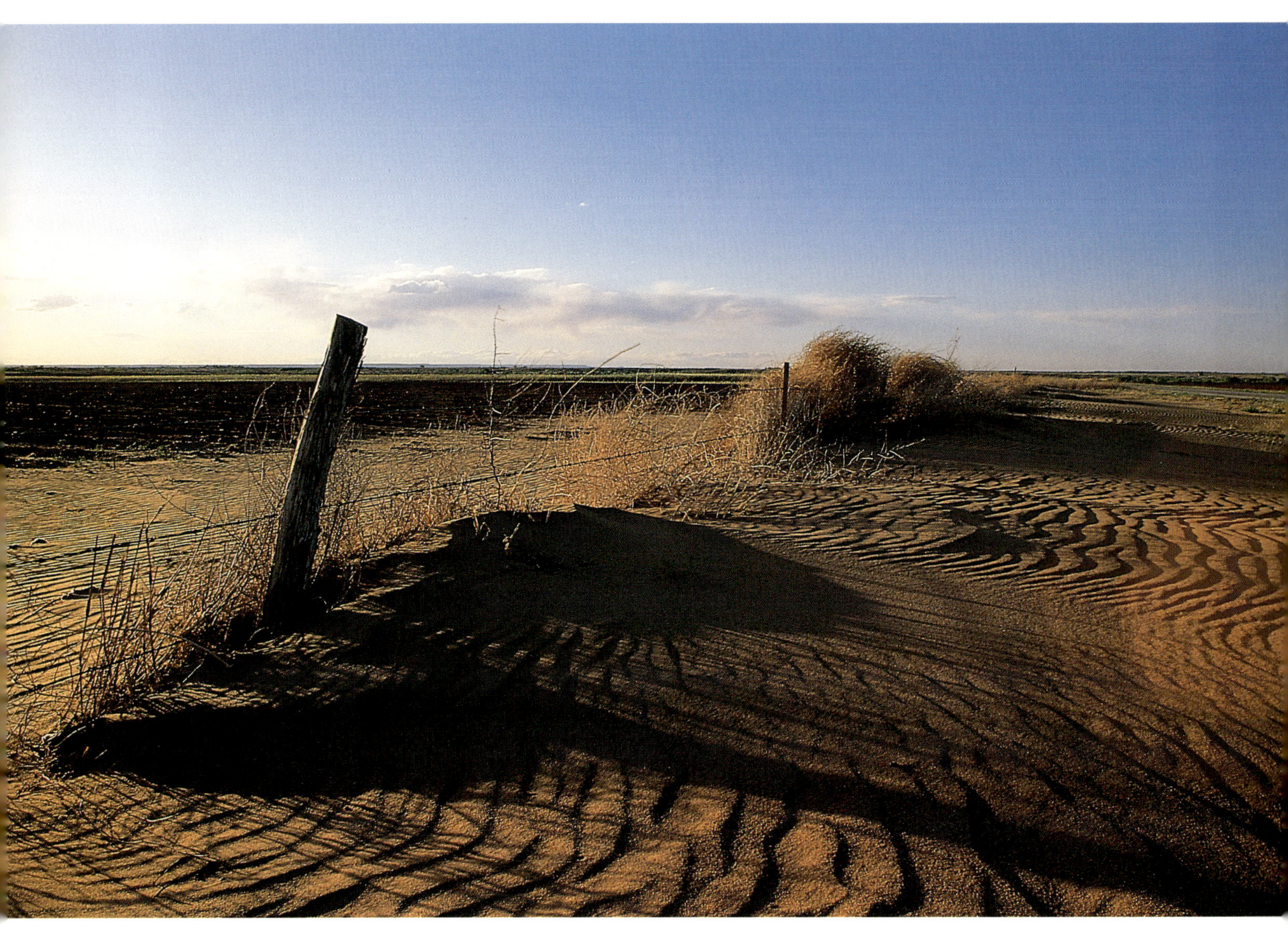

NO MATTER WHERE WE'VE BEEN

I swore I'd never come home
to the Plains, eight hundred acres
and stars so bright they buzzed.

I said I'd work these rows only for sport,
maize for a pair of calves.
Goats and hawks are hobbies, a pond

with bass once in a hundred casts.
Old Uncle Bubba told me
no matter where I've been,

it's home. Our boys make a fortune
dragging home rattlers in towsacks.
The prairie crawls with tarantulas,

hawks in all weather, gliding on thermals.
There's little we could lose, here,
little we could hide. We've almost

stopped pretending clouds are mountains,
here where rain is rare as trees.
If we can't accept these fields,

our souls with all their wind
and cactus, we ought to leave.
Even at night, our shadows sprawl:

that moon is up for hours. On fields
this flat, someone's easy to find
and always calls us friend.

5

THE DUST WE'RE MADE OF

SOARING AT LUBBOCK

We bank and come three-sixty back
and never know we've turned.
These flat plains sprawl to wide horizons,
a million acres for grain and cotton,
a crazy quilt plowed handsome,
no mountains, not even a stream.

Four hundred years ago, Coronado
led soldiers west toward rumors
past that highway, grumbling, his priests
praying to find the gold so they'd go home.
Far off, a herd waits grazing.
That must be how soldiers looked

to buzzards circling over bones
priests saw. The gold they hoped for
was adobe, hunger enough to make them
beg for faith. We bank, now,
falling in a turn toward sundown,
our runway the same wide span of earth.

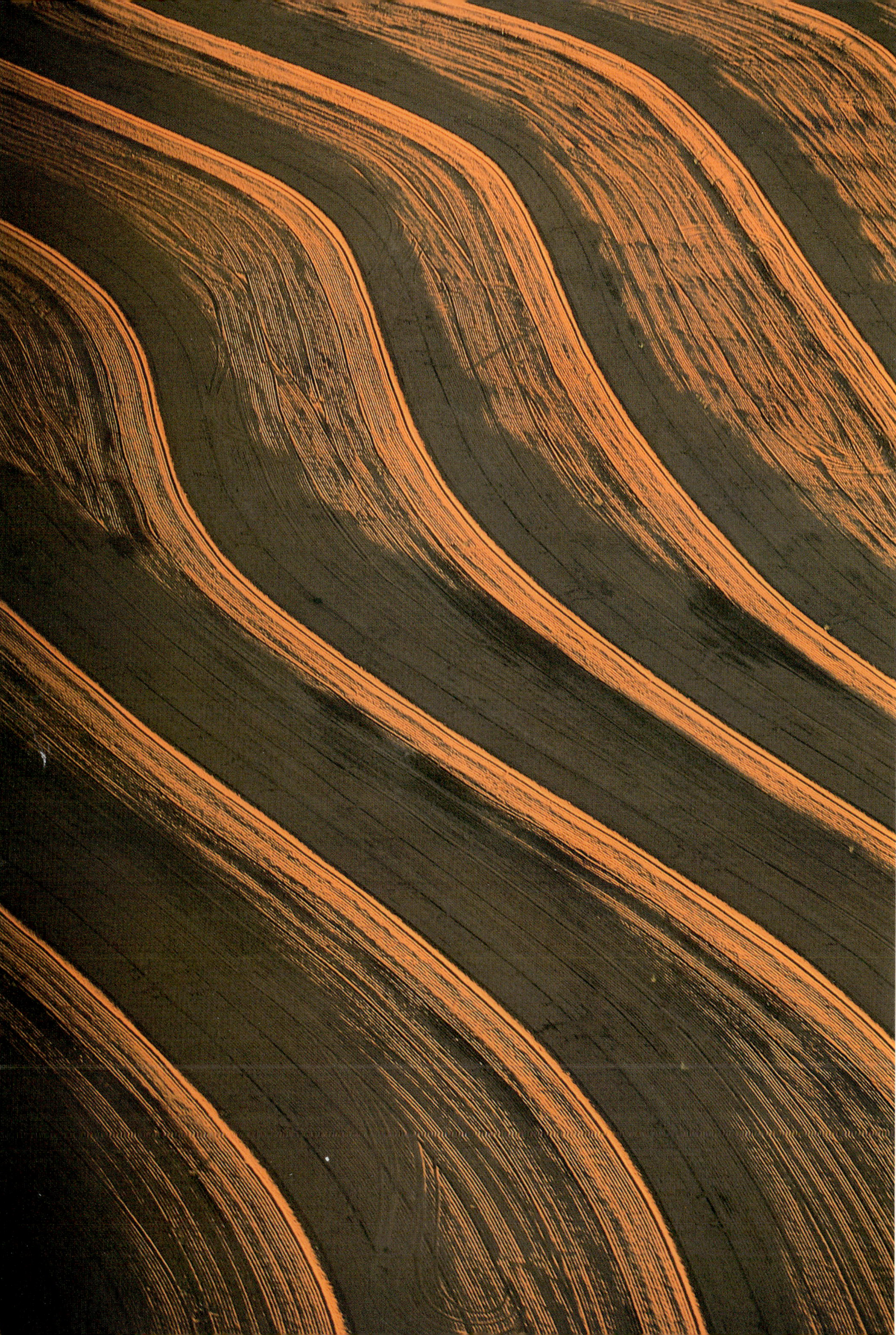

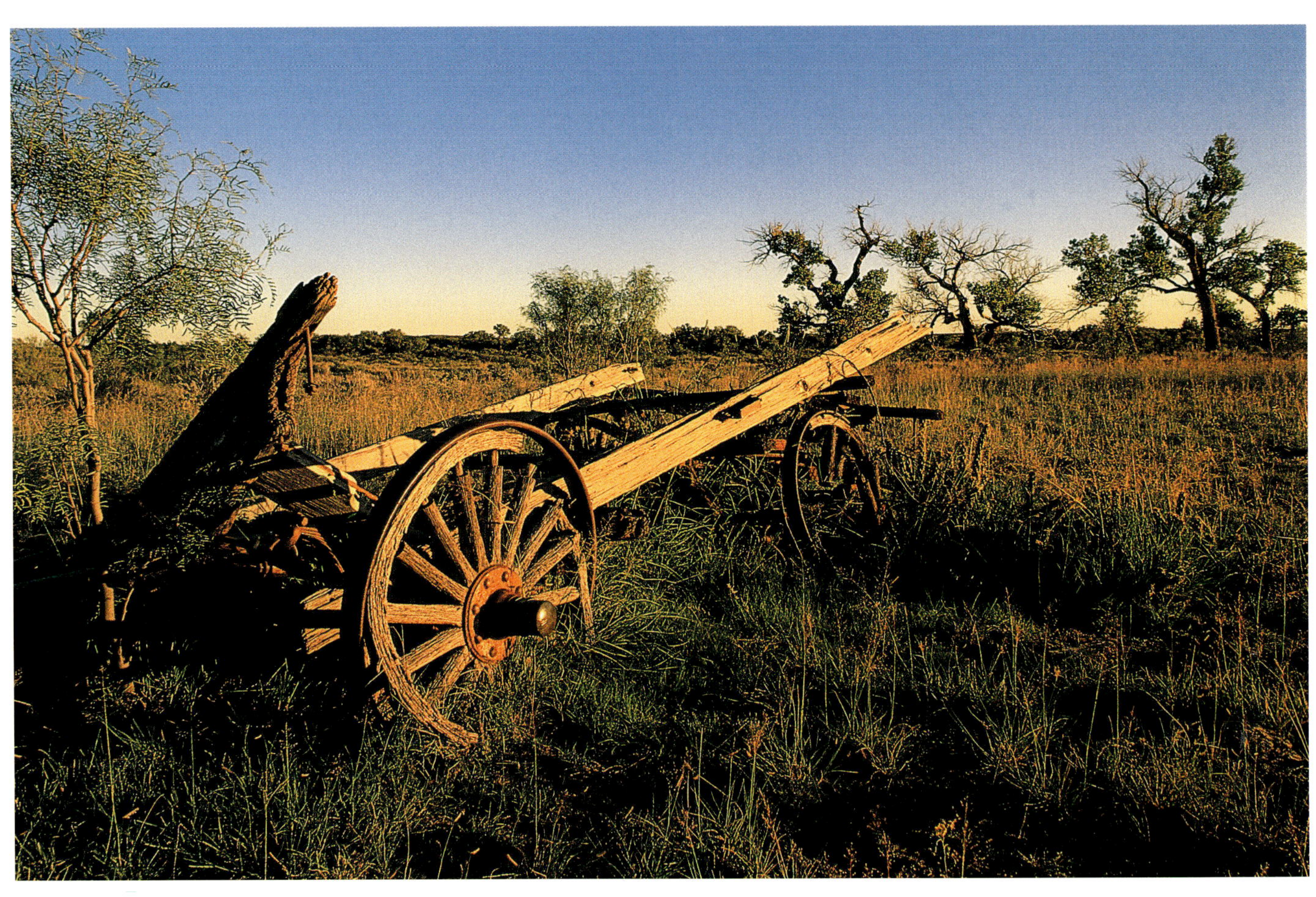

THE ART OF GROWING OLD

It happens when you're rolling oats
around your tongue, like breakfast
after your first baby teeth fell out
or that Daddy pulled, years before you learned
that horses love oats, too. It happens

when you're thinking about retirement
and throw away the daily paper and keep
the classifieds. Or drop the toilet-tissue bar
in the trash and try to shove a new roll
over the empty cardboard, the magazine

you're reading stuck with glue from horses' hooves.
All survivors are naturals in this game.
As long as you breathe, you're practicing,
each year a black belt, easy as licking ice cream
in July, banging your first jalopy fast

down the town's main street, wishing the gang
could see you now—or later in your old,
familiar rocker, or suddenly in a rest home,
hoping anyone would come, you've mastered it,
here's the expert sitting in his chair.

SUMMER NIGHTS

Evenings, when our parents had put away the food,
they'd bring their chairs out on St. Augustine grass
under the shade of Grandmother's magnolia tree

where we climbed through half the jungle scenes we knew,
the sun not ready to settle down anymore than us.
For them, we leaped from higher and higher branches,

hitting the lawn and rolling, flinging ourselves
like all the stunt men we had seen, the world turning dark
like a circus, the gasps and laughter of our elders

proof we were the center ring. Peacocks screamed
in a neighbor's field and someone whispered
Dracula. From then on, scissortails and sparrows

screeched like bats. West Texas echoed screams between us
and peacocks. Without a moon, our eyes turned
into radar. We saw stars fall between the branches,

fireflies too high to reach, the glow of uncles' pipes,
red eyes of things that were not there. And breathing hard,
sneezing, itching from the grass, one by one we fell

before our elders and heard amazing stories of murders
before our time, great-uncles who fought in wars,
houses we never dreamed had ghosts. We listened hard

and heard far in the distance the evening train
to Houston wailing long after any human hand
could have pulled the cord.

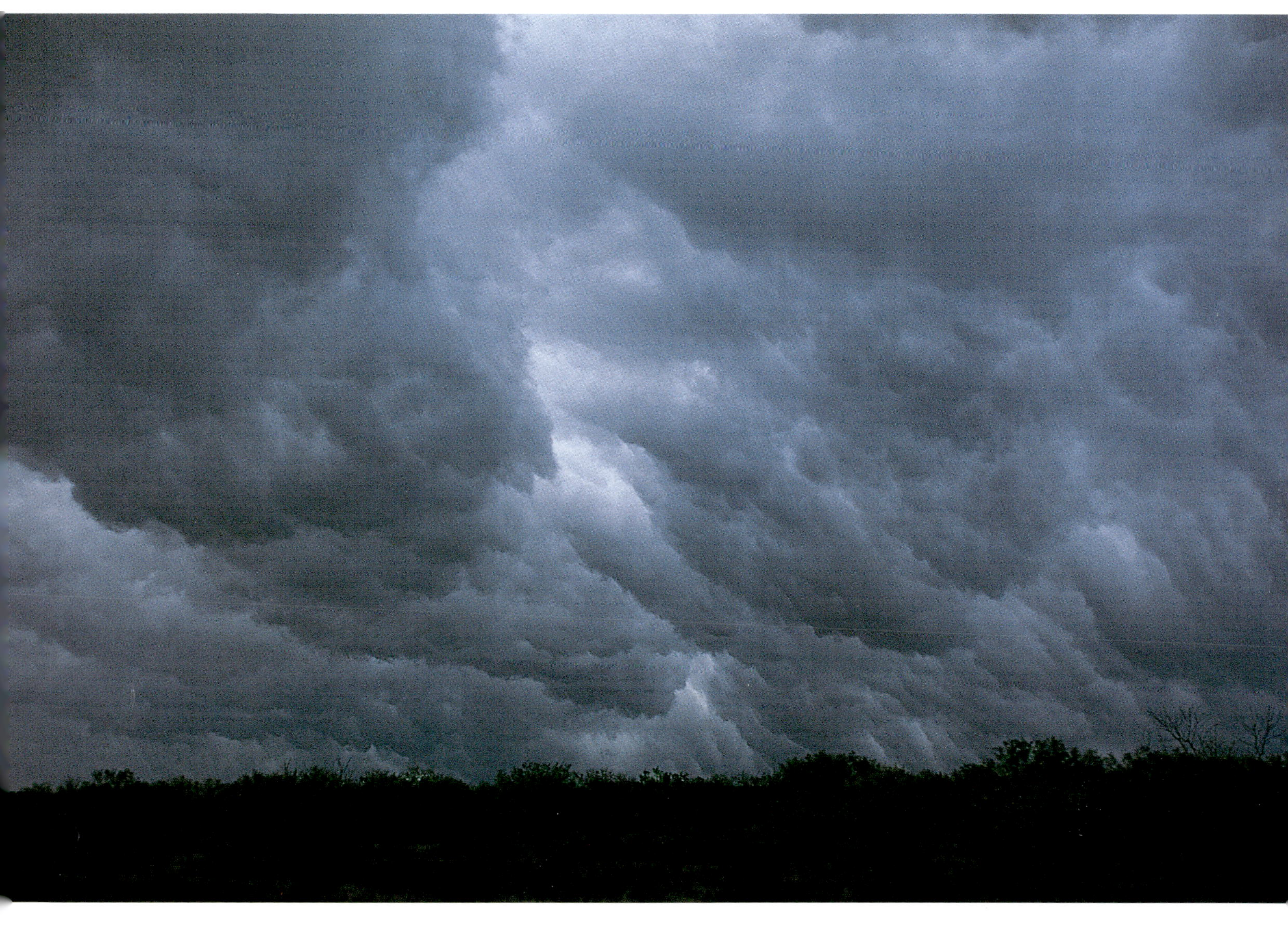

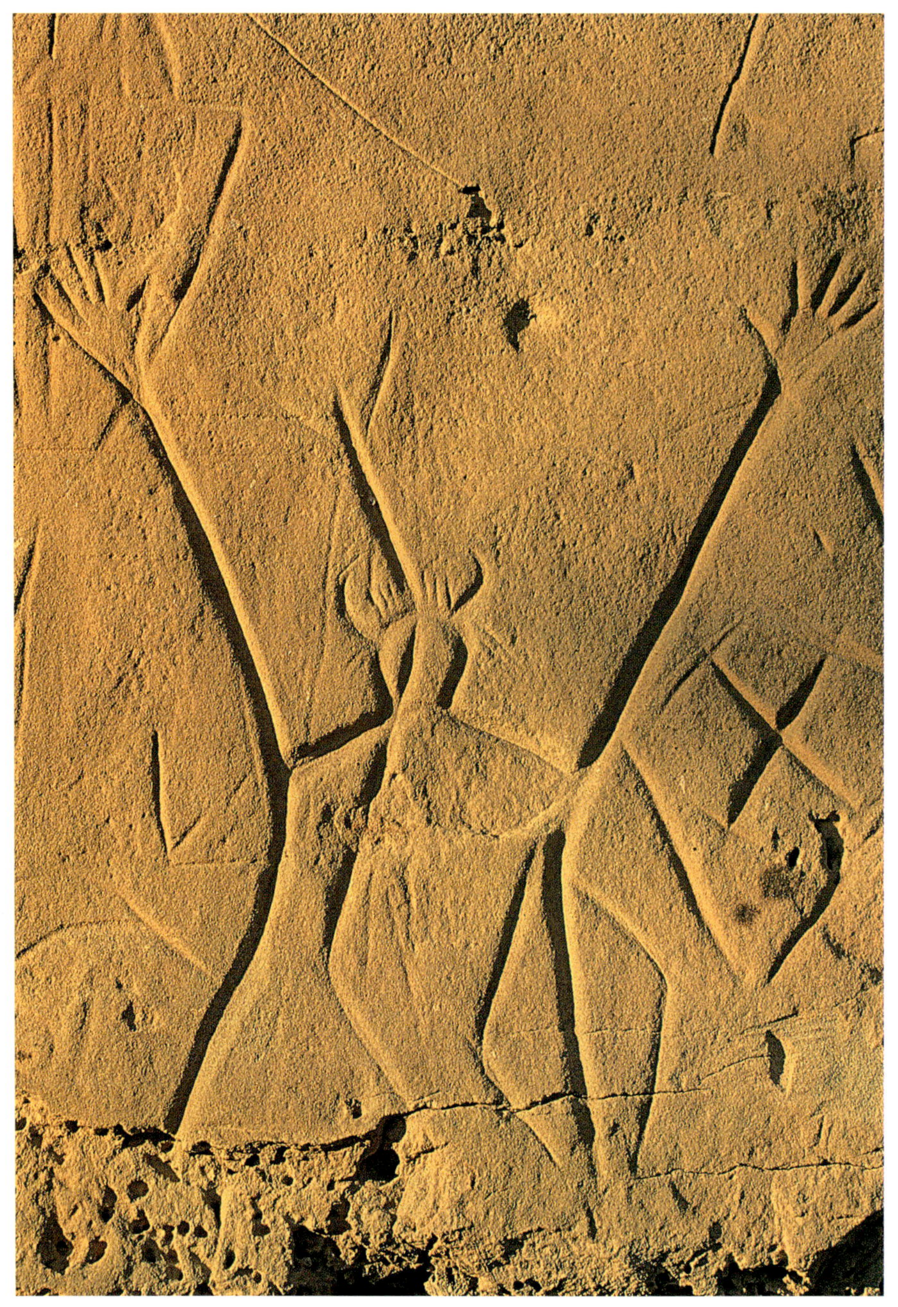

THE DUST WE'RE MADE OF

All summer under klieg lights
we stroke the dirt with trowels.
These digs would disappear, vandals
and idle boys playing plunder: an arrowhead
wedged in a faded Levi pocket, a jawbone mocked

and tossed away like a corncob,
a hand-smoothed bowl crushed to dust by a boot.
We unweave sand like castle tapestries,
thread by thread down to walls that breathe,
that need our touch to live.

We've found bronze kernels never baked,
seen golden ears hung up to dry
on Southwest porches, eaten tortillas
of such crushed corn. Here, people like us
lay down in darkness. We sift the dust

we're made of. What did they fear?
Near midnight on our knees,
we catalog clues for regional museums,
the signs of modest toil, evidence of hope
not seen, the kernels not consumed.

AUNT FANNY AND THE NEIGHBORS' NAGS

Her horses nibbled sugar, our palms barely wet.
The way mares grazed made *horse-face*
not a put-down, after all. *They ate polite,*
Aunt Fanny said, a long-boned widow from Paducah.

When Uncle Joe passed on, she bought a farm
and turned the stalks to pastures, built stalls
for doctors' and lawyers' horses and her own.
Fanny worked magic with ponies and depressed old nags,

trapped all their lives in town back lots. At first,
mares stood in the stalls heads down, stiff lipped
and wooden like Washington's false teeth.
Aunt Fanny talked to them all like daughters

awkward in training bras. Briskly she brushed
and curried, and led them around the pasture,
one at a time, then two, then a herd of old girls
clopping along, wild enough within months

to gallop without coming back sad to the barn
as if beaten or left alone too long. Even us
they let duck under their necks and stroke
and hold, hearing their hearts' deep bumps,

accepting sugar cubes we lifted to gray lips
nibbling, not nipping a finger, old muzzles
quivering, ripples of horse hairs
grazing our necks like fringe.

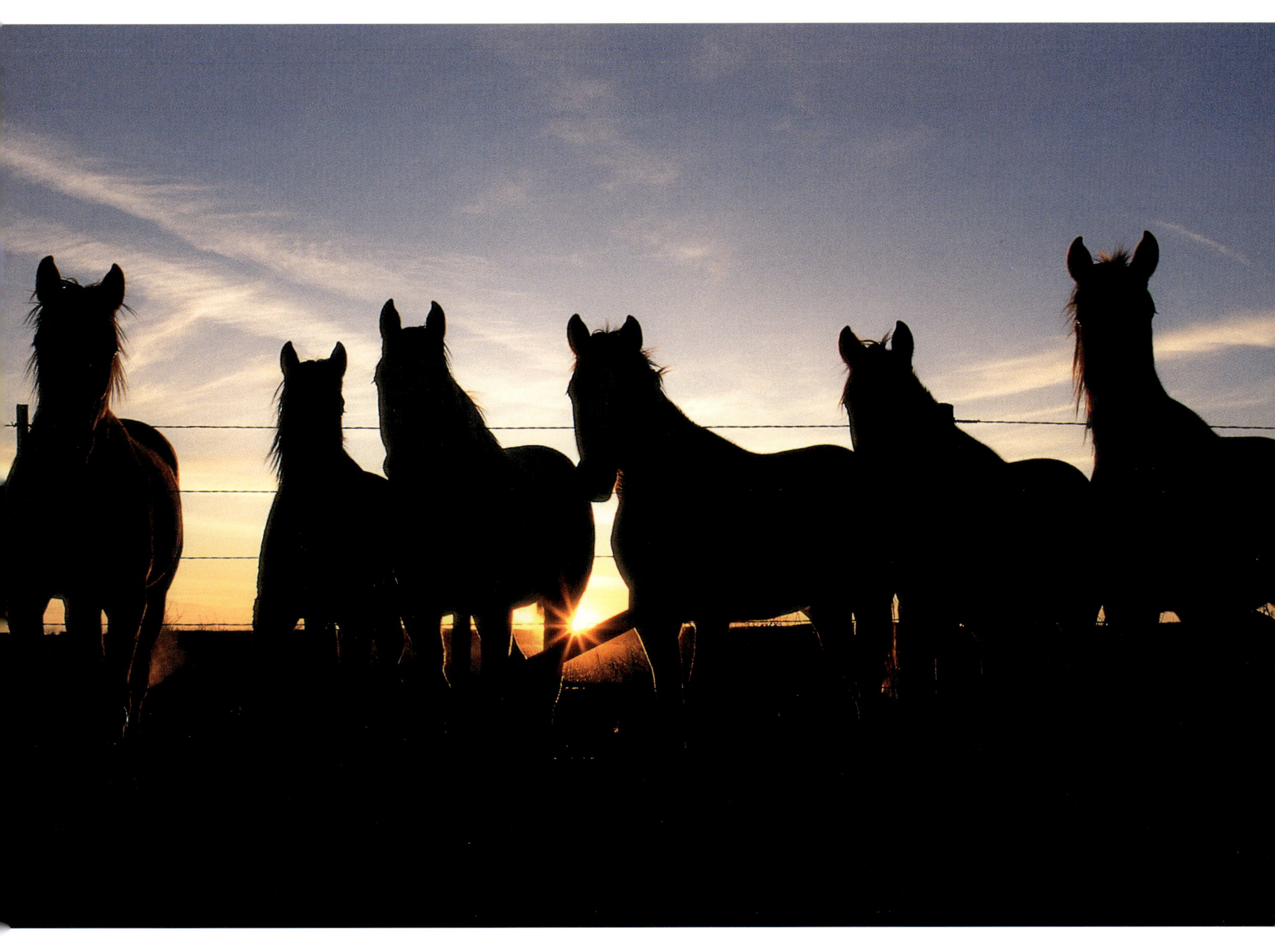

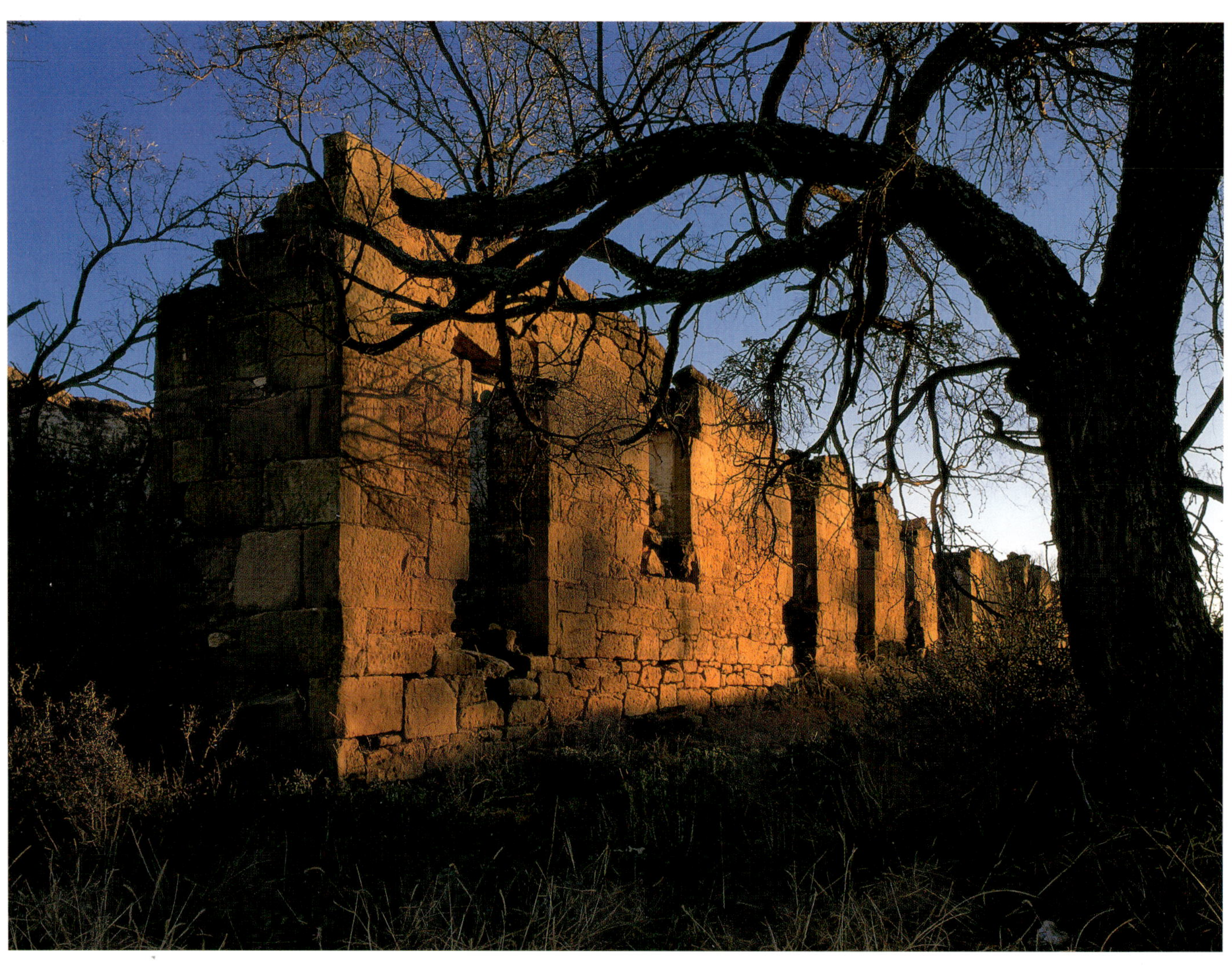

DIGGING IN A FOOTLOCKER

Crouched before dismantled guns,
we found war souvenirs
our oldest brother padlocked in the attic,

a brittle latch easily pried off.
Stiff uniforms on top, snapshots
of soldiers young as our cousins,

a velvet box of medals
as if he fought all battles
in World War II. Bayonets, machetes,

a folded flag, two hand grenades
with missing pins. We picked up teeth
like pennies, loose, as if tossed in,

a piece of something dark and waxy
like a fig, curved like a question mark,
a human ear. We held it up to the light,

wondering how did our brother
learn to kill, what would happen
when we grew up.

BETWEEN THE MOON AND ME

They may have needed calves
more than the wolves, time enough
for caution back at the smokehouse
with meat to last the month.

Grandfather knew what was his, and rode
always with his rifle, ready to die
for his cattle. Living on prairies,
my father said, a man wore the law

in his eyes and guarded his barbed wire
with bullets. I found them
under a board in the cactus, their names
scratched deep with the grain

and simple, fading in the drought
and rains of eighty years. *J. W. McCall
& son, rustlers, 1899.* Deep down,
I found their bones, the skulls

and buckles of their belts
around their backs, coiled like the spines
of rattlers. That night, before I called
the deputy I shot pool with in Dickens,

I took that long Winchester down
from the wall and oiled it, and wound it
over and over in oilcloth, and buried it
under the moon, deep down.

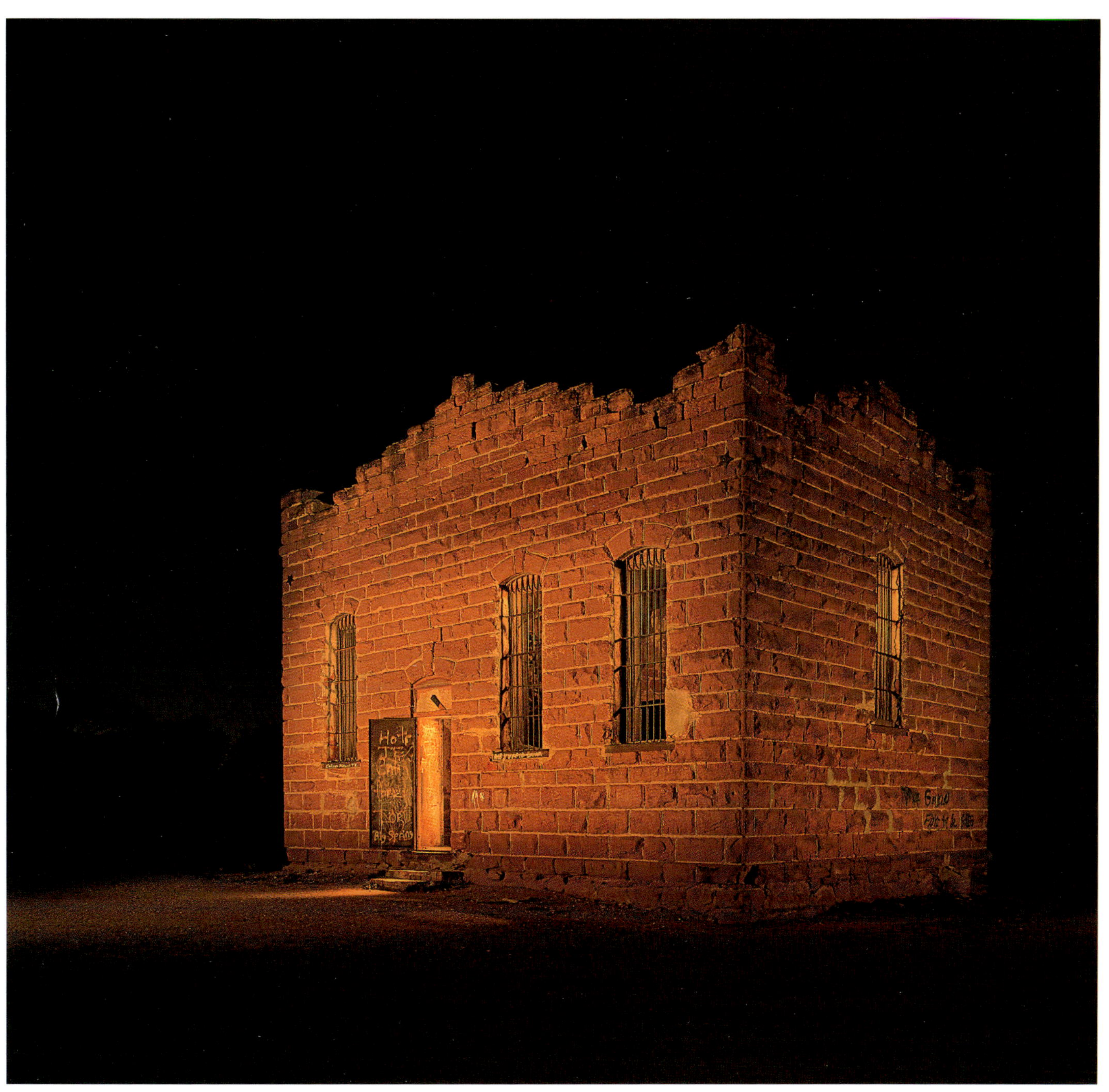

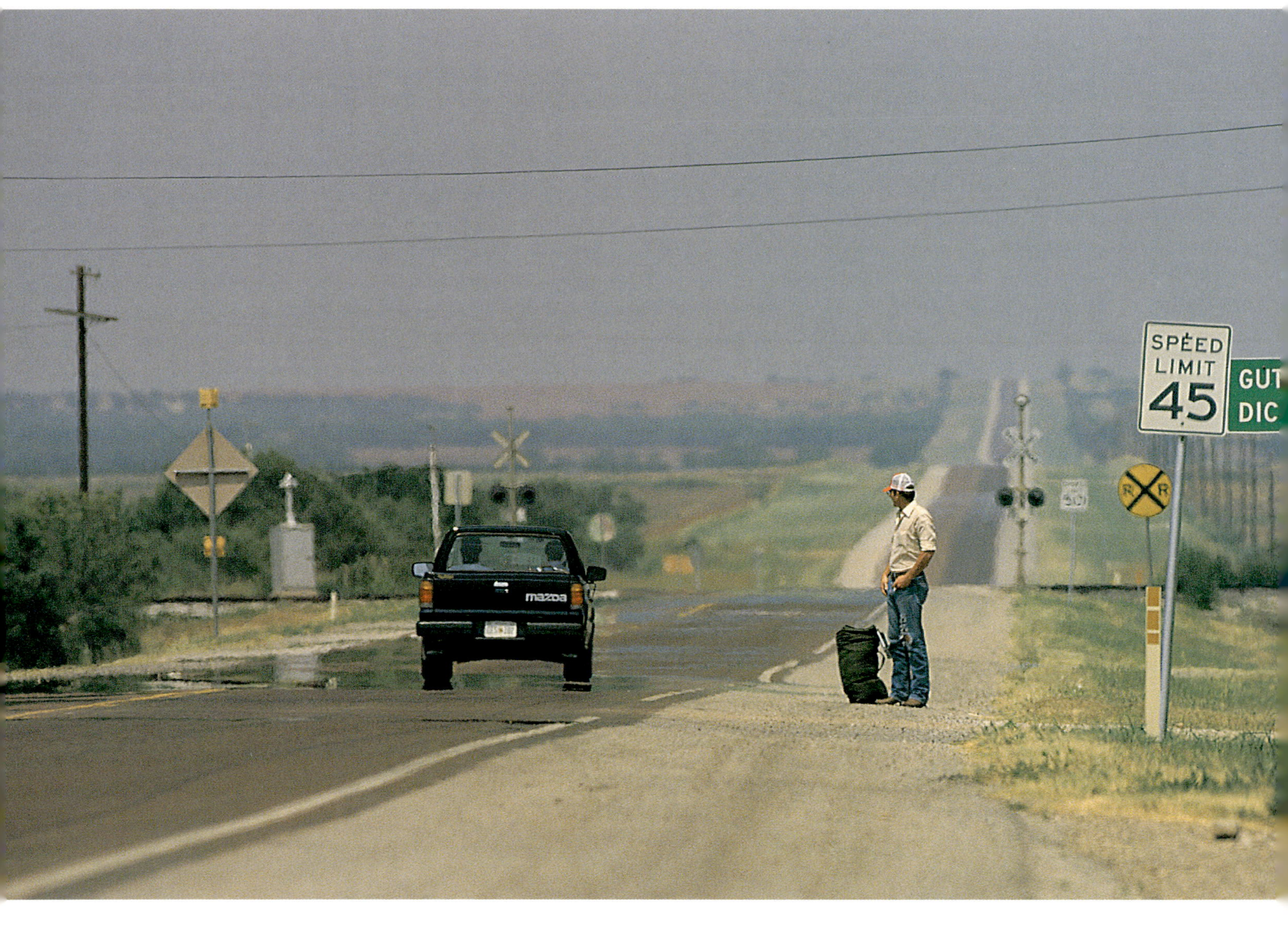
SPEED
LIMIT
45
GUT
DIC
R
R
mazda

SPRINGTIME IN TEXAS

Armadillos drop like dollops
along back highways to Dallas.
They die a mile apart, some belly up,
some like bronzes in Neiman Marcus.

Racing by thickets of mesquite
and live oaks sucked by mistletoe,
I slow to sixty to watch bluebonnets
and Indian blankets dazzle the roadside.

Pickups and cars zip past, a blur of tires
and bumpers daring porcupines
to waddle across, just try it.
We need a chicken to cross the road

to prove to armadillos and skunks
that it could be done. Flat pelts
are closer than a mile apart,
pounded by truckers, meat enough

for crows and buzzards rising
as I approach, polite as diners
in crowded cafes in Guthrie,
Seymour, any West Texas town.

THE SONGS WE FOUGHT FOR

We drank while half the stars came out for us,
Willie and Waylon, Jane and Loretta,
ours in the glow of the jukebox.

Over the laughter and smoke of local men
and women groping for their lives, they sob-sang
all we hoped to know of lonesome love.

Nothing like songs could break a boy's heart
with the draft and a war in Vietnam
drawing him closer daily. Living on dust

and beans all week was bad enough,
and we grabbed for all kind loving we could find.
Slumped under our Stetsons, squinting

in blue smoke layered like gunfire,
we bought pitchers of beer for women
we never hoped to marry. Each time

I took Sweet Darlin's hand and led her
to the dance floor, I felt the world should end
like that, slow-dancing close as we'd ever be

to another in clothes, lost in a sad, sweet
fiddle-rhythm, sliding on polished boots
and humming softly to ourselves.

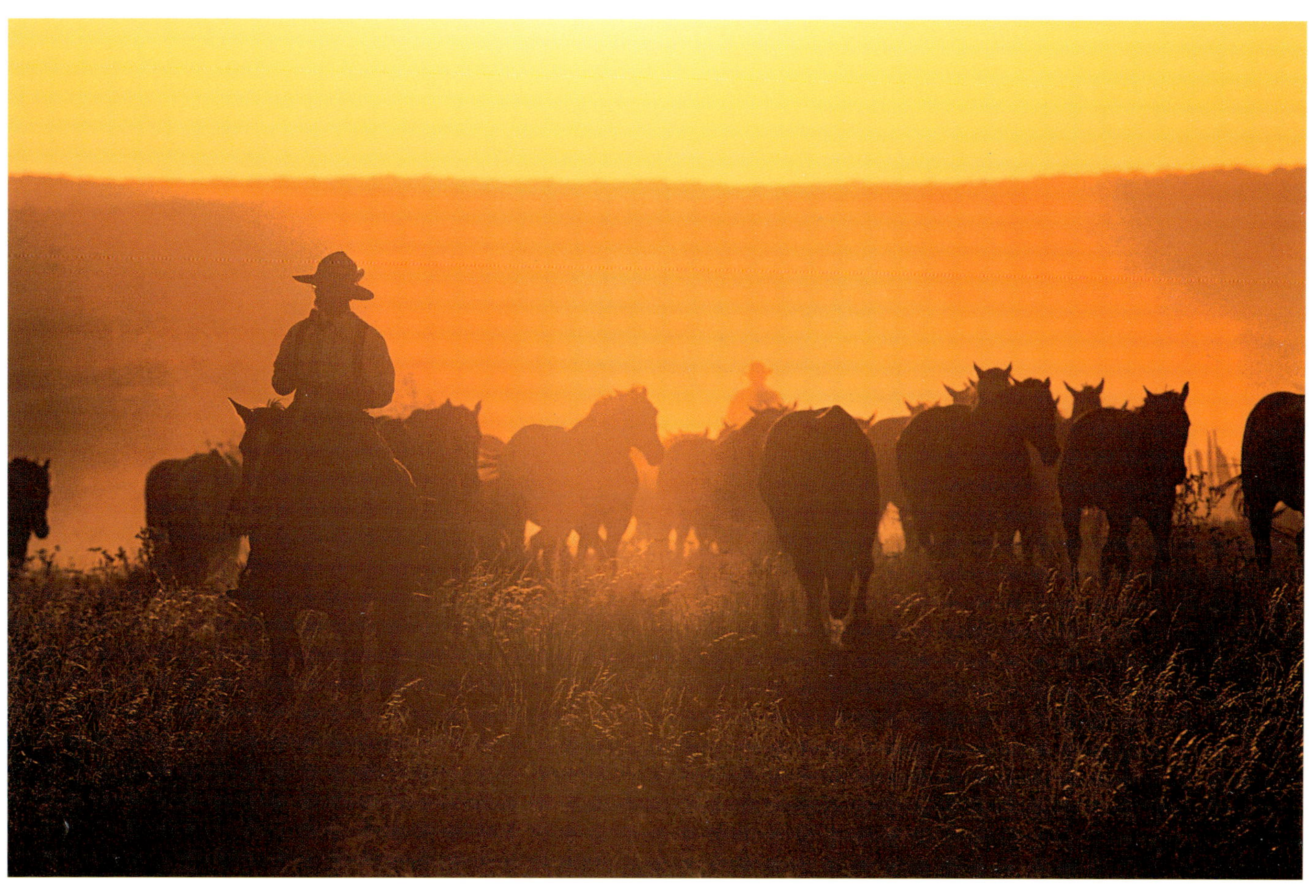

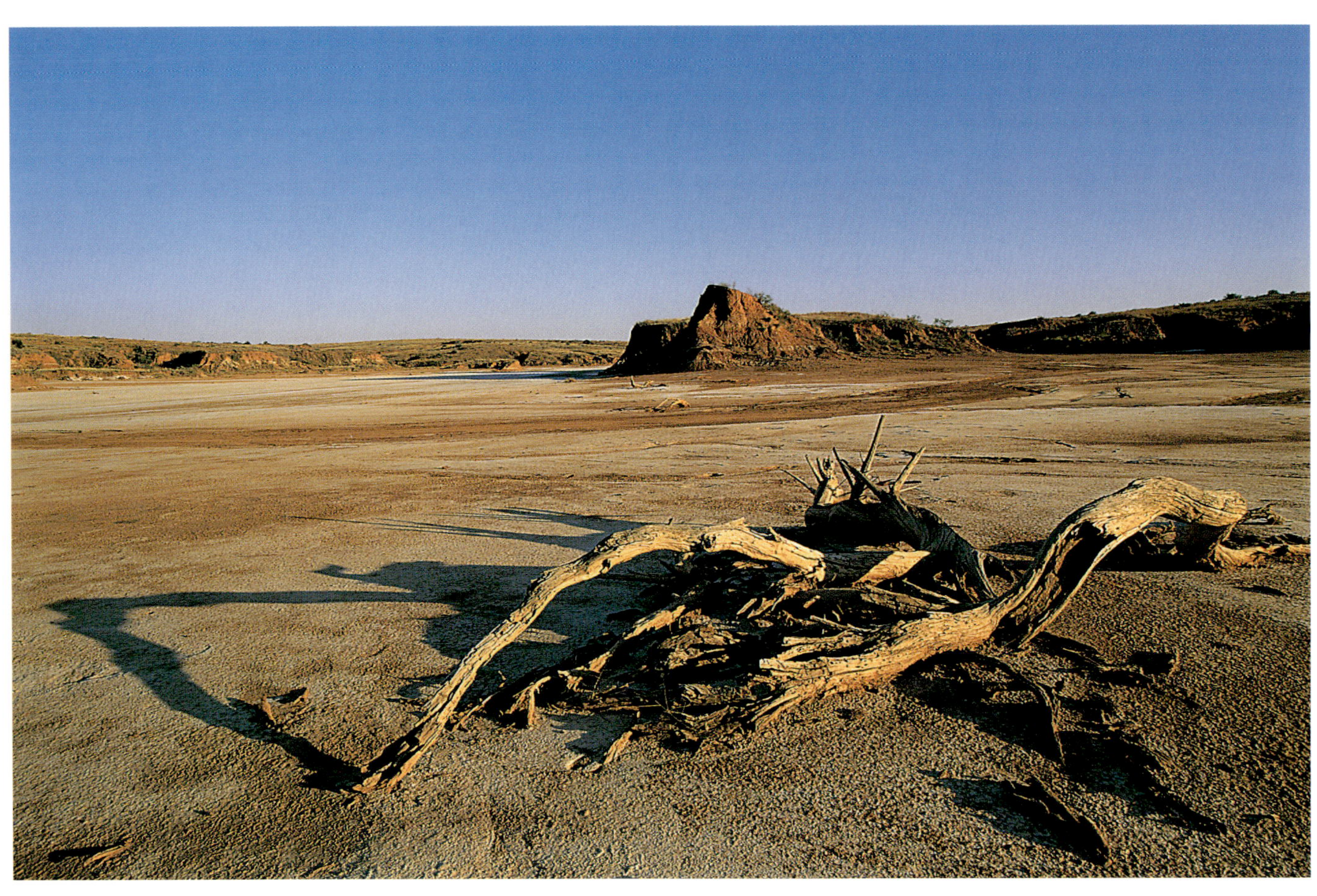

HARVEST

This far out in the country, no dogcatchers ride by,
only cars with pets like rejected hearts. Our stock tank
blesses dogs abandoned by cars with city tags.

Dogs starve if they aren't born hungry for blood,
part wolf, or cute as Disney dogs some farmer's daughter
begs him to adopt. Stray cats survive on mice and birds,

prowling somebody's barn. We're not alone,
here with dry wind to amaze us. Owls wear feathered legs
like chaps, night-riders over sage and cactus.

Cattle bones are witness clouds are dry, plains
where it rains twice a year if we're lucky.
Stiff winds spread fires to playa lakes

where pheasants risk the rattlers. Nothing not tied down
stays in sandstorms that pound down daily from the west.
Little bells lead cows to pasture, time for windmills

to spin their rapture, turning grass to milk.
Sometimes I squeeze a squirt to a row of cats
waiting with mouths wide with fangs. The ranch

is harvest all year long. At night, rattlers
that survive the fires move rippling over fields,
and silent barn owls dive to pluck their staring eyes.

MORNINGS

The dawn jet to Dallas
bursts into sunlight flames,
climbing for distance.
Redstone silos beyond the barn
could still be black. It is dark here.

Tree houses with vines like ropes
prop up the sleep of boys in towns.
Red boxcars bump
and fumble each other
in the freight yard.

Grandmother opens the psalms
on the grit of yesterday's salt.
Nothing outside is singing.
She thinks of friends
awake under quilts

heavy as honey in winter
who search their ceilings
for flames winging toward space.
She pulls the shawl around her shoulders
and reads about still waters.

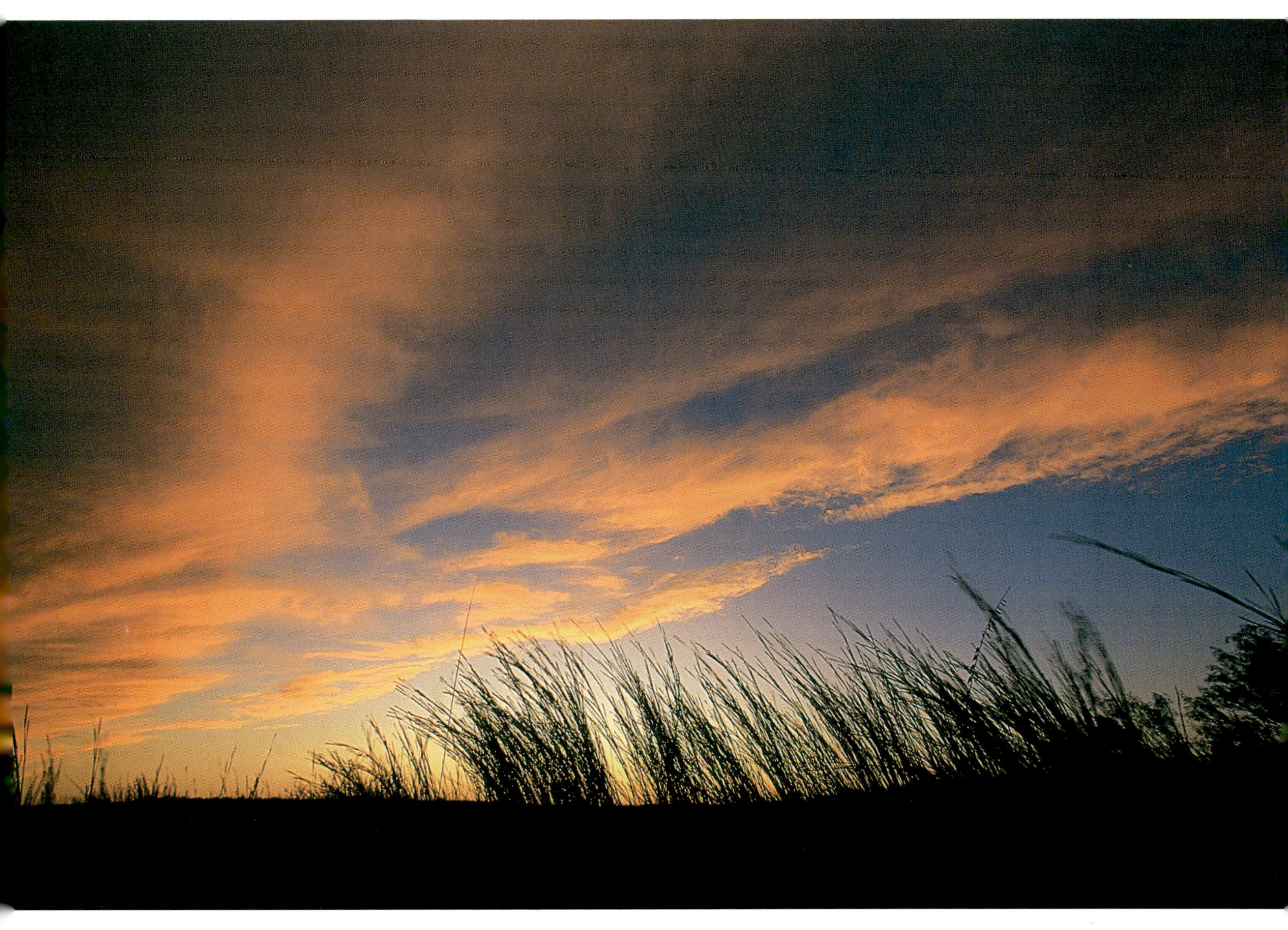

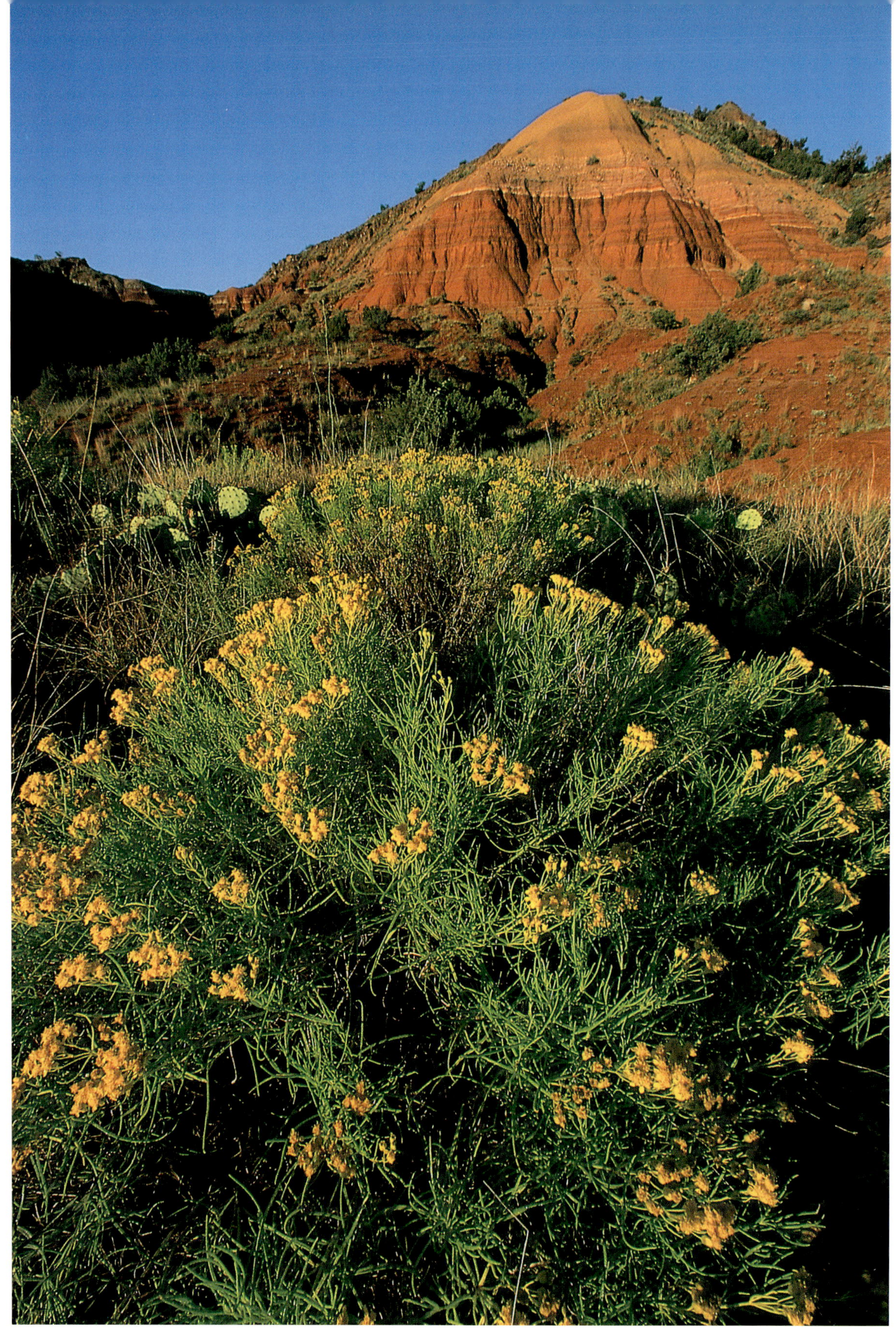

UNDER BLUE SKIES

I see what the horse sees,
a whirling funnel of wings
in slow motion. I know

what I'll find, if I ride there,
the horse not willing to back-talk.
Whatever it was, it's over,

no more desire or fear forever—
a calf that wandered off
down crumbling shale,

unable to bawl loud enough
until it starved. Or only a rabbit
that outlived the rattlers,

the safest death, simply to lie down
under blue skies and sleep, accepting
this as the way, not dreading anything.

HEIRLOOMS

We're down to an anvil and conch,
sea shell and useless steel,
not much from four hard years
of war. Mother's grandmother

blew this shell like a horn,
one steady roar to warn
of soldiers scouring Alabama pines,
two blasts to bring him back.

Feel the smooth, curved shell,
taste the dust of the mouth hole.
Touch the knobs like knuckles,
the wavy edges chipped

before we were born. Rub the nicked,
smooth steel of the anvil.
Grandfather felt the smithy's blast,
watched his father pound red iron

until the muscles bulged,
about to burst. Grandfather touched
those fists, the massive biceps.
Feel the pink bowl of the shell,

slide your hand through the spiral
back to the days of Lincoln,
imagine owning ten burned acres
and a leg a Minié ball took off.

Sniff the Alabama pine,
a thousand miles of powder.
Hold it close and hear an ocean
roll near Mobile, blow it long,

now rapid puffs like a hoot owl—
listen to the ringing steel
on the anvil, the clang of hammers
pounding iron to plows.

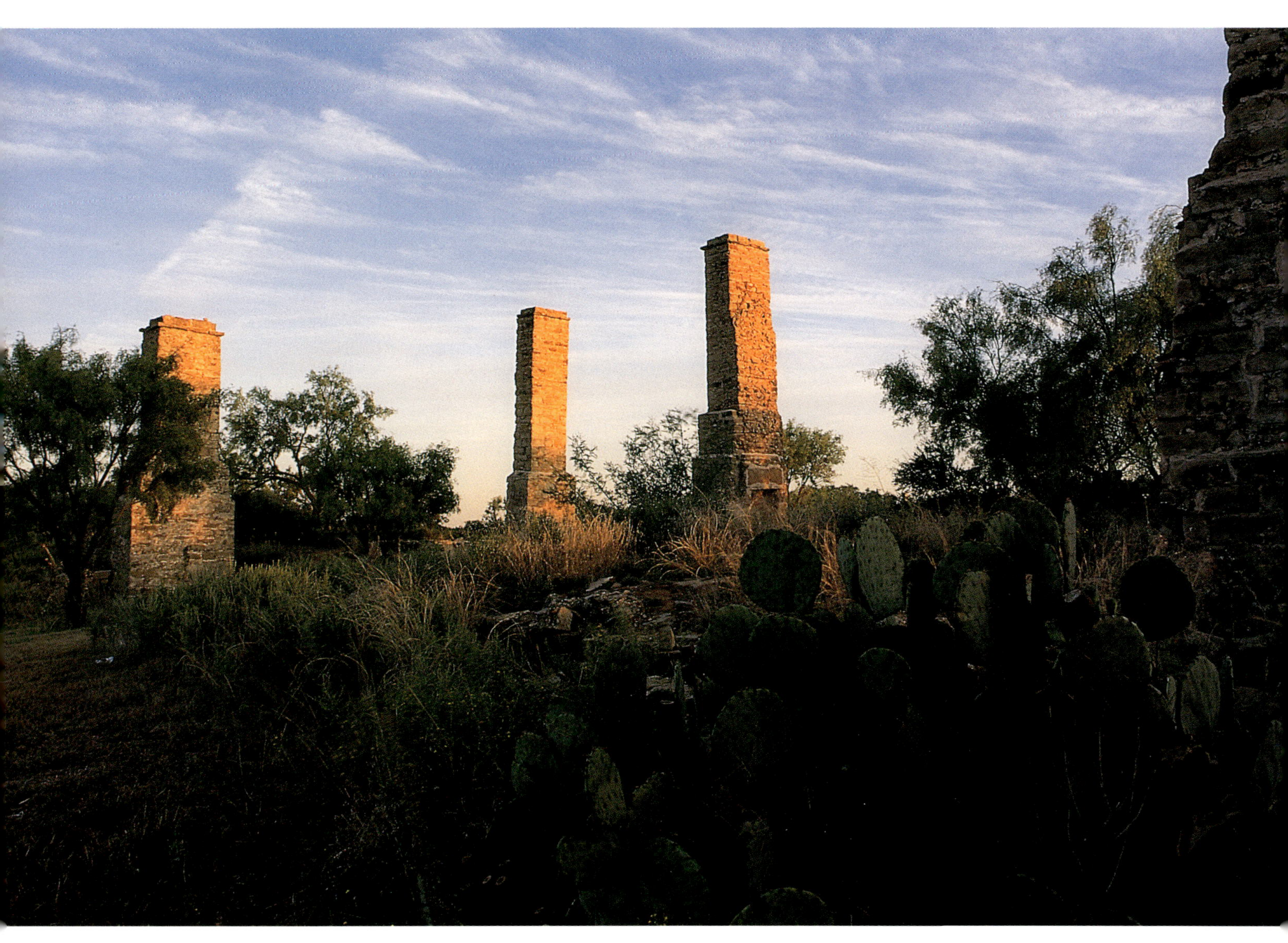

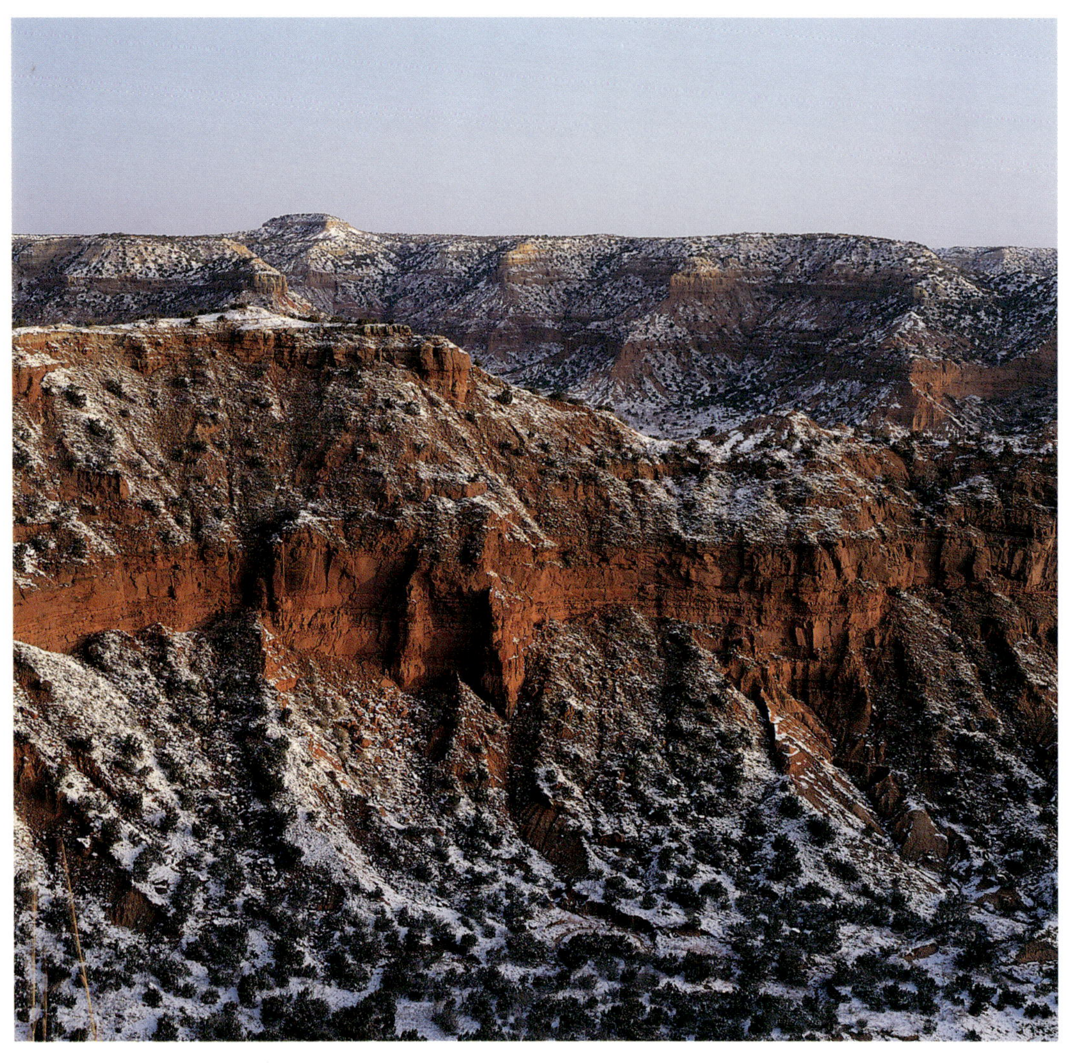

THE PLEASURES OF COFFEE TOGETHER

They'll have to shoot me
if they shoot me down,
our colonel swore.

He leaned back, sipping,
and sighed: *I'd kill them all*
for coffee. How that man

could fly and teach a tight
formation, trying to save us
from rookie mistakes

and missiles. Captured
when his luck ran out,
he lasted years in solitary,

beatings, bones never set.
After they dumped the corpse,
they shipped his dog tags back.

Now, past fifty,
I can't stand coffee at dawn
without my wife beside me.

I'd quit this habit without her.
God knows what I would do
if she were gone.

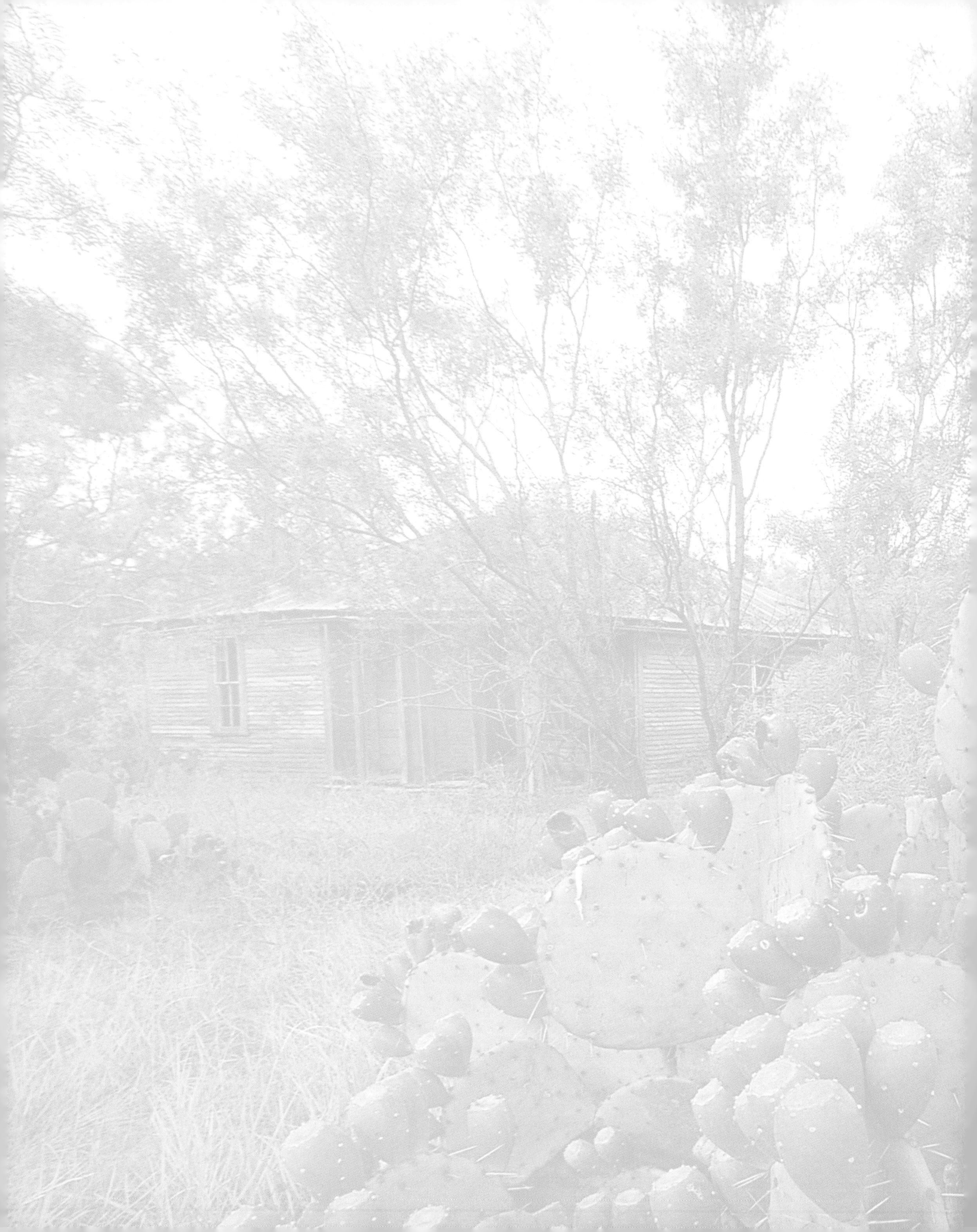

6

GARDENS OF SAND AND CACTUS

CALLING FIRST STARS BY NAME

We live like scorpions in adobe and eat beans
grown in caliche. Two years of drought,
the brittle grass like lichen. If we stand too long
at noon, our boot soles burn. A clean pantry,
coffee and *masa harina* like manna from heaven.
For meat, cabrito and quail, and pronghorns
like fawns we never kill. The ponds dry up

and leave salt rings and stumps. We feed the goats
and keep the windmills turning, the larder stocked.
Good neighbors to the north graze buffalo,
a hold-out herd of eight dark beasts, moody,
hump-shouldered. When we ride to the fence,
they turn away. At night we listen to bobcats
and coyotes crying for rain. We sleep without sheets,

windows wide although there are no screens.
Snakes could burrow over or slide down
through the roof. All summer we plant our chairs
under the only oak and listen to blown sand burn.
We watch for clouds and let our minds glide off
together, calling dusk's first stars by name,
the names of grandchildren we adore.

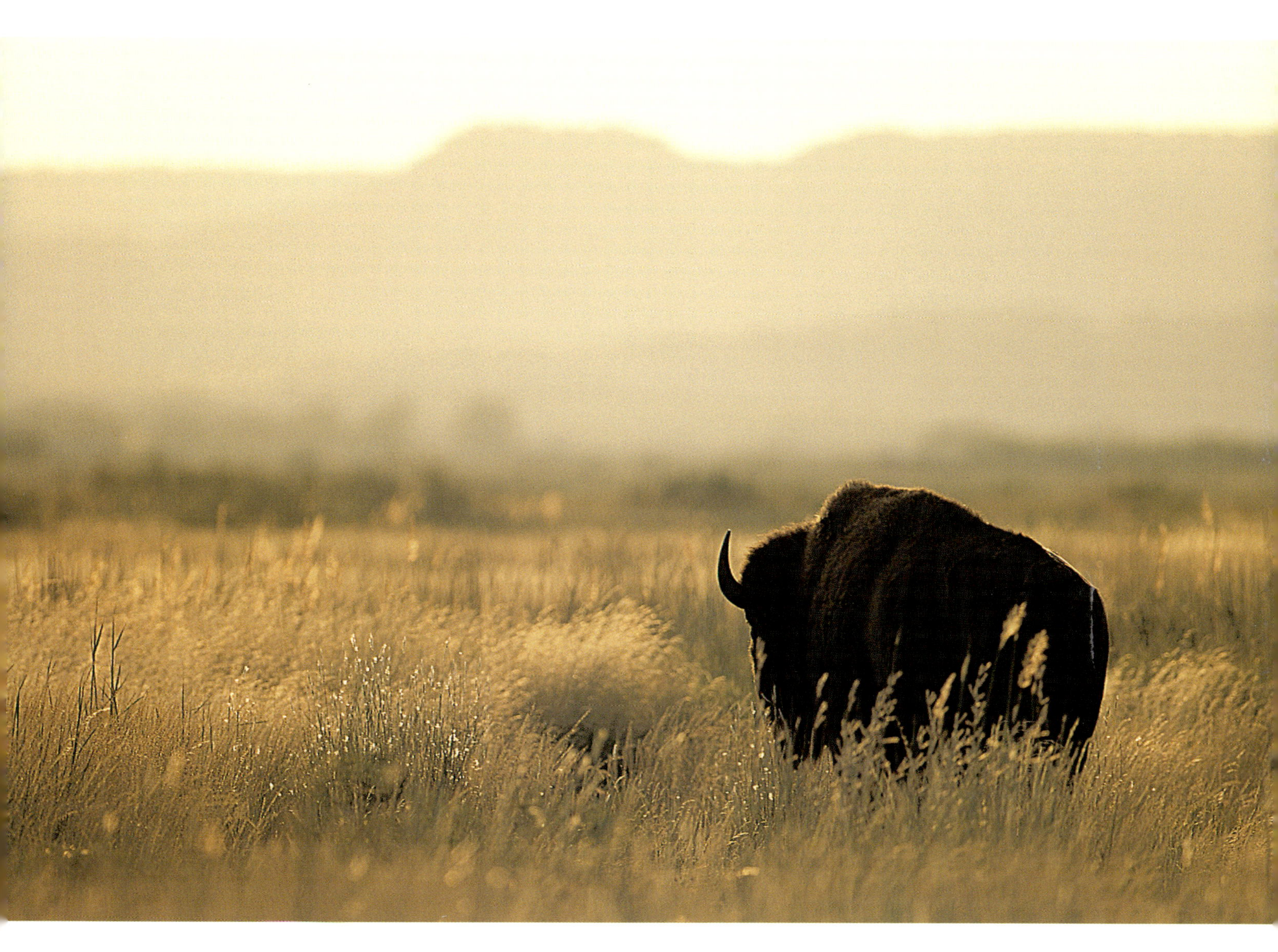

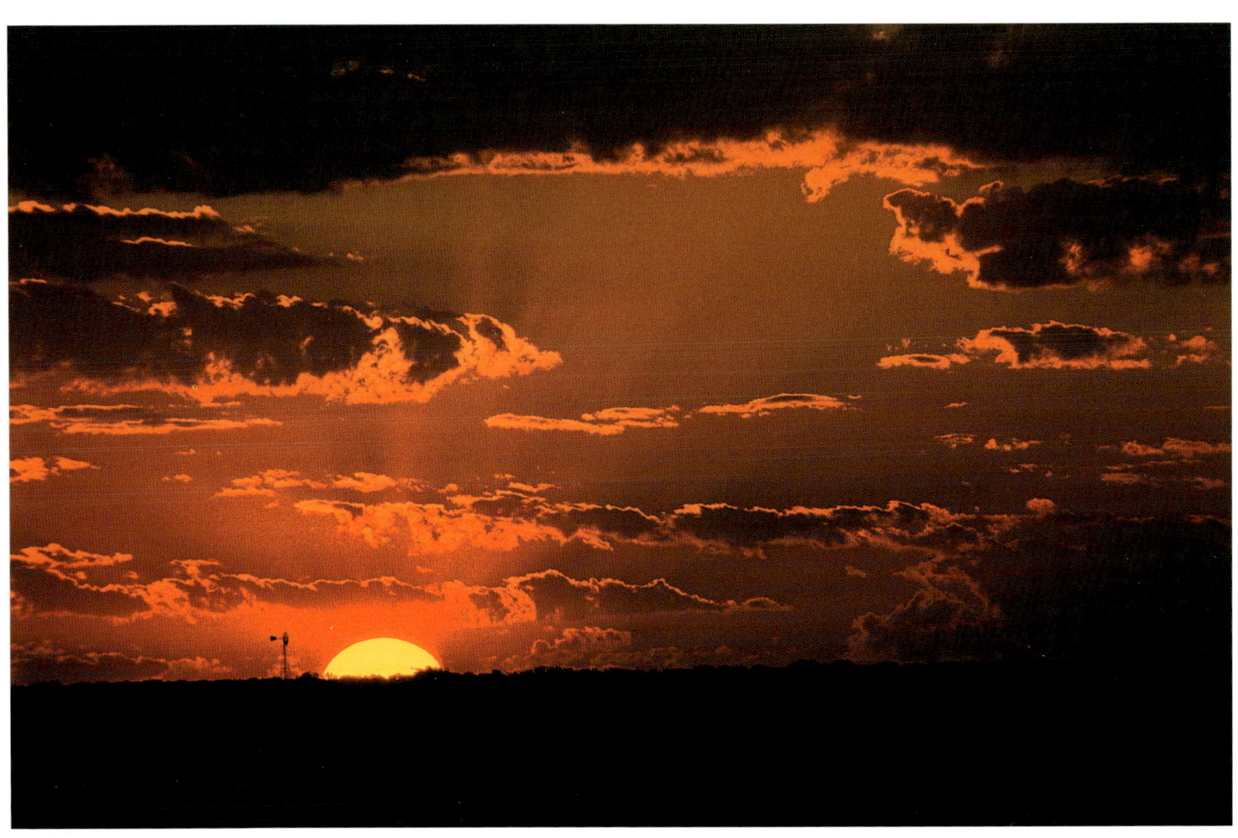

BOWING TO SKIES IN A HAT

I've fenced these fields so many years I'm brown,
chaps and Stetson my disguise. When these are the plains
you ride, you bow to the skies in a hat. Neck and ears

burn anyway, skin cancer bounced from sand to face
no matter how wide the brim. Often at dawn
I see good neighbors in the distance, other vets

back from the jungles, guns slung low and hats
tugged down. I meet them past the corral, or wait
by the windmill grinding its clatter. I see it in their eyes

sometimes, the way snakes go their own way, alone,
not fearing a man or his rifle. Today, we're mellow
after steaks and biscuits, ready to patch barbed wires

and brand, to break strange colts with words,
easy, easy. Maybe memories crawled back to them
last night, wart-faced and haunting, nothing else

on these wide plains like Vietnam. But here together
we're calm, bold enough in boots and Stetsons, men
of the sunburned eyeballs, riding high over rattlers,

taking turns yelling jokes and shouting with laughter,
twisting and creaking in saddles, killing nothing
but time, riding home to our wives after dark.

GARDENS OF SAND AND CACTUS

My wife takes salt for starters, and rusted strands
of barbed wire, the iron Grandfather left.
Chips chunks from a salt block mired in sand,
that tongue-rubbed marble artwork of the West,

anywhere cows roam—not buffaloes that lick
their salt from cactus and the bones of coyotes.
Takes bones, a skull, when she sees one. Takes snakeskin
like twisted strips of film. Looks under yucca

for the best, six feet at least. But fierce
grandfather snakes don't rattle until they're sure,
so she listens before she stoops. Finds horseshoes to pitch,
and curved stones shaped like tools.

Tugging our last child's Radio Flyer in the pasture,
brings pigments back, even the burnt sienna bolus
of owls. Scrapes umber from banks of the Brazos,
however dry, gold dust where bobcats marked the stumps.

Packs, stacks it all. Takes time, fans with her hat,
then hauls that wagon wobbling to our house.
Amazed that she makes gardens of cactus and sand,
I miter frames to hang whatever she's found

and salvaged as art, even rocks she cuts and tumbles
in a barrel grinding like sweet, hand-cranked ice cream,
turning this desert we call home into babies' mobiles,
wind chimes and swings, bird feeders in every tree.

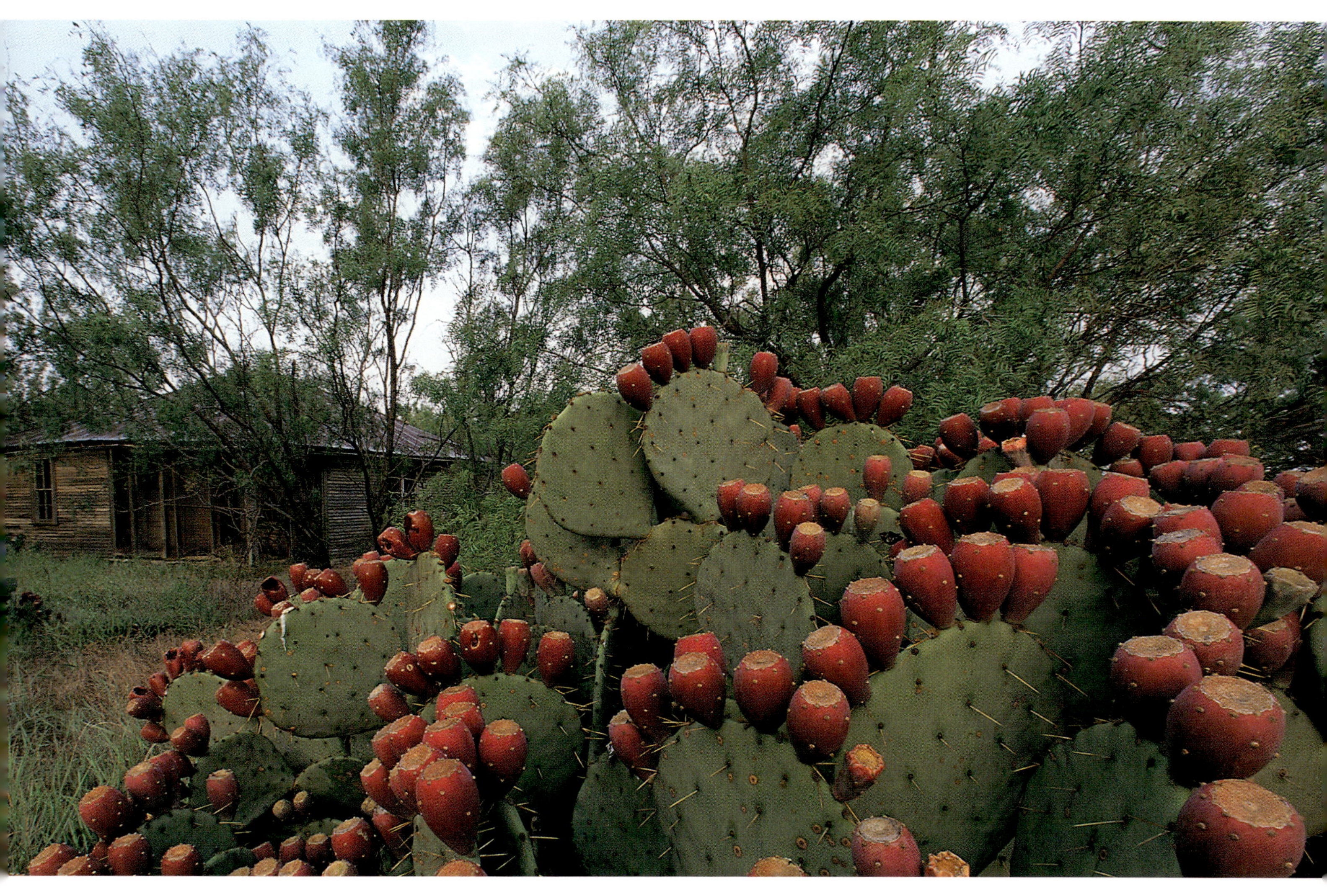

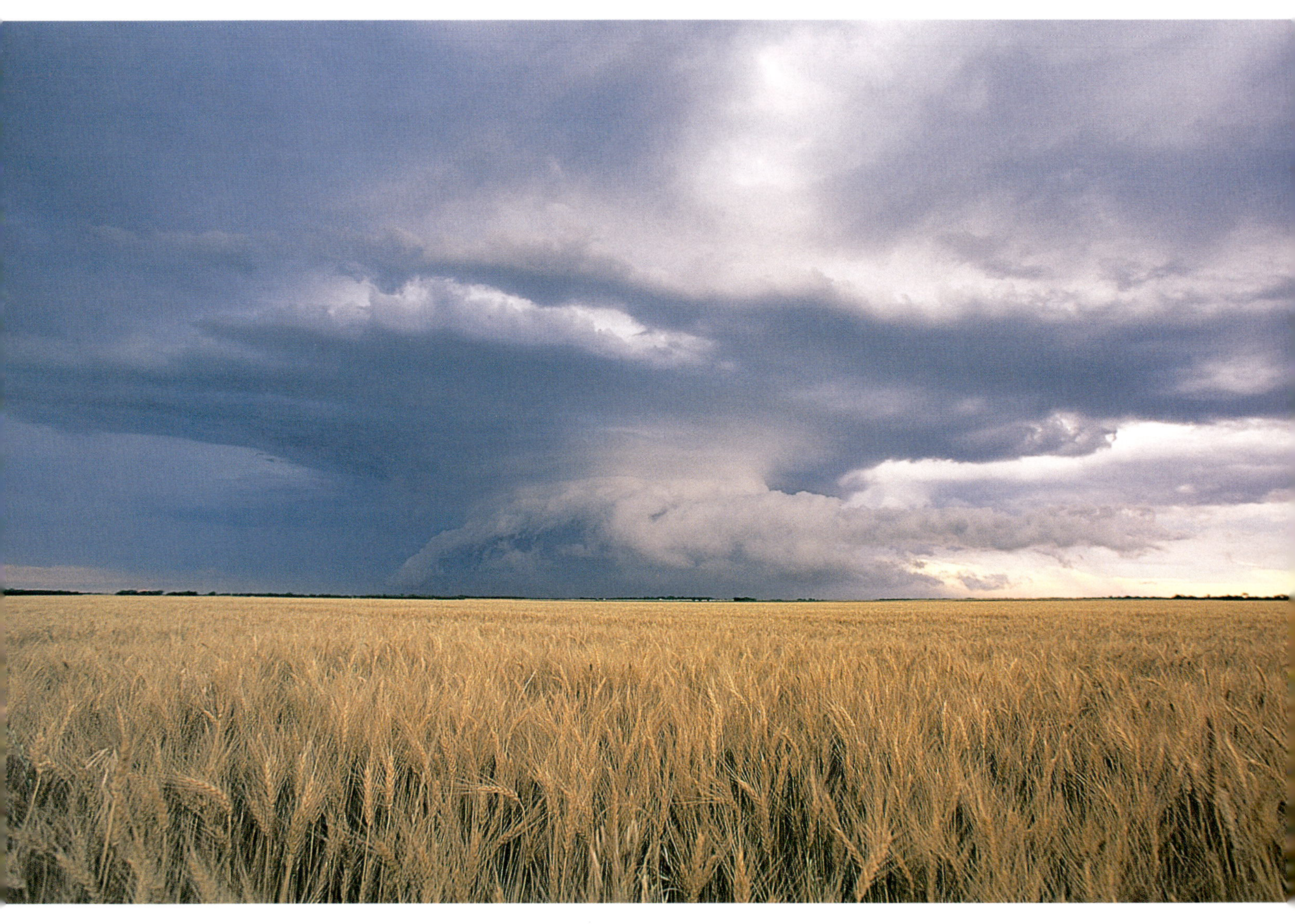

THE FORCE THAT GREW THE GRAIN

I watched Grandfather dip his feet and toes
in a tub of leaf poultice and Epsom salt,
bone weary, the water so scalding hot

steam rose. Eyes closed, he must have prayed
to gods of water tubs to turn hot water to wine
and draw the poison out. He probably thought

of Arkansas forests when he was a boy,
the hand-me-down brogans, blisters popped
and turning hard, ax blade that glanced off

an ironwood log and almost severed his foot.
I saw the puffy scar, albino centipede
down in the snarl of leaves dying the water blue.

Last night, fifteen-below, this deep into spring,
peaches nipped in the bud. When did I last strip limbs
of sappy peach-tree leaves? How many buckets

did I haul, tubs I never knew would ease him along
to here, under a sheet that's flat below the knees—
his hollow cheeks, eyes closed, breath

puffing his rubber lips? How much poison
can one old man endure, gangrene in stumps
of his knees? I lift him in my arms like a doll,

this man who was the wind and stars, a massive man,
the force that grew the grain, that made the bulls behave.
I've seen him slosh and lift a drowning wide-eyed colt

and hobble out of a muddy arroyo, and set it down
and wipe it with his shirt. In World War II,
I watched him put his Sunday hat back on

after others left my father under dirt.
I watched him ride away to feed the herd,
to bear the pain, to make the windmills turn.

WHERE THE TRAIN SLOWS DOWN

Slumgullion and bread fed bums
on Aunt Pearl's ranch by the railroad
in the Great Depression, Uncle Elmer dead.
At first she lost riders and cows,

barbed wire cut down, old cars abandoned
in her pasture, trails trampled past her ranch
by migrants. Windmills and a foreman
old as her father saved the herd.

The bank failed before it foreclosed,
and calves brought enough by fall.
Hobos spread the word for miles by signs
I never saw—*Look for the house ten miles ahead,*

around the bend where the train slows down.
That widow will feed you. I watched them
two at a time, making a trail from the tracks
to her back porch. Hats in hands,

they would ask, but she already had bowls
and spoons, tin mugs for water at the well.
They sat on the porch to eat
or out on the grass under oaks,

then rinsed them clean and stacked them,
found the axe in the stump and chopped
a few thick logs, or raked the yard
the hundredth time that month.

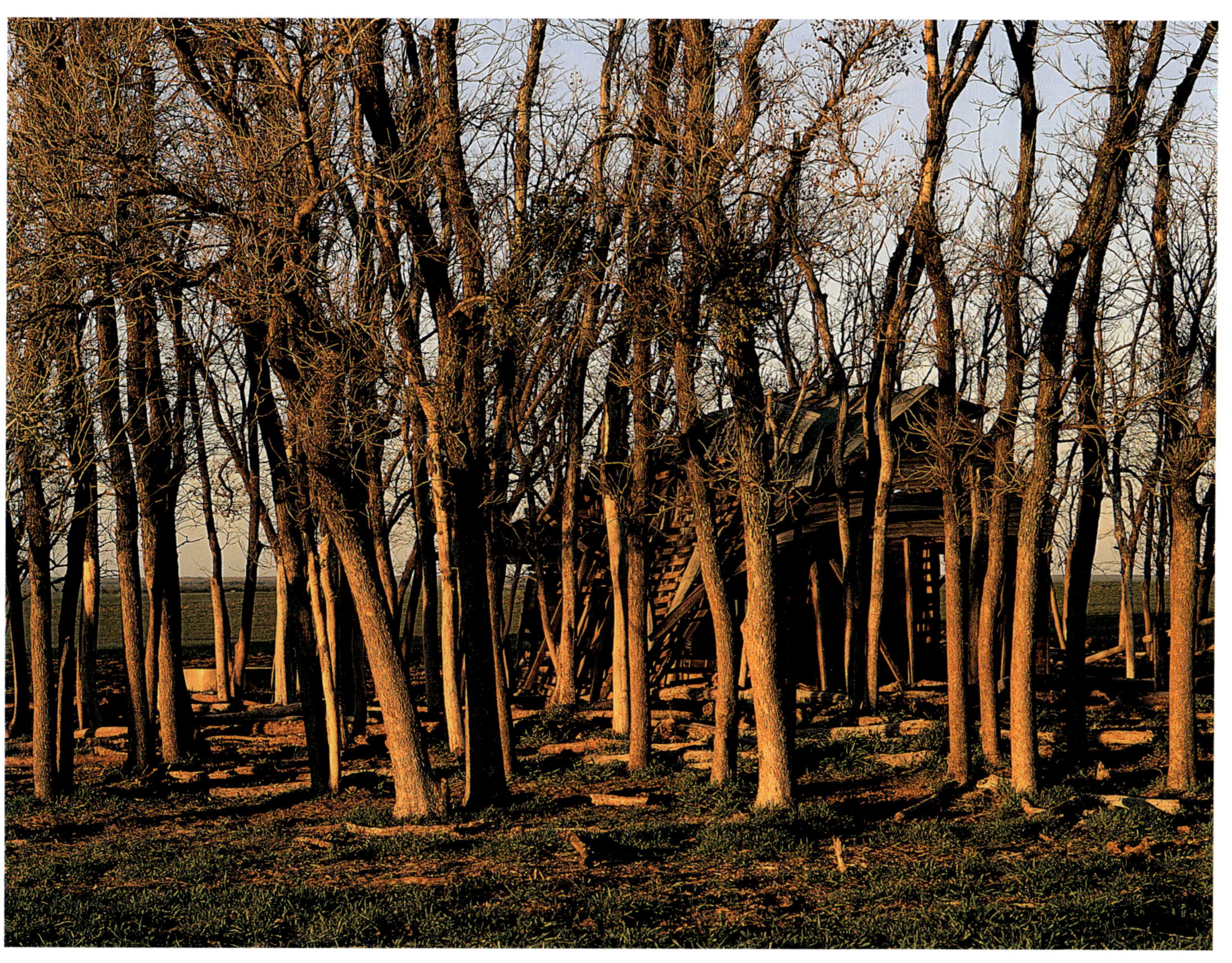

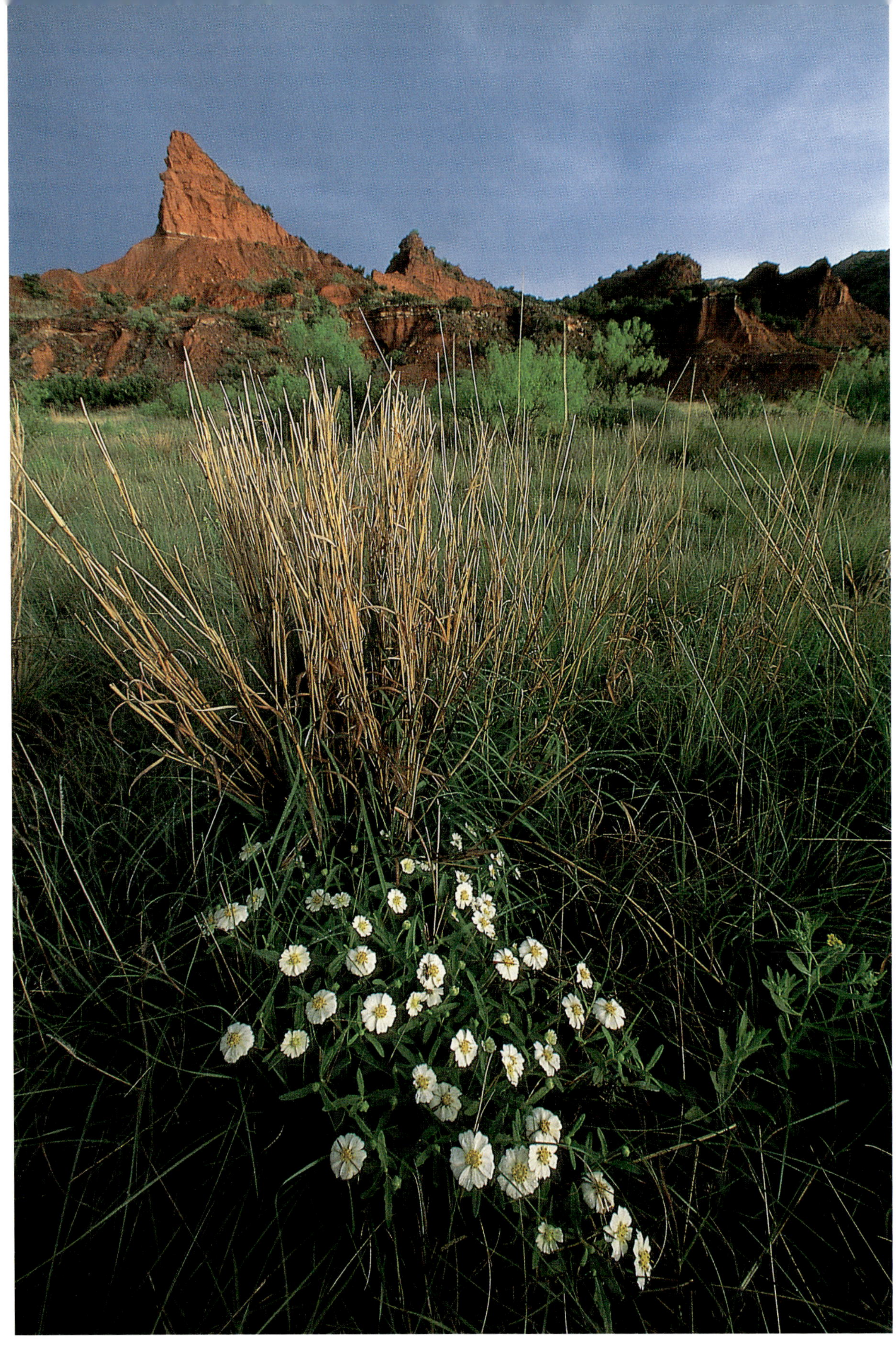

TWO YEARS AFTER WORLD WAR II

Aunt Mabel was coyote ugly in grade school—
I've seen pictures—but a fox
when she got to college in 1940.
She owed all she owned to nature,
no braces or cosmetics on the ranch.

She beat most cowboys on bucking broncs
and bulls, no girls' barrel races for her
in rodeos. She rode off after Pearl Harbor
with the marines, first woman from our county
to enlist. She came back hard

and skinny in a unform, nobody's darling
until Carl from a tank corps rode by,
only one arm but *god!* he could cowboy.
Mother gave her away in the summer church,
big brother handing her off to Carl

while all the kinfolk fanned—what a bride,
pretty as a soldier's pin-up
with a V-neck gown, a left hook
town boys knew. When Uncle Carl
lifted her veil with his only hand

and saw how beautiful a marine could be,
we all saw and applauded,
and the old pump organ played
while Carl and Mabel turned
and kissed while everybody cheered.

WHERE BUFFALO GRASS GROWS LOUD IF WE LISTEN

Out here, cactus is the skyline, a hundred miles of flat.
Turn in a circle and never know you're back,
except for the neighbor's ranch, barns like specks of mica
in the dust, his windmill a semaphore for water, Home.

Deep forests are a myth, black loam and heritage and trees.
The one road into town has highway signs boys use
as targets. The asphalt's cracked, dandelions thriving
as if crews planted them. Rattlesnakes nap

on the shoulders, no trucks along for months.
Jackrabbits limp along like dogs, nibbling grass
and careless weeds, no need to hurry from nothing
that can hide. Slumped on an aging Appaloosa,

I roll a smoke that may take half a day to lick,
to get it right. I dig in deep shirt pockets for a match,
and bite it like a toothpick. I stick the unlit
cigarette like a feather in my hat. I kicked the habit

four years ago after the last grassfire
some trucker started. The butt's for practice,
in case I'm ever bored. My wife saves rattles
for the grandkids, flint arrowheads she finds,

digging strawberry gardens, prying out rocks
for the fish pond, scooping iron and umber
for sand paintings on the patio. Rocking at dusk
that starts at dinnertime and lasts past Halloween,

we talk softly about a coyote a mile away,
one drop of water bulging at sundown from a pipe
over the brimming-full horse trough, the stretch
and shimmer of the drop before it falls.

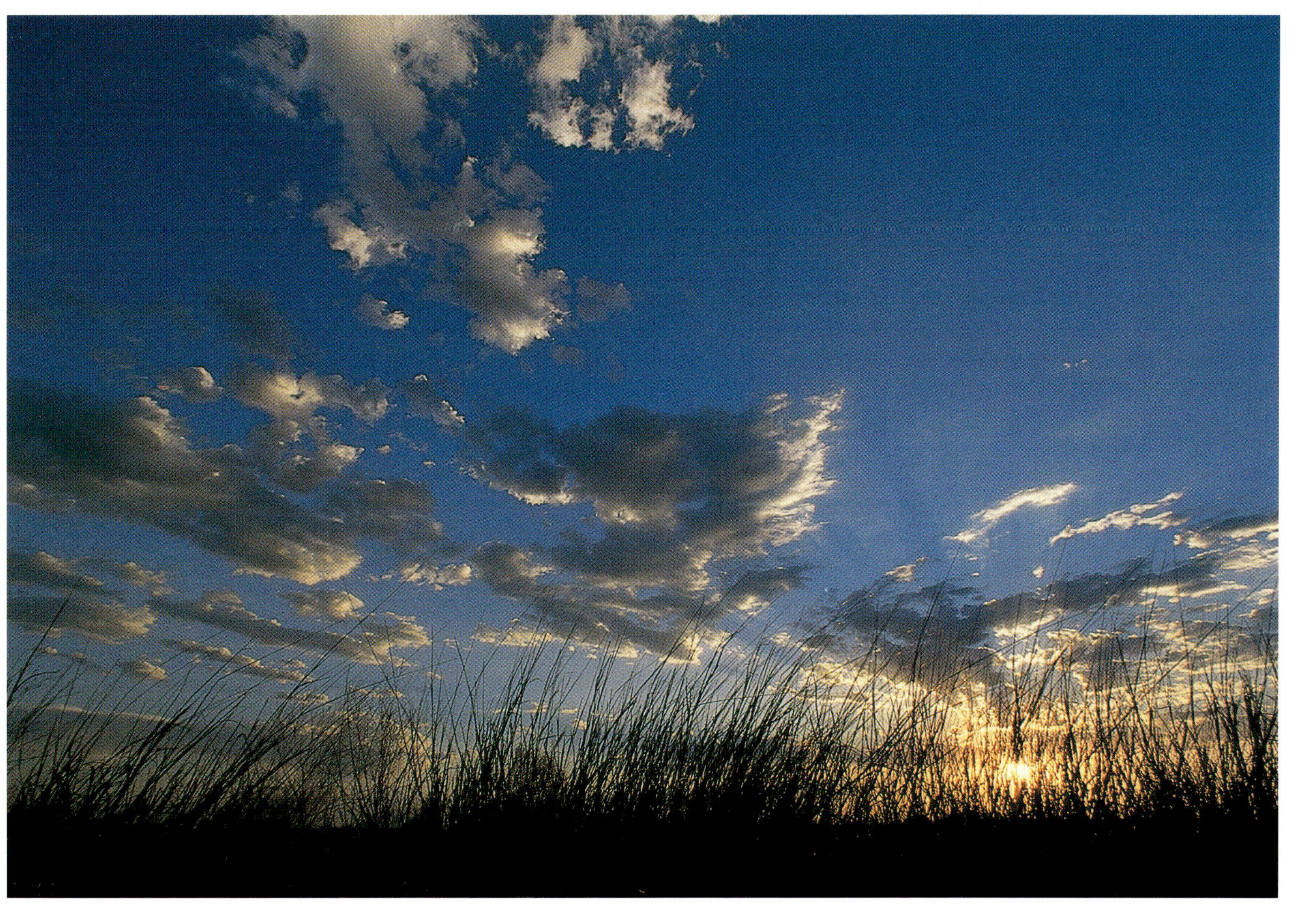

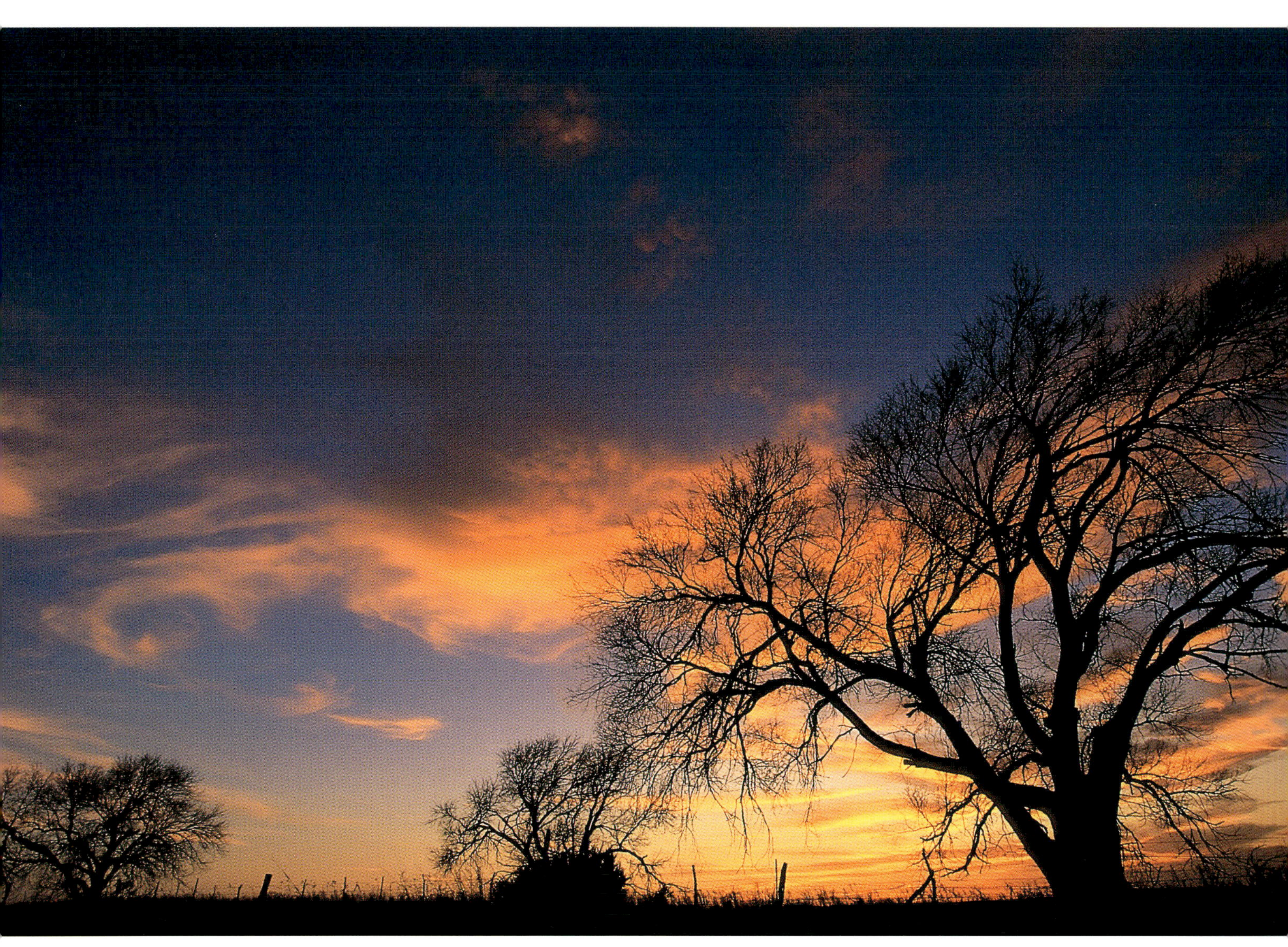

CHAINS WE DIDN'T HANG

Grandpa's mansion was a shack
surrounded by corrals and barns,
a thousand cattle and horses.
Grandpa's ranch was Oz.
Chubby Grandmama spoiled us,
a wand in the kitchen and game room,

presto! our own good witch of the West
telling stories at night by the fire.
Cuddled, we stroked the folds
of her throat that swayed
when she chuckled and hugged us.
Gone, now, only stones and barns,

corrals my wife and I rebuilt,
the last windmills a wonder of pumps.
Nights, we rock on the porch on chains
we didn't hang, wondering how many years
the magic lasts, how long
until our own grandkids come back.

AFTER DECADES AWAY, ULYSSES SOUNDED THE SAME

Some can't leave Texas. Say it once,
it's sweaty and bold as a French tongue.
Texas, sexy as the Alps, Cancun,
Seattle. Decades go by, and the tape's stuck,

spool sticky as glue, the music mellow,
Sinatra at fifty. Some prowl the same
old haunts, so sing, don't throw away
old boots that fit. What can a drifter do

when nothing's sweeter than hometown wells?
Pump water with the same old arm,
deep wrinkles and liver spots.
Dump the bucket in the same locale

and haul it out, crank the frayed rope
creaking on the winch. Go back,
go back even after you've flown
to Spain, Tahiti, the south of France.

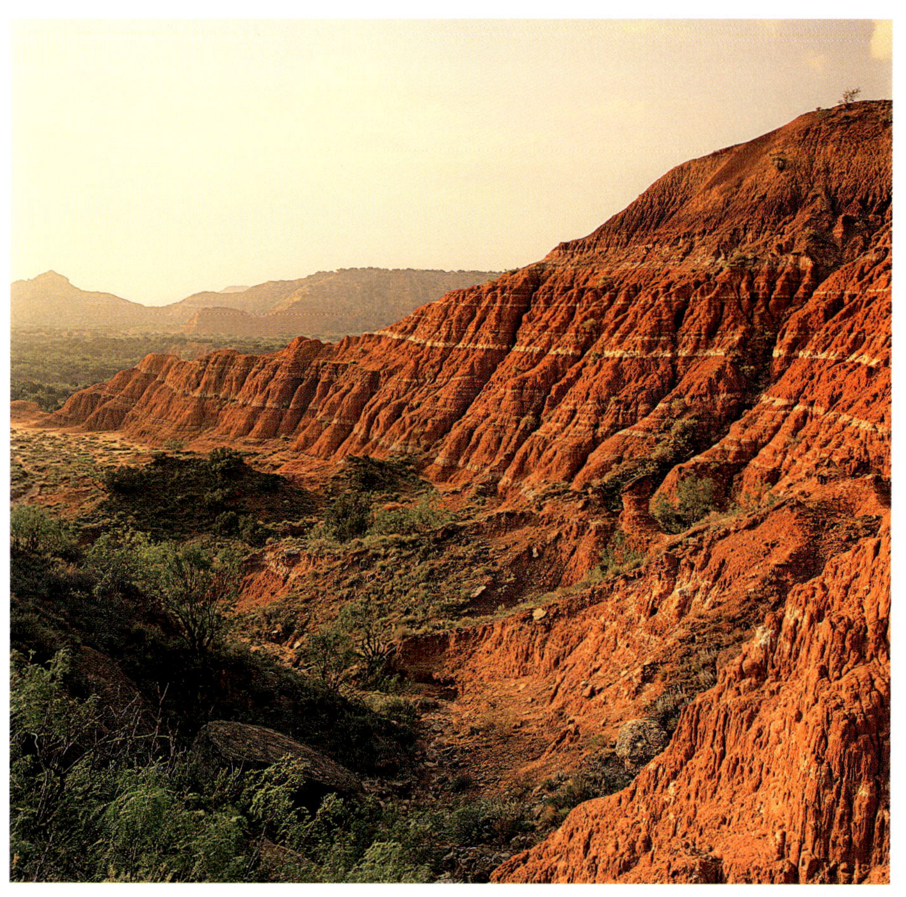

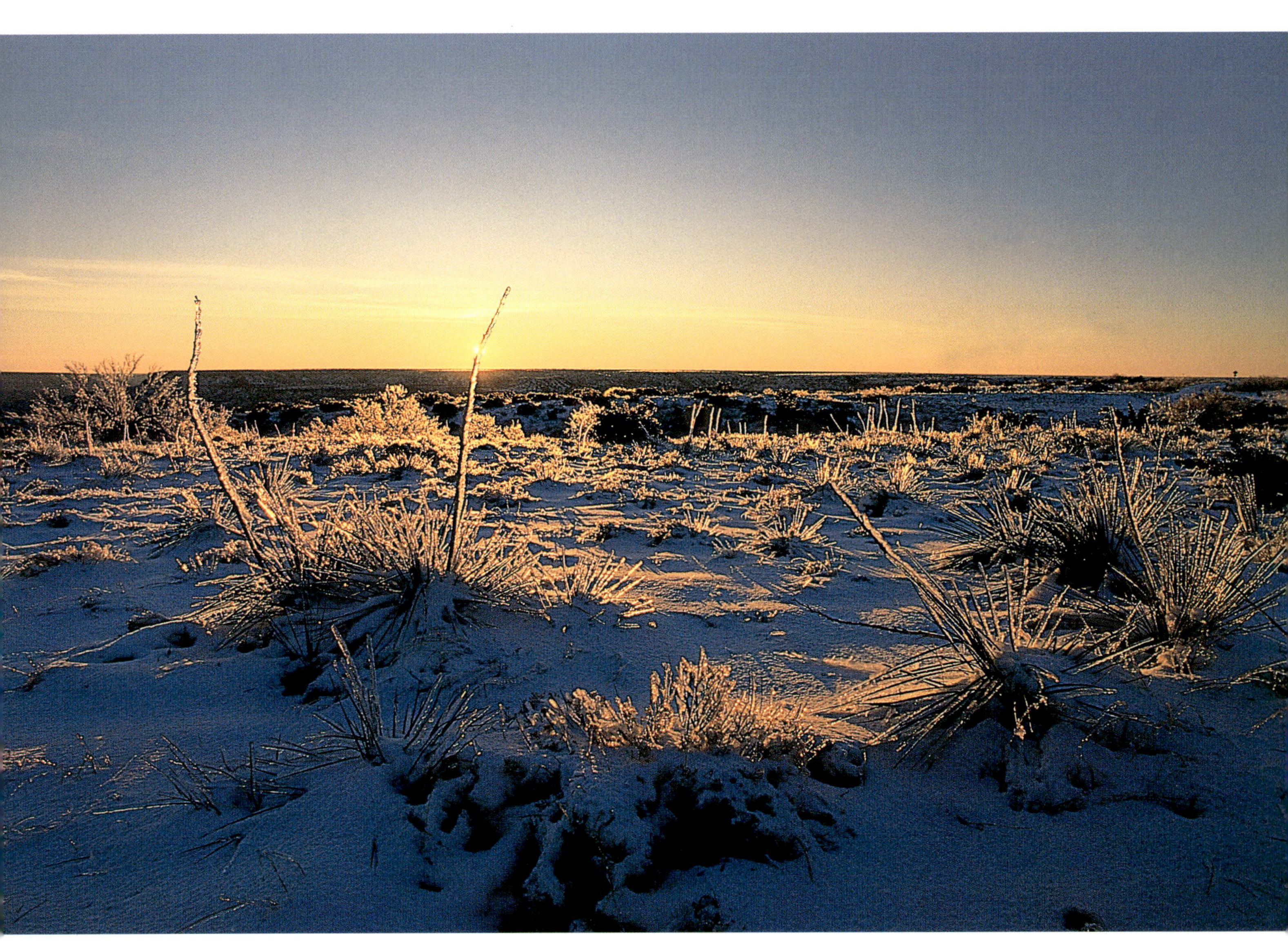

LEAVING THE SCENE

Sleet clicking in the trees, and finches flicking
maize and millet from the feeder. This late in spring,
and still the thin smoke whips from chimneys
a mile away. We rock and watch the dawn,
a ten-watt bulb beyond the clouds. Is all
this sideshow spring a barker's promise of warmth?
Our pears bloomed weeks ago, awnings of green
chiffon. The red oaks bulge, about to burst. Sleet
clicks like thousands of clocks ticking in our sleep.

We take turns leaving the scene with both mugs
to the kitchen for more, draining the urn,
the stiff steam bending as we straighten rugs
and weave back through forty years of furniture,
drapes opened, sleet beating a mute tattoo,
the old oaks wet and dark out to the pasture,

sleet on the steers' flat backs, bowing to dawn
and browsing, always grass and blocks of salt,
the sky nothing they ever watch, no matter what falls,
nothing fat cattle can't endure. We rock
and sip in silence, chairs turned to the porch,
grandchildren far away, knowing whatever force
is coming no one could stop, not even us.

THE WALTZ WE WERE BORN FOR

Wind chimes ping and tangle on the patio.
In gusty winds this wild, sparrow hawks hover
and bob, always the crash of indigo
hosannas dangling on strings. My wife ties copper
to turquoise from deserts, and bits of steel
from engines I tear down. She strings them all
like laces of babies' shoes when the squeal
of their play made joyful noise in the hall.

Her voice is more modest than moonlight,
like pearl drops she wears in her lobes.
My hands find the face of my bride.
I stretch her skin smooth and see bone.
Our children bring children to bless her. Her face
is more weathered than mine. What matters
is timeless, dazzling devotion—not rain,
not Eden gardenias, but cactus in drought,
not just moons of deep sleep, not sunlight or stars,
not the blue, but the darkness beyond.

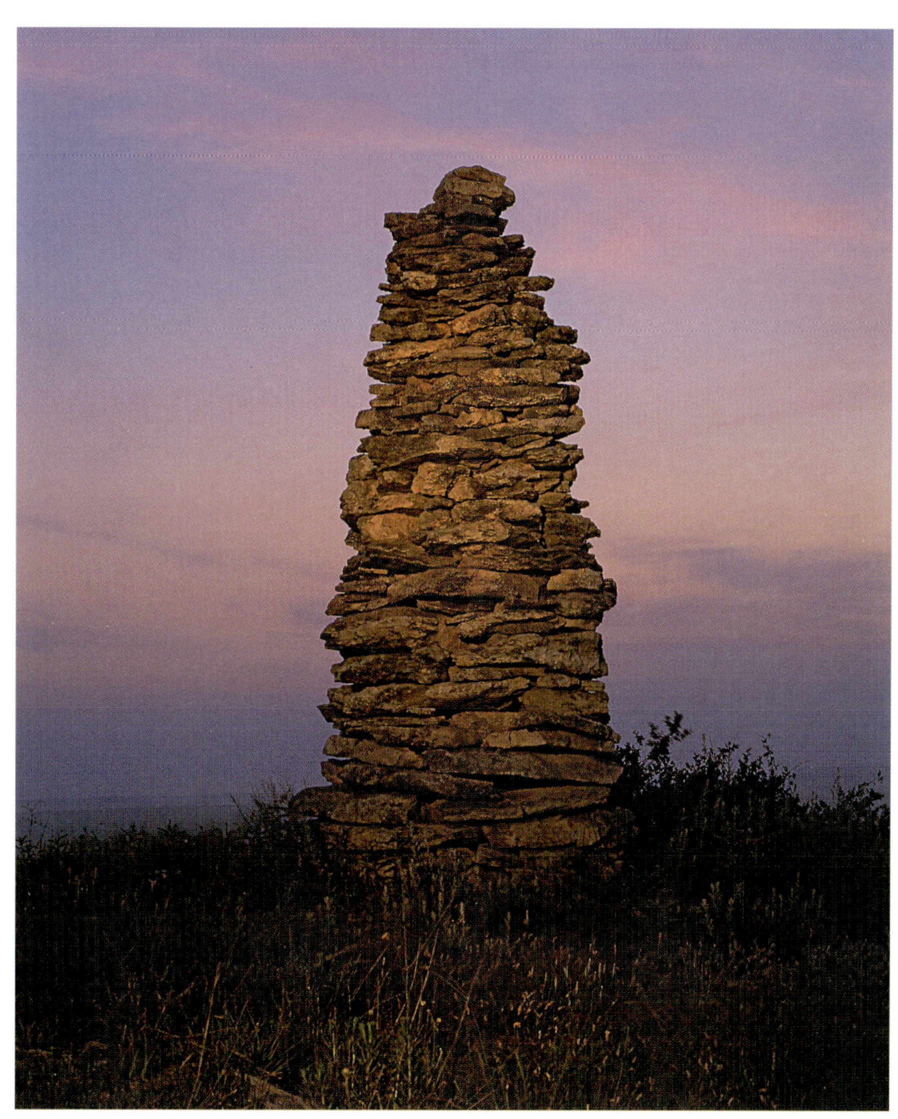

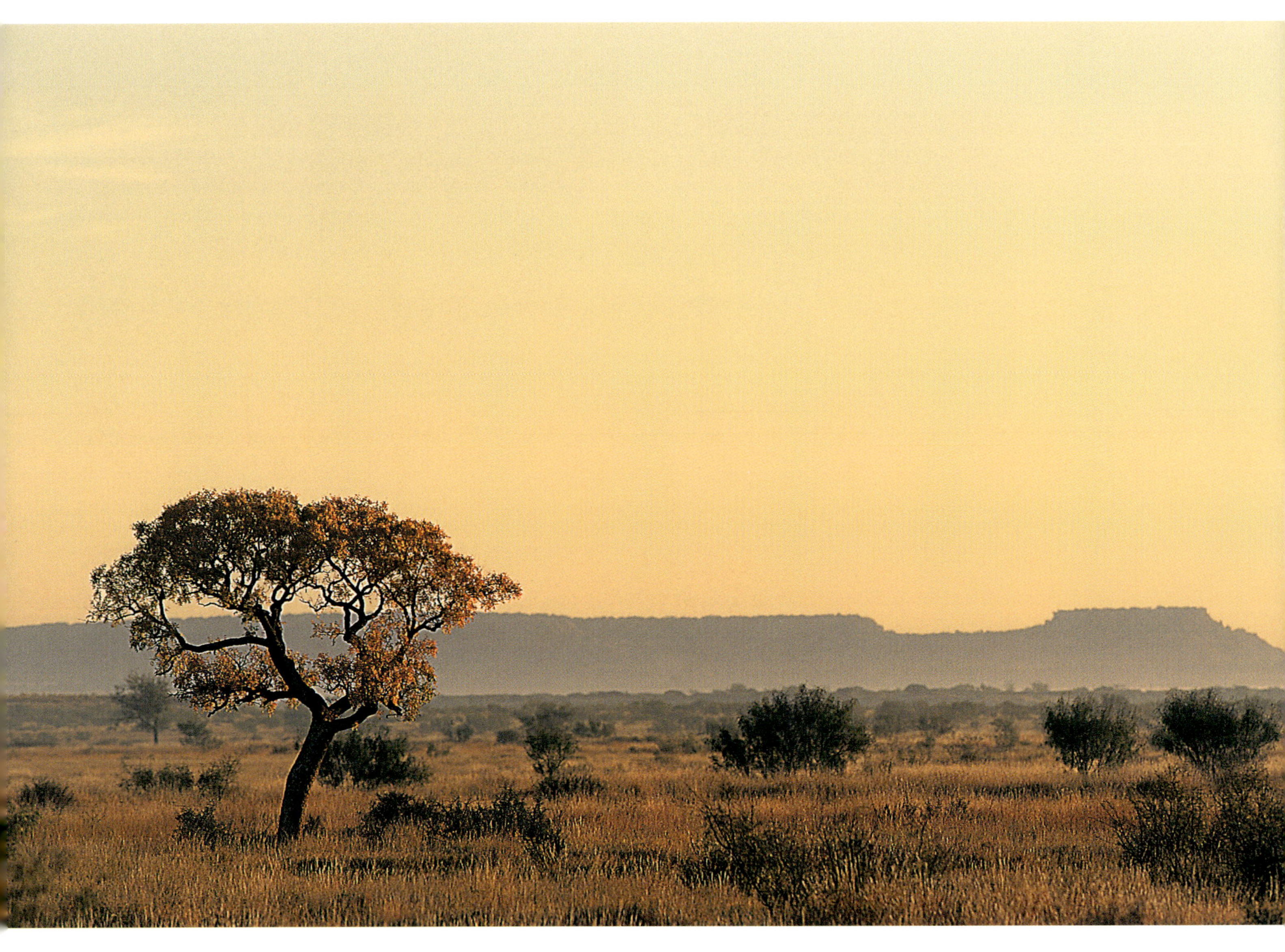

MESAS I NEVER TOOK THE TIME TO CLIMB

I nudge this sweating gelding with my knees.
Old leather creaks as I lean between mesquite
and cactus. Our crops are rattlers and starry skies
we pretend are diamonds. My wife must know I'm coming,
lights bright in the kitchen. We live in a bowl of sand,

ten miles to any mesa. Coyotes prowl at night,
thinking we're fools to roam boldly in daylight.
Dawn, I shove old boots through stirrups
and ride away, content in a saddle, that perfect slap
of leather chaps. Torn gloves I've worn

to brand castrated calves still fit. Hawks see
no farther than I could see from a mesa.
The view is there, if I want it. Today
I found a buzzard in the field, too weak
to flap away. Panting, it hobbled as if on stilts,

others above us wheeling a slow blessing
on flesh. Will it miss the soaring, the glide
toward wide horizons? Someday soon,
I'll cut the fences down and let the bulls run wild.
I'll ride my gelding straight toward a mesa

I never took the time to climb. I'll dismount
and slap the sorrel to send him back to the corral.
I'll look at these flat fields from far above,
the same parched sand and cactus after sundown,
night shining not with diamonds, but real stars.

PHOTOGRAPHY

Note: Unless otherwise noted, all photographs shot on Fujichrome Velvia film.

A ROUND HORIZON WITHOUT A TOWN

1 Part title. See legend for p. 22

2 Sunrise on highway to Matador, Texas
Canon EOS-1N; Canon 17–35 f/2.8L

5 Horseman on the open Texas Plains
Canon F1; Canon 14MM f/2.8L

6 Sunrise and mesquite on the Plains
Hasselblad 501C; Sonnar 150MM

9 Slot canyon on the Rolling Plains
Hasselblad 501C; Distagon 50MM

10 High Plains grassland; northern Panhandle
Canon F1; Canon 28–85 f/4.0

13 Pastore ruins along the Canadian River
Canon EOS-1N; Canon 24MM f/3.5
Tilt-Shift

14 Coyote tracks in the dunes; Llano Estacado
Canon EOS-1N; Canon 24MM f/3.5L
Tilt-Shift

17 Sunrise over Palo Duro hoodoo
Canon EOS-1N; Canon 24MM f/3.5L
Tilt-Shift

18 Panhandle ice storm
Canon F1; Canon 20–35 f/3.5L

21 Winter moon over Palo Duro
Hasselblad 501C; Sonnar 150MM

22 Roll clouds over the Plains; Knox County, Texas
Canon EOS-1N; Canon 17–35MM f/2.8L

25 Big ranch country; Texas Panhandle
Canon F1; Canon 500MM f/4.5L

PRAYING FOR RAIN ON THE PLAINS

27 Part title. See legend for p. 44

29 Drought-stricken landscape near Stamford, Texas
Hasselblad Flexbody; Distagon 50MM

30 Gibson Mill; Pitchfork Ranch
Hasselblad 501C, Distagon 50MM

32 Hoodoo in Tule Canyon; Texas Panhandle
Canon F1; Canon 20–35 f/3.5L

35 Dust devil in midsummer; Knox County, Texas
Canon F1; Canon 20–35 f/3.5L

36 Ancient petroglyph along the upper Brazos; Rolling Plains
Hasselblad 501C; 80MM

39 Rolling Plains snowstorm; Knox County, Texas
Canon F1; 20–35 f/3.5L

40 Fire-killed juniper trees; Palo Duro Canyon
Canon F1; 20–35 f/3.5L

43 Plains dust storm; Knox County, Texas
Canon F1; Canon 14MM f/2.8L

44 High Plains squall line; Texas Panhandle
Canon EOS-1N; Canon 28–70 f/2.8L

47 Summer evening thundershower and lightning
Canon F1; Canon 35–105 f/3.5

48 Mammatocumulus sunset; Knox County, Texas
Canon F1; Canon 20–35 f/3.5L

51 Spring thundershower on U.S. Highway 82/114; King County, Texas
Canon F1; Canon 20–35 f/3.5L

PRAIRIE WAS A TABLELAND OF PRAISE

53 Part title. See legend for p. 68

55 Pate Meinzer, Wyman's dad, posing in the barn; League Ranch
Canon F1; Canon 100MM

56 Old Adams ranch house; Rolling Plains
Canon EOS-1N; Canon 24MM f/3.5
Tilt-Shift

59 Salt Fork of the Brazos, Knox County. Canon F1 with Canon 80-200mm F4.0 lens. Velvia 50 film.

60 Golden retriever and handler; Texas Panhandle
Canon F1; Canon 20–35MM f/3.5

63 Fog over Palo Duro Canyon
Hasselblad 501C; Sonnar 150MM

64 The last wild herd of Southern Plains buffalo; JA Ranch
Canon F1; Canon 80–200 f/4.0

67 Hunter and Pate Meinzer, Wyman's sons. An evening on horseback
Canon F1; Canon 20–35 f/3.5

68 Springtime wheat field in the Rolling Plains
Canon F1; Canon 14MM f/2.8 super wide

71 Caprock escarpment and striated clouds
Canon F1; Canon 14MM f/2.8 super wide

72 Petroglyph at Alibates National Monument; Texas Panhandle
Canon EOS-1N; Canon 24MM f/3.5
Tilt-Shift

75 Hoodoos in the Panhandle canyon land
Canon EOS-1N; Canon 45MM Tilt-Shift

76 Autumn along the Canadian River
Canon F1; Canon 80–200MM

79 Breaking thunderstorm at sunset
Canon F1; Canon 80–200MM

WINDMILLS LIKE CATHEDRAL WINDOWS

81 Part Title. See legend for p. 82

82 Sunrise and windmill in the Texas Panhandle
Nikon FM; Leitz-Telyt 400MM; Velvia 50 pushed to 100

85 Abandoned corrals in the Texas Panhandle
Canon EOS-1N; Canon 24MM f/3.5 Tilt-Shift

86 Driving the horse remuda to wildcat pens on the Pitchfork Ranch
Canon F1; Canon 300 f/2.8L

89 Buffalo trail cut into sandstone near the old Santa Fe trail in the Texas Panhandle
Canon EOS-1N; 24MM f/3.5 Tilt-Shift

90 Sand dunes and artifact
Canon EOS-1N; Canon 15MM f/2.8L

93 Memorial to a fallen cowboy who perished in an accident
Canon EOS-1N; 24MM Tilt-Shift

94 Fog along the Brazos River
Nikon FM; Leitz-Telyt 400 f/6.8; Velvia 50 pushed to 100 ISO

96 Summer evening thunderstorm in the Rolling Plains
Canon F1; Canon 20–35MM f/3.5

99 Earlene Meinzer, Wyman's mother, and her dog Tippy on morning walk; Benjamin, Texas
Canon EOS-1N; Canon 17–35 f/2.8 lens; Kodak 100G

100 Elevated view from abandoned windmill tower in Knox County
Canon EOS-1N; 24MM TS f/2.8

103 Fallen windmill and water tub once owned by the XIT Ranch; north of the Canadian River
Hasselblad 501C; Distagon 50MM f/4.0

104 Badlands in Knox County
Canon F1; 20–35MM

107 Palo Duro in snow
Hasselblad 500C; Planar 80MM f/2.8

108 Rippling sand dune along fence line near Matador, Texas
Canon F1; 20–35MM f/3.5L

THE DUST WE'RE MADE OF

111 Part title. See legend for p. 122

113 Furrowed field near Snyder, Texas; aerial view
Canon EOS-1N; Canon 70–200MM f/2.8L

114 Old wagon remains along the Canadian River
Hassleblad 501C; Distagon 50MM

117 Thunderstorm in Knox County, Texas
Canon EOS-1N; Canon 28–70MM f/2.8L

118 Native American petroglyphs on sandstone panel in Garza County, Texas
Canon F1; 50MM f/3.5 macro

121 Young colts at sunset in King County, Texas
Canon F1; 20–35MM f/3.5L

122 Original walls from the barracks at old Fort Chadbourne
Hasselblad 501C; Distagon 50MM

125 Abandoned nineteenth-century jail in Clairemont, Texas
Hasselblad 501C; Distagon 50MM

126 Hitchhiker on the outskirts of Benjamin, Texas
Canon F1; Canon FD 500MM f/4.5L; Kodachrome 64

129 Remuda on the Pitchfork Ranch; Dickens County
Canon F1; Canon FD 300MM f/2.8

130 Salt flat in King County, Texas
Canon F1; Canon 20–35MM f/3.5L

133 Sunrise in Knox County, Texas
Canon EOS-1N; Canon 17–35MM f/2.8L

134 Springtime in Palo Duro Canyon
Canon F1; Canon 14MM f/2.8L

137 Chimney remains at old Fort Phantom; Nolan County
Canon EOS-1N; Canon 24MM f/3.5 Tilt-Shift

138 Dusting of snow in South Prong Canyon at Caprock Canyon
Hasselblad 500C; Distagon 50MM f/4.0

GARDENS OF SAND AND CACTUS

141 Part title. See legend for p. 147

143 Buffalo beneath caprock escarpment
Canon F1; Canon 500MM f/4.5L

144 Plains sunrise near Canyon, Texas
Nikon FM; Leitz-Telyt 400MM; Velvia pushed to 100 ISO

147 Disheveled homesite in Benjamin, Texas
Canon F1; Canon 14MM f/2.8L

148 Tornadic thunderstorm in Knox County, Texas
Canon F1; Canon 14MM f/2.8L

151 Old German homesite near Rhineland, Texas
Hasselblad 501C; Sonnar 150MM

152 Wildflowers in Caprock Canyon
Canon F1; Canon 14MM f/2.8L

155 Sunset over the Rolling Plains grassland; King County, Texas
Canon F1; Canon 20–35MM f/3.5L

156 Elm trees and sunset; Foard County, Texas
Canon F1; Canon 20–35MM f/3.5L

159 Spanish Skirts; Palo Duro Canyon
Hasselblad 501C; Planar 80MM

160 Winter dawn; High Plains
Canon F1; Canon 20–30MM f/3.5L

163 Stone monument of unknown origin; Foard County, Texas
Hasselblad 501C; Planar 80MM

164 Autumn soapberry tree; King County, Texas
Canon F1; Canon 80–200MM f/4.0

The authors and Texas Tech University Press are deeply grateful to the Helen Jones Foundation and the CH Foundation, without whose generous and timely support this work would not have been possible.

Designed by Laine Markham and Barbara Werden, this book was typeset in Adobe Jenson created by Robert Slimbach. Jenson captures the essence of Nicolas Jenson's roman and Ludovico degli Arrighi's italic typeface designs. The combined strength and beauty of these two icons of Renaissance type result in this elegant typeface.